Making the Bear Dance

A NATURALIST'S JOURNEY INTO THE WORLD OF WILDLAND FIREFIGHTING

by

Jeff Connor

NORTH STAR PRESS OF ST. CLOUD, INC.

Library of Congress Cataloging-in-Publication Data

Connor, Jeff, 1949-
  Making the bear dance : a naturalist's journey into the
  world of wildland firefighting / by Jeff Connor.—1st ed.
      p. cm.
    ISBN 0-87839-165-7 (alk. paper)
    1. Connor, Jeff, 1949- 2. Wildfire fighters—West (U.S.)—
  Biography. 3. Wildfires—West (U.S.)—Prevention and
  control. I. Title.

  SD421.25.C65 A3 2001
  634.9′618′092--dc21
  [B]   2001044164

The stories are actual events but names have been changed or not used to respect the privacy of friends.

Cover photo courtesy
Alaskan Type I Incident Management Team

ISBN: 0-87839-165-7

First Edition: September 2001

Printed by Versa Press, Inc., East Peoria, Illinois

Published by
North Star Press of St. Cloud, Inc.
P.O. Box 451
St. Cloud, Minnesota 56302-0451

For Brooke, Ryan, Paddy, and Cayley

Dedicated to all wildland firefighters who have been on the front lines and especially the 600 plus firefighters who have paid the ultimate price fighting fires since 1910.

Introduction

Wisdom is Treasured by the Few
Knowledge by the Multitude
            —The Tibetan Book of the Great Liberation

*T*he siren echoed off a nearby cliff as a patrol car drove rapidly down the main street with its overhead lights flashing. The officer turned off the siren and spoke over the loud speaker, telling everyone to evacuate the town. Local citizens, their cars full of cherished possessions were leaving, heading towards safety. One car stopped near where I stood by the side of the road. The driver rolled down his window and said, "Good luck. Please protect our town." In the backseat sat a small girl about five years old. She clutched a teddy bear and cradled her dog. Tears in her eyes, she was clearly frightened. I smiled to her and told her not to worry. A tear welled up in one of my eyes, and it took a lot of will power not to let it start rolling down my cheek. I watched them drive off in the line of cars and pickups. My fire crew, standing next to the bus, and I exchanged looks; no one quite knew what to say.

I glance towards the sun, barely visible in the smoke-enshrouded sky. The smoke, a strange yellowish green color, with the sun barely visible as an orange ball, looked surreal in the early afternoon light. In twelve years of wildland firefighting I had never seen anything like it. Glancing to the south, flames from the Hellroaring Fire that had burned into the North Fork Fire billowed up over the top of a ridge. The fire beast was galloping hard in our direction, heading directly for the town of Gardiner, Montana.

The time was early September 1988, and my crew and I had been on the fire line in and around Yellowstone National Park for almost three weeks. This was the third fire we had fought. We started out in Colorado on a small twenty-acre fire and ended up on a fire well over 100,000 acres in size. We also saw action on the Huck Fire in the Grand Teton Wilderness just south of Yellowstone and now on the Hellroaring Fire on the north boundary of the park. We were suppose to be on "R&R" at Chico Hotsprings for a couple of days, but, after just one day, we were called back to the front lines. A cold front, with winds better than sixty miles per hour, pushed the fire towards the town of Gardiner. Mammoth Hotsprings, to the south, had already been evacuated, and some of the citizens moving through Gardiner were Park Service and concession employees from there. As the vehicles drove by us, the folks inside looked tired and scared. The fires in Yellowstone had been burning out of control since late June.

My bus was parked outside the Incident Command Post. A Forest Service employee came out and directed us towards the high school. Our job was to hold the line, preventing the fire from getting into town. There were six hand crews, including one hotshot crew, along with ten engines. We were the last bastion, the "defenders of the Alamo." Hundred of families were relying on us.

The strong winds made it hard to stand upright, and the flames were eating through sagebrush and pine trees, getting ever closer. Just when it started to look like the gates of hell were going to open and swallow us, the wind shifted, and I noticed for the first time that there were clouds overhead, not smoke. The clouds were lower to the ground. The ridge just south of town engulfed in flames had clouds flowing over the top like fog coming in from the sea. The temperature fell, and flakes of snow began to fall. The greater Yellowstone finally would get relief. The threat that had been ongoing for two months neared an end. The fires would continue to burn for a couple more months but not at the intensity of the past few weeks.

Later that night as snow blanketed the ground, the residents of Gardiner and Mammoth Hotsprings began to return. No homes had been lost, and there was relief but also anger. Many held hard feeling for the National Park Service, blaming them for this fiasco. In reality, the fires were no one's fault. Nature was doing what it did best in time of drought. Burn. Started by lightning as well as by a careless logger, the fires of Yellowstone followed a pattern thousands of years old. Only in the last 100 years had people crowded into areas that had evolved with fire and tried to imagine that fire had a different meaning, not one to admire and behold as a wonder of Nature, but one of horror and fear. People feared the beast that roared and consumed all in its path.

The next day as we left town, people waved, and signs appeared in store windows, thanking the firefighters for all the hard work. I felt proud to be part of a chapter in the history of the National Park Service. It is not uncommon to have firefighters portrayed as protectors of the forest, protectors of Bambi, homes, and human lives. For most who have never been on a fire line, the image of Smokey the Bear comes readily to mind with the statement, "Only you can prevent forest fires." Pictures of blackened forests or burned out ruins of houses are shown on the news while, in the background, firefighters dressed in yellow and green battle with the fire beast. When I was a kid, I saw firefighters on the five o'clock news fighting a raging fire and thought, "I want to do that." When a wildfire becomes the bad guy, the villain burning homes and making the bear dance, firefighters then become Sylvestor Stallone, Arnold Schwartzenager, Mel Gibson, and Bruce Willis—heroes to people whose lives or communities are threatened. Over my twenty-four years as a wildland firefighter, knowing that I protected someone's home or a community has made my chest swell. "Yes!" I yell, while beating on my chest with my fists. "I am an American, a firefighter, and damn proud of it!"

Of course, there is another side to the glittering coin. As a wall of flame 100 feet high heads in my direction, burning thousands of acres in a blink of an eye, I have found myself thinking, "Holy shit! What am I doing here?" I can't even count the number of times I had to retreat to get out of the way of racing flames or the many other times I stood my ground along with other firefighters, taking the beast by its horns and throwing it to the ground. I have been on wildfires as in Yellowstone, where whole communities were evacuated and my fire crew and other firefighters were the only ones staying behind. I have watched families drive away from their homes with a car full of what possessions they could grab, the kids in the backseat crying, holding onto the family dog—all fearing for their lives. Tears have come to my eyes knowing that we probably will not be able to save all their homes. Tears also come to my eyes in joy after saving one house, one cabin, or one barn after several hours of hair-raising firefighting. It is all worth it when I see the smiles or tears of joy of children or adults when they return to find their home still standing.

Unfortunately, because of years of fire suppression, heavy fuel build up, and homes being built in dangerous areas, it has become more common for families to have tears of sadness when they return and see their house burned to the ground on a blackened landscape.

When we do save a home, we become heroes, but other times — especially when buildings are burned — we are blamed for the loss. In Yellowstone National Park in 1988, we became the bad guys when whole communities blamed the National Park Service for letting "out-of-control" fires threaten their communities, burn their homes, and supposedly destroy Yellowstone National Park, the jewel of the National Park system. When people's livelihoods or homes are threatened, they easily forget that forest fire is a natural part of the world — like a hurricane or tornado. No matter what resources we throw at some fires, we just cannot stop them. The yin and yang of firefighting is that, by suppressing fire for decades, fuels build to dangerous levels. Combined with global climate change because of fossil fuel burning, and with more people building homes in places where they should not, disaster looms. When homes are built in foothills or dense forest, defending them jeopardizes homeowners' lives and those of the firefighters. Homes are being built in areas where fire is a natural component of the ecosystem, forcing firefighters to suppress fires when they should stand off to the side and let fire do what it is supposed to do. Building a home in a dangerous area with volatile fuels is the same as building on a beach exposed to hurricanes. The reality is, "Not *if* a fire (or hurricane) is going to occur, but *when*." Fires like those in Yellowstone in 1988 did not get put out by firefighters, even with the gargantuan effort made to do so, but by a change in the weather, even though millions of dollars had been spent and thousands of firefighters battled the beast. Yellowstone had experienced similar fires previously, but then no permanent towns existed. It will see similar fires in the future.

Being raised in a military family, I easily compared firefighters to soldiers who put their lives in jeopardy, but, unlike the Armed Forces, firefighters battled on American soil instead of in some far-off foreign land. Some firefighters have been on hundreds of fires over a course of twenty years. Friends I know who were in the military and then became firefighters often describe similar feelings when they faced hostile enemies trying to kill them and a large wall of fire bearing down on them. They get that same sick feeling in the stomach and bowels. Once during the 1988 Yellowstone fires, one of the firefighters on my crew, who had served in Vietnam, had a bad day when the Huck Fire burned over our fire line causing us to scramble to safety. During the height of the blow up, he experienced a Vietnam flash back. The stress of firefighting, lack of sleep, physical exhaustion, extreme fire behavior, helicopters flying overhead, and the danger had overwhelmed him much as in the war, bringing back memories he had suppressed years before.

Lives are occasionally lost fighting fires, similar to the military. Over the years, friends have not come back alive from an armed confrontation in a foreign country, and, similarly, some did not come back alive from battling a raging forest fire on our own lands.

A lack of sleep is what I hate the most in firefighting. I am an eight-hours-a-night type of guy when it comes to sleep, and rarely do I ever get more than six while on a fire an often less than that. It is not uncommon to go twenty-four hours or more with little sleep, little food, sometimes little water, and physically demanding conditions. I have gone as long as thirty-six hours with no sleep, forty-eight hours with maybe an hour or two. The lack of sleep is cumulative and over a twenty-one-day assignment, it wears me down faster now than it use to when I was younger. Being tired makes me more susceptible to colds and other complications. In recent times when I came back from a two- or three-week assignment, I have bronchitis or a cold from breathing smoke and ash. Sore muscles, poison ivy or poison oak, red eyes—all part of firefighting. I have witnessed firefighters fall asleep standing up; vomit uncontrollably from breathing too much smoke, ash, and carbon monoxide; get burned from falling hot branches; knocked down by falling trees and had to run like hell from walls of flame. All this comes with the territory.

For those who love the adrenaline rush, danger always lurks over the hill. I have been evacuated off a mountain top by helicopter with a wall of flame not too far behind, had to run to a safety zone a number of times, and even once been shot at for building a fire line into someone's marijuana patch in Northern California. I have never had to deploy my fire shelter, but I have thought about it a couple of times. I have seen brilliant maneuvers stop a fire dead in its tracks and also seen blunders that endangered the lives of firefighters. I have been on fires where over a million dollars a day were spent with thousands of firefighters constructing or holding fire lines and been on fires where I was the only person involved.

Of the thousands of wildland fires started each year, lightning is often the cause. This incredible natural phenomenal—beautiful to behold—is also very dangerous. I have witnessed lightning blow a tree apart as if it had been dynamited, completely envelope a tree in a white ball of electricity, igniting the top of the tree. I have seen first hand what lightning does to humans and have great respect for it and also fear, especially when caught in a storm above the treeline on some mountain top.

Many times over the years, I have wondered why I returned to do it all over. The stress of being in danger day after day on large project fires or worrying about a fire crew for whom I am responsible wears me down. Some firefighters' careers have seen many fires with a moderate to high "pucker factor"—very dangerous. Many fires are small, less than one acre in size, and are not very dangerous, but a small number end up huge, many thousands of acres with extreme fire behavior. Those I dread. I am now fifty-two, and the older I get the more I worry.

Meanwhile, as wildland fires seem to become more dangerous, politicians cut the federal budget, and firefighters like myself are retiring. In 1995, Congress reduced the budget by downsizing every federal agency. This reduced the number of firefighters available to fight fires. The next year, 1996, was the second most severe fire season in the twentieth century on federally managed lands. Because of downsizing, fewer federal firefighters were available to fight the fires. One fire had only two fire crews (forty firefighters) on a fire that burned thousands of acres. Also many permanent federal employees, like myself, who are not full-time firefighters but have a lot of experience, are getting older and go out less, while fewer permanent jobs are available for new employees to take our places. In the year 2000, after another severe fire season, Congress recognized its mistake, particularly when constituents began losing their homes to wildfires, and more money began to filter back into the program. There is now more money than ever available for managing fire and hazardous fuels and a bigger emphasis on prescribed fires—physically reducing hazardous fuels and trying to reestablish an ecological balance after so many years of fire suppression. There is also a big push to allow young firefighters to work directly with experienced firefighters so they can learn from them. However, each year the fire seasons seem to be getting worse. The year 2000 saw the worst fire season since the firestorms of 1910. Over seven million acres burned, and over a thousand homes were destroyed. Eight firefighters lost their lives and four million dollars were spent. About 29,000 firefighters were involved, including fire-fighters from Canada, Mexico, and Australia.

The 2000 season started off disastrously with a prescribed fire in New Mexico set by the National Park Service. The fire quickly went out of control, burning through the nearby community of Los Alamos and destroying 240 homes. Everyone screamed about the danger of prescribed fires, and the government placed a ban on them. Three months later, the state of Montana was burning as well as many other western areas because of lightning-started and human-caused fires, and the government said we needed to do more prescribed burning. Federal agencies found themselves in a position of "Damned if you do, and damned if you don't." The National Park Service could still not do prescribe fires in 2001 west of the 100th meridian. The fire ban was finally lifted in June. In 2001, once again thousands of fires have started, millions of acres burned and communities evacuated. Each fire season since 1994 has appeared to be worse than the previous one.

Over the years, I have enjoyed traveling around the country bat-tling the beast. I like seeing new mountain ranges, valleys, mesas, or plateaus and visiting states such as Idaho, Montana, Wyoming, Washington, Colorado, New Mexico, and California. I've seen some of the wildest areas of the West, many square miles of open space lacking human dwellings, areas where fire-influenced vegetation and wildlife have developed over thousands of years. The beauty I have seen in these places has left fond memories. I think back through the twenty-four years to the many times I have watched the sun clouded in smoke setting behind a mountain or ridge with incredible displays of differ-ent shades of orange and violet. Then I've been on the fire line all night and watched the sunrise shrouded in smoke the next morning, a large red ball trying to burn through early morning haze and smoke. During the night, I've watched a full moon rise over a valley while I stood high on a ridge or mountaintop digging a fire line or back burning. Smoke filled the valley below because of a temperature inversion and looked like low-lying clouds on a cool fall day in the hill country of New England. Listening to the wind blowing through the needles of a pine tree, observing a far off lightning display from a thunderstorm, listening to the sound of an owl calling at night, and the welcome sound of water flowing in a river, stream, or small brook—all moments of beauty that have occurred on fires many times over the years. I've also been on fires in the fall with cold mornings, cool crisp air, and aspen or cottonwood trees in a brilliant yellow display. Grass, turning from green to yellow or browns, creates a multi-colored landscape not unlike the foliage change in Minnesota or New England and became etched in my memory. I've heard bull elks bugle their mating calls, keeping track of their harem of cows, oblivious to fires raging nearby and have seen buffalo in Yellowstone National Park idly walking through a meadow filled with low lying smoke, while pine trees burst into flames along the edge of the meadow. Sometimes I've seen wildlife behave as if nothing is happening while the forest burns nearby—salmon spawning in a stream, moose nonchalantly feeding on willow, elk and even buffalo in meadows bedded down, grazing or walking slowly, showing no concern about flames or smoke. At other times I have witnessed wildlife running in panic from a wall of flame. Once, a bear with its back smoldering from fallen ash ran down the fire line causing firefighters to scatter. Most of the time, the wildlife gets away, but sometimes they don't, and occasionally I find the burned carcass of a hapless animal that could not move fast enough or found itself trapped by flames.

Some fires display incredible behavior. Fire whirls fifty to 100 feet high dancing across a burning meadow, hissing, and whistling, scattering burning debris, and starting hundreds of small spot fires. These mini-tornadoes of flame mesmerized me into a dream state, beckoning me to dance with them. Once, late at night, looking down from a hilltop into a valley of about 5,000 acres, I saw everything below me on fire—thousands of small fires, like the campfires of some giant army bivouacked in the valley below. Walls of flame licking at the starlit sky above have left me with the sensation of heaven and hell coming together. The roar from the flames of hell have been so loud I had to shout to be heard. Sometimes I envision fire as the force of evil fighting the forces of good; death, and then rebirth—the ultimate battle. The fires of the armies of life and death find harmony because fire, while it destroys trees, is actually the rebirth of forest and meadow: it is the phoenix rising from its own ashes. The blackened landscape often within one year turns into acres of wildflowers, ferns, and grasses. Young tree seedlings emerging from the ashes of their ancestors, whose fiery death provided them with the nutrients for life. Observing this in the wilds of America, I can only believe fire has a place in the scheme of things. In a sense, fire is right. It's good for the vegetation and wildlife that evolved with it.

The pleasurable images will always be etched into my mind and leave me with a warm glow in my heart, a tear in my eye, and a smile on my face. However, the sad or frightening images sometimes rear their ugly heads in nightmares, drenching me in a cold sweat. This is the yin and yang of firefighting.

Sometimes in the early morning hours while on a fire, just before sunrise when I am the weariest, the eerie glow from burning trees casts a red-yellowish color through heavy smoke making me think of Dante's *Inferno*. The gates of hell open for a short time until the sun causes it to close. While on a fire at night in California, I once heard a strange whistle that sounded human coming from a dense stand of burned-over woods. I wandered through the forest in ash a foot deep and finally found a fifty-foot standing tree on a ridge top. The tree had been burned—burned through its middle—leaving a hollow core from the base of the trunk to the burned-out top. Hot coals inside the trunk were sucking wind into the hole in the bottom, and heated air was flowing out the top much like a stovepipe. This was the source of the whistling sound that could be heard from a long distance away.

I have enjoyed the camaraderie of fellow firefighters, men and women who rely on each other for support; the mixing of races on large project fires—Hispanic, Native American, Caucasian, Black, Asian—working side by side; the laughter, smiles, Hacky Sack games, football played at fire camp; the cheering of a fire crew watching a favorite football team on *Monday Night Football* on a television powered by a gas generator and picked off a portable satellite disk under the night sky many miles from the nearest town; the chatter after a hard shift on the fire line while sitting at the dinner table, everyone covered with dirt, ash and smelling of smoke, talking about the day's work or telling war stories of battles with the fire beast—wars won and lost.

As I write, I look out a window of my house at the Flatiron Mountains just west of Boulder, Colorado. Pine trees cover the sharply inclined slopes except where granite rock cliffs prevent any trees from growing. From my house I have watched wildfires burn the slopes and destroy nearby homes. Fires—the Black Tiger Fire and Old Stage Coach Fire—have burned nearby. Wildfires are always on the minds of those who live in and near Boulder. I live at the doorstep of the Rocky Mountains, only twenty to thirty miles east of the Continental Divide. The backbone of North America rises to better than 14,000 feet. Majestic trees blanket the mountains up to tree line, which is about 11,500 feet. I can vividly recall the image of huge trees hundreds of years old in some forested western glen with sunlight beaming down through their needles in smoke-filled rays. I have stood at the base of these trees looking up towards the sky through the canopy high above. Feeling the trees' energy, I felt compelled to hug one of the biggest trees, borrowing some of its energy to recharge myself to do battle with the fire beast burning nearby. Sadly, sometimes I would return to find that fire had passed through the grove, and ancient trees had succumbed, were completely burned, blackened, their naked branches reaching into the smoky sky.

Once on a fire in Idaho while descending from a mountaintop, I passed through a magnificent grove of old firs and pines while a fire raced up the mountain, one ridge over from me. I had to walk quickly because of the fire, but I wanted to linger under the canopy of these beautiful trees. I wanted to stop and stretch out beneath them in the cool grass, and watch clouds slowly drift by overhead. Because of the steep terrain and no trails or roads nearby, I was probably the first human to pass beneath those trees in many years, if ever. Sadly, as I left the grove, the fire jumped the ridge. It burned into that beautiful grove, killing all the trees. I returned several days later and walked through ash a couple of feet deep beneath the dead, blackened trees with fire-scorched bark sloughing off the trunks. The stark white heart wood lay exposed. I know deep in my heart that other trees will replace those burned, that they might grow as tall and as beautiful as the ones I saw, but it will be way beyond my lifetime before they ever reach the height of the giants that I saw. I just wish I had had a little more time to enjoy them on that beautiful autumn day.

If fires were allowed to burn as Nature planned for them and not suppressed, perhaps the fire that took that magnificent grove might have only been a ground fire and the trees only slightly scarred. In a forest that is in ecological balance with fire, many of the older trees bear fire scars but live.

Firefighting—"the good, the bad and the ugly" of it—I have experienced it all. There are thousands of others who have seen the same things I have, had similar experiences, tell similar stories. Some have seen more fires than I and put their lives on the line more times, but we are all brothers and sisters, bonded together by danger. When my firefighting friends and I get together around a campfire with a few beers, the stories start. We might say, "Do you remember the Hellroaring Fire, the Chicken Complex, Happy Camp, Deadwood Reservoir, the Swedlund Fire, the burning bush?" The stories go on and on. Our kids sit and listen wide eyed; our spouses sometimes roll their eyes and say, "Here they go again."

So, is firefighting glamorous? To me it was—in my younger days when I was full of piss and vinegar—but not as much anymore. Nowadays it seems more dangerous to me. I go out less often and find more pleasure in spending my summers at home with my family. Glamour ends when people die, and I have seen that happen too often over the years. I remember a teacher in the seventh grade giving us the depressing statistics on how many of us would live to be twenty, thirty, forty and fifty years old. Sadly those statistics have been close to reality in the loss of friends and acquaintances I have experienced over the years.

Looking back over the past twenty-four years, I think about the many times firefighters have been on television and in newspapers. Our fifteen minutes of fame. I have to admit the old chest has swelled a few times over the years. One might ask, "If I had to do it all over again, would I?" Without hesitation.

1

The Teacher can point the Way
The Path is for one and all;
The means to reach the Goal must vary with the Pilgrim.
— Tibetan Yoga

Utah 1976

July is often the beginning of the monsoon season in Utah. The days start out clear and hot, the sky so blue that if I looked straight up the blue turned black, and I swear I could see stars. Small cumulus clouds build during the morning from hot air raising from the desert and mix with the cool air over the mountains or high plateaus creating large thunderstorms. By mid-day these grow large enough to bring rain as well as lightning, the harbinger of fire. My firefighting experience started in 1976 while working as a naturalist at Bryce Canyon National Park. After graduating from Bard College in the spring, I received a phone call from the chief park ranger wanting to know if I was interested in a seasonal job. There was no hesitation in my reply. My soon-to-be wife and I headed West into the sunset. During the five days we spent traveling across the country, my excitement rose as we left the eastern deciduous woods and entered the Great Plains of the Midwest. Finally, the Rocky Mountains began to peek over the horizon while crossing the eastern plains of Colorado. The snow-capped peaks were visible from 100 miles away. Driving through Denver, we quickly climbed into the foothills up into the high country. We camped that night along the shores of Lake Dillon and woke the next morning to a late spring frost. The eastern United States was well into summer, but at 9,000 feet, snow still blanketed the ground. We drove along I-70 over passes where snow lay thick. Patches of grass, with the first wildflowers beginning to bloom, dotted south-facing slopes.

The highway finally met the Colorado River, the main artery for the West. As the highway followed the river, the landscape began to change from spruce and fir to piñon/juniper and finally to high desert scrub. We knew we were in one of the more remote areas of the lower forty-eight states when we entered Utah and saw a sign that said no gas or services for the next 110 miles. Driving 110 miles in New England, we could drive through three states and pass countless towns and cities, let alone gas stations. The highway passed through the Cisco Desert surrounded by mesas and mountains covered with pine, spruce, and fir. The colors of exposed rock and soil were gray, red, purple, and white with rills and gullies formed by the infrequent rains. The view of mountains over 100 miles away made my heart soar as free as the golden eagle we could see circling in thermals over the desert. After living five years in New England where the world is closed in with forest and dense urban areas, the desert felt open and exposed.

Driving through Moab, Utah, and into the heart of slickrock country — the land made famous by Ed Abbey — we passed by Arches National Park. I had been reading *Desert Solitaire* and thought about working at Arches; little did I know that years later I would. We ended up in Capitol Reef National Park for a night, camping in a apple orchard. The next day, we crossed over a mountain and the Escalante River. Sandstone rock painted in desert varnish. We finally climbed out of the desert and entered the orange-and-red-rock country of Bryce Canyon.

The beauty of Bryce Canyon National Park I found breathtaking. The job was perfect — spending the summer hiking, horseback riding, giving guided walks and evening programs. At least once a week I was assigned to the south end of the park called Rainbow Point, a scenic viewpoint at the highest elevation in the park, providing panoramic views of Grand Canyon National Park to the south and Escalante Canyon to the southeast. The desert areas of Escalante and Lake Powell shimmered in intense heat several thousand feet below, while I stood in the cool mountain air surrounded by spruce, fir, and ponderosa pine at Rainbow Point.

The geologic history of the world lay exposed at Rainbow Point. The area contains some of the youngest known rock in the West, then, thousands of feet below along the desert and into the inner gorge of the Grand Canyon 100 miles to the south, some of the oldest rock on the planet lies exposed. Many of these layers of increasingly older rock are within view at Rainbow Point. The visibility at Bryce Canyon is usually so good that one can see from there to Grand Canyon. One cannot actually see *into* the Grand Canyon, but the forests of the North Rim are visible. However, there is a special place, one of my sacred places scattered around the country, just outside Bryce Canyon, where I can actually look into the inner gorge of the Grand Canyon with a pair of binoculars.

For the three summers I worked at Bryce Canyon, every Fourth of July friends from the park, my fiancée, and I would drive up to Rainbow Point to watch the fireworks display in Page, Arizona. Page lay about ninety miles away, but with the great visibility we could easily see the fire works and the lights blinking on the smoke stacks at the Page Power Plant. Rainbow Point was also a great place to go after dark to watch summer thunderstorms. Sometimes I could see ten or more cumulonimbus clouds scattered across the desert looking like giant jelly fishes floating in an ocean of air, some many miles away. Lightning in the clouds flashed from ground to cloud or streaked across the sky—all in silent splendor since the storms were so far away. Sitting out on a rock at the viewpoint arm in arm with my lovely fiancée, we would watch Nature's own fireworks display, while, at the same time, gazing up above us to a diamond-studded sky. No artificial lights or haze clouded the night sky, and all the billions of stars were visible above us with an occasional meteorite flashing across the sky. The only sound would be the wind gently blowing through the trees around us or the soft hoot of a great horned owl.

One particular day in July, the temperature reached to the low eighties, which was hot for 9,000 feet. Looking off towards the Escalante River to the southeast, the sandstone shimmered in the heat; temperatures in the desert simmered around 100 degrees. By lunchtime, cumulus clouds had begun to build, looking like white fluffs of cotton gently floating overhead. By the middle of the afternoon, the clouds had built to dark, ominous-looking thunderheads. Near the end of the afternoon guided walk, the wind suddenly picked up, blowing hard from the west as a thunderstorm approached the viewpoint. A roll of thunder caused me to look towards the west. The sky had taken on a deep purple, almost black, color. I could feel the humidity rising, smell rain coming and also ozone. Lightning would soon be striking near the viewpoint. Rainbow Point is notorious for lightning, and the last thing I wanted was to have one of the visitors on my walk fried. I shortened the guided walk, getting the visitors back to the viewpoint before the lightning and rain reached us. Park visitors have been killed by lightning at Bryce Canyon. Just as we returned to the parking lot, small hail stones began to pelt us, followed by rain, with lightning snapping across the sky. Thunder reverberated in the air around us. I took shelter along with a number of visitors in the information kiosk at the viewpoint. Lightning bolts starting hitting the ground and trees around us, the crack and boom heard the same instant the flash lit up the sky. The bolts hit so close, several visitors' hair began sticking straight out from the static electricity. One bolt hit a tree no more than 100 feet from the kiosk, causing some visitors to scream. The storm only lasted about fifteen minutes before the rain tapered off, the wind died down, and rays of sunlight began to poke through the clouds. The orographic thunderstorm moved off to the east, sending virga rain (which never reaches the ground) to the desert below.

Once the danger of lightning had past, I walked out to the viewpoint to have a look around, enjoying the smell of wet spruce, pine and fir. Not far off to the west, I saw a low-lying cloud with a strange bluish tinge to it. I was thinking, *Man, that sure is a strange-looking cloud*, when I saw a telltale lick of flame reach above a treetop. Forest fire! The lightning had started a fire! My heart started racing, and the adrenaline began pumping. My first wildfire, and I was the only park ranger on the scene. I grabbed my portable radio from my belt and called headquarters eighteen miles away. I was so excited the first word that came out of my mouth was, "Fire!" I swallowed and said into the radio, "The forest is burning. I need help!"

In a calm voice, dispatch called back, "Who is this, and where is the fire's location?"

Excited, I yelled, "About one-half mile from me!"

There was a moment of silence, then, in a calm voice but with a little irritation, the dispatcher said, "Who and where are you?"

I yelled back into the radio, "Jeff, at the viewpoint. The fire is burning just below me!"

Once again a moment of silence, and the dispatcher said in a voice with more irritation, "What viewpoint?"

I yelled, "Rainbow Point. Send help. I'm heading for the fire!" *My God,* I was thinking. *A forest fire is burning in the park. I have to put it out and save the trees, the wildlife. What would Bambi think if I failed? Meanwhile, dispatch is bothering me with mundane facts like who and where I am. They don't even know where I am. What's wrong with them?*

I ran to my patrol vehicle, opened the trunk and started pulling out my fire gear.

In 1976 the Park Service was not really up to speed on firefighting. Seasonal employees were not given formal fire training, so I did not really know what to do other than use water and dirt to put a fire out. I learned that in Boy Scouts. At the first of the summer, I was issued a Nomex shirt and pants, a hard hat, and a pair of Nomex gloves, and that was it. No one gave me a fire shelter or said we had to have fire boots or discuss safety or what to do if one encountered a fire. Each patrol vehicle did carry a shovel, a bladder bag full of water, and a pulaski—a tool similar to an ax but designed by a firefighter. It has the blade of an ax for cutting trees or shrubs on one end and a flat blade for digging up grass and dirt and cutting roots on the other—a great tool for digging a fire line through heavy brush. The bladder bag is a four-gallon rubber bag with a quarter-inch-diameter hose about three feet long attached at one end with a nozzle. By pumping an apparatus above the nozzle that is carried on the back like a backpack, a firefighter can spray a mist of water to cool down small flames.

I put on the gloves, yellow Nomex shirt, grabbed the shovel, pulaski, and bladder bag and headed back to the viewpoint. By this time, a crowd had gathered, watching the smoke and occasionally seeing a small flame through the trees. Everyone saw me coming and moved aside, leaving a path for me. As I passed through the crowd, I heard a low murmur about the firefighter, and I thought to myself, *This is cool, the firefighter heading to the front lines, everyone cheering me on. Yeah, our hero!* I kept waiting for some beautiful female to burst out of the crowd and fall at my feet holding onto my ankles. She would have tears in her eyes and say, "I want to have your children." "Sorry ma'am," I would say, "but I have to go battle a raging forest fire."

Without looking at the smoke or acknowledging the visitors, I stepped off the path and headed into the woods in what I thought would be an easy jaunt to the fire. Fifteen minutes later, I found myself lost in a dense forest with heavy underbrush, hardly being able to walk. I had no idea where the fire was, I could not smell smoke or see flames. Thirty minutes later, I decided I better head back up hill and find some place to spot the smoke and get my bearings. An hour had passed since I stepped off the viewpoint, and I showed back up at the same place. The crowd that had sent the hero on his way was smaller but seemed curious why the hero was back. The smoke was still visible, the fire not out. Why had this great firefighter, this macho, good-looking, cool guy showed back up at the viewpoint with the fire still burning? I was hot, sweaty, covered in dirt and had a few scratches from the thick underbrush. The cool, macho firefighter who had left the viewpoint was now a humbler man.

Meanwhile, back at headquarters, the cavalry had been gearing up, all two of them. By the time I had stumbled back to the viewpoint, the troops were just arriving in the park wildland fire engine. Seeing me at the viewpoint, they walked over. Though they looked me up and down, seeing me, the rookie, sweaty and dirty, they at least had the courtesy not to say anything and turned their attention to the fire. Both had fought forest fires before. The permanent employee, Joe, pulled out a map and compass, oriented the map and took a compass bearing towards the smoke.

Duh, I thought, *a compass and map. I should have used mine*, which were in the pocket of my fire shirt. I had forgotten I even had them.

Joe looked at the map and said, "This dirt road two miles below the viewpoint will take us to within a 100 yards or so of the fire. We can then traverse along the contour of the hillside without having to climb up or walk down to it." Looking at me he said, "It is better to approach a fire from the side or below, with the wind to your back, not from above since the fire could blow up and burn up hill, killing you in the process."

Of course, I, the cool, macho firefighter, had started walking into the jaws of death, heading downhill towards the fire in thick vegetation with no safety zone, no place to go if the fire had blown up. I was thinking I was lucky to still be alive. In just a few minutes, I had learned several valuable lessons. Do not just jump off the side of a road into thick brush without figuring out where the hell I was and where the hell the fire is burning. Do not walk downhill to a fire with lots of unburned fuel between me and it, and, by all means, keep my cool. I had for the past hour been running around like Chicken Little yelling, "The sky's falling! The sky's falling!"

We reached the fire after a short drive in the engine and traversed across a steep slope. We found a large ponderosa pine with the fire burning near the top of the tree and slowly creeping down its trunk, still thirty feet off the ground. I was carrying the bladder bag and immediately pointed the nozzle at the flames and began pumping water up the tree. Joe set his chain saw down, watched me, and said in a calm voice, "What are you doing?"

I yelled back over my shoulder, "Putting the fire out!" The pitiful stream of water was not even reaching halfway up the tree to the flames.

Joe said, "Hold on there, honcho. Take a break and save the water. We'll need it later."

Ah, the humble Jeff, the I-have-no-idea-what-I-am-doing Jeff. I sat down and waited, wiping sweat and dirt from my eyes. Joe, calm as if nothing out of the ordinary was happening, slowly got the saw ready, put on the protective gear, and then sized up the tree.

Joe, a veteran firefighter, had fought a number of fires over the years and knew that a fire in the top of a single tree was not going to go anywhere. The rainstorm had dumped enough rain to soak the forest. The sun was setting and the temperature dropping. There was little chance anything other than the one burning tree would ignite. On the other hand, I had been thinking if we do not put this fire out immediately the entire world would ignite into one huge flaming inferno. The other more important thing Joe knew that I didn't know was that we just went on overtime. Joe was not in any big hurry to put this fire out. We needed to be safe and aggressive with fire, but it wasn't going anywhere, and, hey, overtime money was gravy. Looked good on the next paycheck. Anyway, Bambi would probably be happier if we let the fire burn a few trees; it would open up the dense forest, allow some browse to grow. Deer don't eat trees or at least they prefer other things.

We spent the next hour clearing some dense vegetation away from where we needed to drop the tree. Joe cut the heavy brush and small trees while the two of us cleared out the grass and other vege-tation. Meanwhile, it had grown dark. The burning top of the tree lit up the surrounding woods like a big candle. The torch of the Statue of Liberty beckoning to everyone all around. In the dark, while watching the flames, I realized for the first time that this fire had actu-ally been started by lightning and not some careless human striking a match. That fascinated me. My first wildfire, not a campfire burning inside a ring of rock or fire grate in a campground. I wondered what our ancestors thought about fire before they started using it for heat-ing and cooking. Did they run away in fear, or did the flames and the heat fascinate them? Something that was good and not bad? Watching the flames suddenly made me hungry. I wish I had brought some marshmallows.

The ponderosa had a trunk about forty-eight inches in diame-ter, the tallest tree on the hillside. It towered above the other trees, and I could see why this tree had been hit by lightning. Joe started up the Stihl chain saw with a twenty-eight-inch bar and lined it up with the base of the tree. He began to cut, with Fred and I backing him up as spotters. Sawdust and pieces of wood began to fly, covering our heads and shoulders. I wished the tree hadn't had to be cut down, but the policy of the 1970s was to put out all fires. We had no other way to put out this one. Joe use to be a logger, cutting trees for a lumber company in the Pacific Northwest before he joined the Park Service. To him this ponderosa pine was nothing compared to the giant fir and redwoods of California. In twenty minutes, using the saw and some wedges, Joe neatly dropped the tree into the area we had cleared. One hour later my first wildfire was out. We had kicked the fire beast's butt. Later in my career, on other fires, I would learn that we had only kicked a baby fire beast's infant tush that night. I would encounter far larger butts, some that would kick mine.

I learned a lot on that first fire even though it was a one-tree fire. I at least lost my virginity on a small fire; some of the rookie fire-fighters from the crew I took to Yellowstone National Park twelve years later witnessed some of the most intense fire behavior I had ever seen. Some of my crew had never been on a fire before and did not know what to expect; they were as naive as I was in 1976. In 1988 it was my job to calm down the kids chomping at the bit to take on the beast. They had the shit scared out of them when the beast bit back. The beast fooled me in 1976; I thought that firefighting was a piece of cake. Since 1976, I have had a lot of fire training and seen a lot of fires. Fire training and a physical endurance test is now required of all firefighters; there should never be another case of an over-eager, rookie, dingbat firefighter running off into dense woods towards a forest fire with no idea what he or she is doing.

2

The Phenomena of Life may be Liken unto a Dream, a Phantasm,
a Bubble, a Shadow, the Glistening in Dew, or Lightning Flash;
and thus they ought to be Contemplated.

—The Buddha in the Immutable Sutra

Utah 1977

Since my job was only seasonal at Bryce Canyon, I accepted a job during the off season as a school teacher in a private school in New York, teaching environmental education. Environmental education was another dream job, and I loved working outdoors in the deciduous woods during the fall. The red leaves of maple trees and oranges of oaks with cool clear mornings and a sapphire-colored sky only seen in October was my favorite time of year. For several weeks, after returning to New York from the wide open views of the West, I had this strange, restless, almost claustrophobic, feeling that I did not understand. Being in a classroom , I found myself uneasy and jittery. Going outside did not seem to help. The feeling slowly began to fade away. After my first month of work, I had a long weekend, and my wife and I drove to Cape Cod, Massachusetts. On our first night, we took a long romantic walk along a beach and sat out on a rocky point, watching a full moon rise over the water. It was then that I realized what that uneasy feeling had been. Back in New York there was no wide, panoramic view, everything was closed in because of the trees. Seeing the moon rise over the water made me realize how much I missed the openness of the West.

Once I understood the problem, I felt better. I knew we would be back at Bryce Canyon the following summer, and I dreamed about working full time in a national park someplace in the West. I enjoyed my teaching job, but it did not give me the freedom or diversity that I had at Bryce Canyon. Though I did get to work outside every day, using the outdoors as my classroom, I could not wait to get back to Utah. The winter months passed slowly but finally gave way to spring. The day school let out, we again headed into the sunset. My spirit soared when, once again driving across the plains of eastern Colorado, I saw the rocky mountains slowly rise into view.

That summer, I spent a large portion of my time working alone in the back country, monitoring golden eagles and other raptors, fixing fences, riding horse patrol, conducting a breeding bird survey, as well as giving guided walks and evening programs. As for wildland fires, the park had only a few that summer, none of them large in size. As fires go, they were not big except that one of them became a major crossroad in my life.

When reflecting back on one's life, each of us can probably think of decisions or events that were pivotal in changing the direction our lives were heading. There have been several in my life, where I chose one path over another. I do not believe our destiny is preordained but can be controlled by our actions, thoughts, or events.

There have been four big events in my life. The first was leaving Texas Tech University in Lubbock, Texas, and moving to New England, living in Maine in the summer and Cape Cod in the winter. The second was when I tried to be a hermit in a log cabin in Maine during the winter. I got cabin fever and decided to go back to school. The third was meeting the love of my life, now my spouse of twenty-three years, in the woods of Maine, and the last big event occurred while on a small fire at Bryce Canyon National Park in 1977.

While on road patrol at Bryce Canyon in late July 1977, the day started cloudless with the temperature quickly rising as the morning progressed. My road patrol shift started before dawn, and I watched the sun rise over a plateau twenty miles to the east. The first rays of the day bathed the rocks around me in red. A hermit thrush sang its harmonious song from a nearby thicket. All felt right with the world, and I was probably the happiest man alive at that time. I got out of the patrol car and spent a few minutes doing some Tai Chi.

By the middle of the day, clear skies gave way to cumulus clouds that quickly built into thunderheads. Just before my shift ended, a thunderstorm moved overhead, producing little rain but lots of lightning. The relative humidity was probably in the teens before the rain, and most of it fell as virga. Because of the amount of dry lightning I saw hitting the ground, I decided to drive to a viewpoint and check for fires. I parked at the end of the parking lot, next to a large, standing ponderosa pine that had died years ago. With the thunderstorm still overhead and lightning striking in the area, it seemed unsafe to get out of the car. Suddenly, in a brilliant flash of light and an instant boom, a lightning bolt had hit the snag. Branches blew off the top and crashed down onto the patrol car. Instinctively, I ducked below the dash. The branches were not large enough to dent the car or break windows, but my heart pounded in my chest such that I thought it would explode. I had seen the result of trees hit by lightning, seen trunks splits right down the middle and both sides fallen, almost as if Paul Bunyan had split the tree with one mighty chop. After the branches stopped falling, I looked up. The top of the snag was burning. Hungry flames ate into the dry wood. But, before I called the fire into dispatch, it started to rain. The fire was quickly extinguished, leaving only a small wisp of flame and smoke.

I moved the patrol car a safe distance and watched the few remaining red coals and tendrils of smoke fade away. This happens with most lightning-caused fires. Most never have a chance to be born, a miscarriage of the fire beast. The storm moved on, and I got out and walked over to the railing. Below the rim, off in the distance, I saw two thin columns of bluish smoke. Lightning had started two fires about a mile apart in a piñon/juniper forest. This time, instead of grabbing the radio and screaming into it as I had the previous summer, I was mister cool. I pulled out the map and made sure of my location and the fires'. Calmly, almost in a whisper, I called dispatch. *Ah, the veteran firefighter*, I thought. *Not the rookie anymore.*

Dispatch called back, saying only two of us were available that day for initial attack. I was to gear up. The other person called on the radio and said he was on his way to my location, E.T.A. thirty minutes. If more resources were needed, we were to call. Instead of running off to battle, I waited for the other firefighter, watching the smoke columns. They were small and not growing. They appeared to be one-tree fires. Once the other firefighter arrived, we stood at the railing and planned our attack. The fires burned at the top of a ridge jutting out from the plateau about two miles from our location. The map indicated no roads nearer the fires than our present location. Because both appeared to be one-tree fires, we decided to split up, each taking a fire. Each of us had a shovel, pulaski, and a bladder bag full of water. This time before I took off from the viewpoint, I pinpointed my fire on a map and laid out the best route to get to it. Unlike the year before, I did not get lost in the woods. About one hour later, I found myself at the base of the ridge just below the fire. Amazing what a topographic map and compass can do.

With the sky cleared overhead to only a few small clouds, the afternoon had again turned hot and dry. As I suspected, the fire was burning at the base of a single piñon tree. Since I was down in the bottom of a ravine, I started up the ridge towards the fire. While climbing, I glanced up and noticed that one of the small clouds had grown a bit bigger and darker, but nothing like the thunderstorm that had started the fire. I did not think much of it other than it was causing some erratic winds. I could see the flames kicking up, looking for more fuel to burn. But, along that ridge little understory vegetation grew, and the trees were spaced such that the fire had nothing else to burn. There was little chance this fire was going anywhere.

I reached the fire and took off the bladder bag, deciding to save the water. Using the pulaski, I started scraping the burning coals away from the tree and spreading them around beneath the tree on bare ground, and using the water sparingly, I covered the coals in wet dirt. This year when I first arrived at the park, all the seasonal help received some fire training and learned about the basic fire triangle made up of oxygen, fuel, and heat. If any one of the three is removed a fire will go out. Water cooled the fire, and dirt deprived it of oxygen. While working, I forgot about that small dark cloud above me. I stopped to wipe some sweat from my eyes, when suddenly, without warning, in a brilliant flash and a loud clap of thunder, a lightning bolt hit a piñon tree about twenty feet from where I stood. I happened to be looking in the direction of the tree and saw the flash. The lightning bolt knocked the top of the tree off, and either an electrical shock passed through the ground or my being startled made me lose my balance. I fell over backwards, rolling part of the way down the ridge, until stopping against a shrub. "God damn that was close," I muttered, "twice in one day." Of all days to almost be hit by lightning; this day I happened to be particularly paranoid.

The day before while on road patrol, I had received a report over the radio about a visitor being hit by lightning at Bryce Point. I was not far from Bryce Point, so, with my patrol lights flashing, I drove there in a couple of minutes—first on scene. The victim had been unfortunate enough to be walking back to his car when a lightning bolt hit a tree next to him. The electricity passed down the trunk of the tree and arced from a dead branch to the side of his head, passing down the left side of his body into the ground. When I arrived, he was lying on the sidewalk on his back with several people kneeling next to him. Most of his clothing had either been blown or burned off, and pieces lay around him. Later, I was told he had been wearing a leather hat, but the biggest piece of leather we could find was the size of a fifty-cent coin. It looked like he had stepped on a land mine. I also found out he use to have a full beard and a thick head of long hair, but when I saw him all that was left was singed stubble close to the skin. Each strand was blackened and curled. The smell of burned hair and flesh and the sweet smell of blood hung in the air. The lightning had even burned his eyebrows.

Blood oozed from his mouth and ears, and, because he was on his back, he was actually drowning in it, with a gurgling sound coming from his mouth. He was fighting for air. His eyes were open, but he was in shock, mumbling incoherent sounds and not responding to my words. I rolled him to his side and saw that he had first and second degree burns down his left side. Even on his side he was still choking, so I reached into his mouth to clear his airway. I pulled out teeth and bone. His mouth had been shattered by the blast. I almost gagged a the sight of the blood, bits of bone, and teeth in my hand. I thought he had little chance of living. His pulse was weak, his skin cold and clammy—he was in shock.

It took only about fifteen minutes, though it seemed forever after I had arrived, that the park ambulance drove up with two emergency medical technicians onboard. We got the victim on oxygen, strapped him onto a stretcher, loaded him into the ambulance and headed for the nearest hospital, thirty miles away in Panguitch. I drove the ambulance while the EMTs worked on keeping him alive.

He had lost a lot of blood but was still breathing when we reached the Emergency Room and the doctors and medical staff took over. After he was whisked away into the emergency room, the three of us sat on the floor letting the tension from the past hour drain away.

I found out later the man did survive, but had lost most of his teeth, had to have reconstructive surgery on a shattered jaw and had permanently lost his hearing. The blood coming from his mouth was mostly because he had ruptured some alveoli in his lungs. His lungs had actually been filling with blood. The blood coming from his ears was due to ruptured eardrums. He was lucky to have lived.

Now here I was, the very next day getting knocked down a hill by a lightning bolt. Lying part way down the ridge, all I could think of was what lightning had done to the guy the day before. The last thing I wanted was to end up as toast. If I had been hit by lightning, no one would have seen it happen, and I could have lain on the ground, drowning in my own blood for hours. I jumped up from where I was lying and ran down to the bottom of the ridge. "That fire can burn all it wants. I'll be damned if I am going to sacrifice myself," I said to myself. Bambi and the other wildlife in the area will just have to thank me later for saving them. I looked up. The cloud that had tried to kill me was still small and innocent looking. I was thinking maybe the big enchilada in the sky was pissed off at me. It sure seemed like someone was trying to tell me something.

I sat in the bottom of the drainage for thirty minutes until not a single cloud loomed above me. Finally, constantly looking all around and expecting some lightning bolt to be lurking from behind a tree, I walked back up the ridge and starting working on the fire again. I was just nervous enough to believe that any minute a lightning bolt might come shooting out of the clear blue sky, leaving my body parts spread all over the ridge top. I finally got the fire cooled off, with no visible smoke left in the air. When no clouds appeared, I finally began to relax. I leaned against the base of a nearby tree and waited through the rest of the burn period that day to make sure the fire stayed out. It was peaceful to just lie with my back against the trunk of the tree and enjoy the last couple hours of the afternoon. I began thinking what a great job I had, working in the outdoors, getting paid to do something I would probably do for free. I worked in a national park that millions of people come to visit on vacation. I had lost count of the number of times park visitors had said I was so lucky to be working in such a beautiful place. While sitting up on the ridge, I realized I was indeed content with my life. The pay was not the greatest, but the benefits sure were. Then I began to think about the guy hit by lightning and how close I had come to getting blasted into oblivion. I thought may be I need to be a little humbler and appreciate the great life I was living day by day instead of hoping for something better in the future.

I realized that afternoon while sitting under the tree that I really wanted to spend the rest of my career working for the National Park Service and not be a school teacher. It was a great way to spend one's life, getting to do such a variety of things. One day doing a patrol in the back country, another day giving an evening program or fighting a forest fire or monitoring an eagle nest. Working for the National Park Service, I still could spend a considerable amount of time educating the public on a variety of topics, so, in a sense, I would still be a teacher.

Using my bare hands I checked the trunk of the burned tree and the ground around it for any heat. I used up the last of the water in the bladder bag to give everything a good soaking. The sun was beginning to slowly sink behind a mountain off to the west, and it was time for me to start walking out. I called my partner, who was on the other fire and asked if he needed any help. He called back, saying his was out, so no assistance was needed. I decided to follow the ridge back up to the top of the plateau, where my vehicle was parked, instead of the way I had walked in. About one hour later, I was nearing the top. I stopped to take a look around. Only a sliver of sun could still be seen, and the sky was turning from blue to black. The rock all around me had changed from orange and white to a dark red. There was no wind, and it was so quiet, the silence left a ringing in my ear. I heard a faint soft whistle and looked to my left to see a golden eagle flying towards me, following the late-day thermals along the edge of the plateau. Reflecting the last bit of sunlight, the mane on the back of its head showed a brilliant gold, almost white, giving the bird a mystical appearance. The gold from the mane left a trail of stardust just behind the bird as if someone waved a sparkler around on the Fourth of July. The eagle's wings were spread out six feet wide and not beating; the bird expended no energy as it glided on the last warm air of the day. The source of the whistling sound had not been a call but the sound of the air passing through the feathers of its wings. The great bird soared past me at eye level with one wing tip so close I could see the intricate detail of each brown feather. I could have reached out and touched it, but I was so mesmerized that I just stood there. When the eagle came abreast of me, it turned its head, and the two of us made eye contact. I could see a golden glint in its dark brown eyes. The yellow line between its lower and upper mandibles seemed upturned in a smile. I shuddered, closing my eyes, suddenly visualized myself flying, the world beneath me. I felt as if I had entered the body of the eagle and could see the world through its eyes, watching the land pass beneath its wings. I felt no fear from the eagle, only warmth; it seemed to accept me as an equal. A feeling came over me, and I sensed the eagle saying, "You belong here, my friend." I realized at that moment I did belong there.

I opened my eyes. The eagle had turned its head back towards the last rays of the setting sun, and it passed on along the ridge and out of sight around a bend. I felt a cold chill go down my back, making the hairs on the back of my neck stand up. I knew at that moment that I would get a permanent job working for the National Park Service and that my vision would come true. I would dedicate my life to protecting the eagle and its brothers and sisters with all my heart and soul.

Looking towards the setting sun, with the shovel in one hand and the pulaski in the other, I raised both arms above my head, a silent tribute to Mother Earth and all her creatures. The last rays of sunlight disappeared, the sky darkened, and the first stars began to twinkle in the sky overhead. A tear rolled down my cheek; I was home.

With a warm glow in my heart, I turned and continued up the ridge to the top and the patrol car. "Whew, what a day," I said to myself. Sometimes it takes a lightning bolt or two to make me realize the path I am on is leading in the right direction. The fear of being lost on a wandering path disappeared; I finally found myself in friendly territory.

3

I Meant to do My Work Today
but a Brown Bird Sang in the Apple Tree
and a Butterfly Flitted Across the Field
and All the Leaves where calling Me
and the Wind went Sighing over the Land
Tossing the wind to and fro
and a Rainbow Held its Shining Hand
So What Could I do but Laugh and Go

— A Children's Song

New Mexico 1979

I did become a permanent employee with the federal government, not with the National Park Service, but with the Bureau
of Land Management (BLM). I worked for the National Park
Service as a seasonal employee, and I went back to teaching at the private, but just before Thanksgiving I received a phone call from the
BLM, asking if I was interested in a wildlife biologist position as part
of a team conducting a wildlife survey on eleven million acres of BLM
land in New Mexico. My wife and I left New York when school let out
for the Christmas holidays, and I drove west to the Chi Desert.

Working as a public servant for the federal government does
have its advantages, one of which is not always being stuck behind a
desk. There were many days that I spent on top of a mountain or deep
in a canyon inventorying the public domain of New Mexico. Working
in the "Land of Enchantment" with several other biologists, we

30

would sometimes head out of town on Monday and not come back until Friday. During the week, we would camp out under the stars, rising before dawn to do bird transects and follow up with small mammal, reptile and amphibian transects. We sometimes stayed in towns with names like Magdelina, Datil, Pietown, Quemodo, Grants. These towns still bore evidence of the wild cattle ranching era of the 1800s. New Mexico still had cowboys who walked bow-legged from years of being on horseback. Folks who lived in these towns or on a remote ranch miles down long dirt roads, were third or fourth generation ranchers, rugged as the land on which they lived. Many ranchers in New Mexico only own a portion of the land they ranch, leasing the rest from BLM or the United States Forest Service. They are an independent lot and often did not take kindly to young college kids like myself, trying to tell them how to manage the land they have known all their lives. They wanted to be left alone, but, since they leased land from the federal government, they had to put up with us. I always treated these people with respect and honesty and became friends with a number of them. One individual I got to know was a living legend, a remnant of the Old West.

South of Grants, New Mexico, twenty miles down a dirt road lived an old cowboy who use to be a deputy, a bounty hunter in the early 1900s, and a rancher later on when he retired. No one knew how old he was; he could have been 100 years old for all I knew. His face was as wrinkled as a prune and as rough as sandpaper. He had a long gray beard that hung to his stomach. The middle of it was stained permanently brown from tobacco juice. He wore a black ten-gallon cowboy hat, dusty and sweat stained, always had on a greasy leather vest that was years old, and wore a pistol strapped to his waist no matter where he went. He kept a big knife in his boot. He had an old four-wheel-drive GMC Jimmy and always drove right down the middle of the road. The locals on the same roads looked out for him and moved to the shoulder when he drove by. He never budged an inch. He also kept a pistol in his glove compartment, a rifle on his dashboard, and a shotgun in the back seat.

There were many stories about this old cowboy — told by other ranchers or by him. How many were actually true, I had no idea. The stories were about the bad guys he had hung, and the gun battles he had been in. He had been wounded once in a gunfight, and on his right shoulder he had a small round scar from a bullet. He claimed that another deputy had dug the bullet out with a red-hot knife by the light of a campfire. He now lives in a small cabin with his wife and a few dogs. The yard was full of broken down trucks and rusted equipment. I use to stop at his cabin and spend time talking to him when I needed to enter his ranch. When dealing with cattle rustlers or thieves, he told me he had no problem taking someone in dead or alive. One story I heard in a local café in Grants had him riding into Grants on horseback leading a pack horse with two bodies draped over its back. Some claimed he had thousands of silver dollars buried in the walls of his cabin. When I knew him, he would often lapse into the past, speaking of it as if it were the present. He liked government employees, but I was wary of him because he carried so many weapons and sometimes would lapse into moments of silence when he seemed to be someplace else. I feared he might be thinking me a cattle thief or crook and bring me in dead or alive strapped over the back of a horse.

During the third winter I worked for BLM, the old cowboy disappeared from his cabin without taking a horse or his Jimmy. A couple days passed before his wife reported him missing. She said it was not the first time he had wandered off into the wilderness. A half-hearted search by the local sheriff and deputies produced no results, and, after a few days of searching in snowstorms and below freezing temperatures, everyone thought he was dead. No one as old as he could have survived. Most thought he had wandered off into the vast roadless area between Grants and Quemado to die.

I spent time driving dirt roads in the El Malpais and hiking out into the lava flow looking for him, but I did not find him either. Unbelievably, after being missing for almost two weeks, he showed up in Quemado in a snowstorm almost a hundred miles south of his cabin. He was half-starved and hypothermic, muttering that he had been on the trail of some bad guy. He had his pistol and rifle with him and nothing else. Wearing only a wool shirt, pants, the dirty vest, cowboy boots, and his hat, he didn't even have a coat or gloves when he stumbled into Quemado. He had slept on the ground in the dead of winter, living off game he had shot for two weeks.

He passed on in 1984, a chapter of the Old West dying with him. I wish I had spent more time listening to his tales.

Just out the back door of the old cowboy's cabin stretched a large lava flow called the El Malpais. I surveyed wildlife and explored numerous lava tubes in the El Malpais, laying the groundwork for what is now a national monument. Even though I still dreamed of working for the National Park Service, little did I realize that some of the inventory work I did, would lead to the creation of a national monument.

A co-worker of mine, an archeologist, spent the same time working with a crew surveying the land for cultural resources, while my crew inventoried biological resources. All of us were young and full of piss and vinegar. We loved our jobs. After a hot, dusty day of work my *compadre*, the other archeologists, biologists, and I would usually meet down a dirt road somewhere in the El Malpais. After a few beers, someone would get out a guitar. We would throw steaks directly on the coals of piñon and juniper wood campfires and eat them with jalapeno beans and salad. When the moon came up over the nearby extinct volcanic craters, we would end up dancing naked like the humpbacked flute player of ancient times, dancing around, over and through a roaring fire with burning ash billowing up into the sky. We were wild banshees, scaring ghosts and wildlife for miles around. Sometimes the old cowboy would show up and spend the night with us, telling us stories about the Old West. He would sleep on the ground without a blanket. The cool didn't seem to bother him.

Also working for the BLM, my duties included firefighting. I took many training courses and worked my way up from a firefighter to a qualified chain saw grunt, water pumps expert, engine boss, and squad boss. One evening during my first summer in New Mexico, two of us were sent to mist net for bats at a tinaja southwest of Socorro. There had been some thunderstorms in the area that afternoon but no reports of fires. Heading out, I was not thinking about firefighting and wore flip-flops, shorts, and a T-shirt. The only fire gear in the truck was a shovel and a pulaski. We drove down a dirt road, turned around a bend, and discovered, all by itself, a burning bush. Just this one bush, burning. *Uh oh,* I thought, *God is speaking to me again.* Last time it was lightning, this time a burning bush. This was getting serious, Old Testament type of stuff. I was afraid God was going to send me a new set of commandments and send me on a quest to save all the sinners of the world. All six billion of us.

Using the radio in the truck, I called dispatch and reported the fire. Their skepticism was evident; they did not quite believe there was a wildfire consisting of only one burning bush, but they told us to put it out and to monitor it for a couple of hours. I pulled the shovel out of the truck and walked over in my flip-flops, dug the shrub out of the ground, turned it upside down and buried it in its hole. This took all of ten minutes. My co-worker and I spent the next couple of hours drinking beers and watching the sun set behind a nearby mountain range. Sometimes firefighting can be pretty hard work.

After two hours, we called dispatch and told them the fire was out and continued on to where we were going to catch bats that night, setting the mist nets out shortly after dark. As the sky darkened, the stars began to blink on one at a time and then by the millions. With no air pollution, the night sky took my breath away. The Milky Way looked like a river flowing across the sky. The night was quiet enough that we could hear the faint clicking of the bats, calling out their echo-locating sounds as they flew over the tinaja in search of insects and water. The nets set up over the small tinaja out in the desert among creosote bush and ocotillo cactus, began to snag them. We kept the nets up all night and checked them every half-hour. In the desert these tinajas are critical to bats and other wildlife, and the bats feed on insects that concentrate around the springs, and they drink from the pond while in flight. The mesh of the nets was too fine to allow the bat's echo-location to warn them of where it was. We caught about fifty bats of six different species—a busy night.

Bats are fascinating animals: flying mice with poor eyesight but great hearing. One of my favorite species—the hoary bat—is one of the larger bats in North America with orange to red coloration on the underside of the wings. When we caught them, I could hear them screaming from quite a distance away, ripping and tearing the fine mesh of the net. Sometimes they would chew their way through the net before I could get to them, and extracting them from the net was always a challenge. They would chew on my fingers and had sharp teeth, mandating the use of gloves to keep them from turning my hands to a bloody pulp. Even through leather gloves, although they could not break the skin, they could bite hard enough to hurt. Bats come in all sizes from that of a robin to a small mouse. Our job was to identify the species, sex them, and then let them go.

Quite by accident while on a ten-acre grass fire, three of us rediscovered one of the largest concentrations of Mexican free-tailed bats in New Mexico. We had been dispatched to the fire in the early afternoon. We found it burning near the edge of a large lava flow, one of the many found in New Mexico. Like the El Malpais, some of these lava flows have tubes and caves formed when lava cooled on the surface, but was still flowing underneath. Once the lava stopped flowing, hollow tubes had formed, sometimes miles long and big enough to accommodate a bus.

Driving a Type V engine, we arrived at the fire a couple of hours before sunset and drove around the fire perimeter with two of us in back with hoses, cooling down the fire with foam and water. There was no need to dig a fire line. The fire was contained by sunset, so we took a break, sitting on hoses on top of the engine, eating supper as the sky darkened. Just when it was getting dark, I happened to notice two dark funnel-like clouds off to the south. The sky was clear so they weren't tornadoes, and the air seemed stable, so they could not have been dust devils. Curious, I jumped off the engine, walked to the cab and retrieved a pair of binoculars. Looking through them, the funnel clouds resolved into millions of bats spiraling a couple of hundred feet up into the sky, where they then leveled off and headed west towards the Rio Grande River. I was astounded. Our wildlife team had been surveying the area for bats for almost a full year, and we had no idea such a concentration of bats existed anywhere near us, other than at Carlsbad Caverns National Park about 150 miles to the southeast.

The columns of bats appeared to be at least a couple of miles out into the lava flow, with no obvious road towards them. Walking through the lava flow at night would be too difficult, so we decided to wait for another day to find out where the bats lived. Besides we were assigned to the fire and could not just go wandering off chasing bats. After mopping up a few remaining hotspots, we left the fire around midnight and drove into town.

When I got to the office after sleeping for five hours, I began digging through the files, looking for anything that might mention this particular bat cave. In the bottom of a file drawer, I found an old topographic map dated 1923, that had an X on it, marked in the middle of a lava flow. Next to the X were the handwritten words "bat cave." The map showed no road leading to the area. I showed the map to the two other guys who had been on the fire, and we all became as excited as if we had found a treasure map with an X indicating "dig here." We asked around the office if anyone knew of a bat cave, but no one else knew anything about it. An adventure was about to begin.

A couple of days later, we loaded a four-wheel-drive truck with mist nets and gear and left town, driving southeast along a two-track dirt road. Once we got to the edge of the lava flow near where the fire had occurred, we started scouting around for a road or trail that might head in the direction we wanted to go. Since no topographic maps indicated a road, we thought we might have to walk in. Hiking over several miles of sharp lava would not be easy. Also trying to find the cave on foot would be like looking for a needle in a hay stack. It didn't help that the name of this lava flow was Jornada Del Muerto, meaning Journey of Death—not exactly encouraging. We had hoped a road or at least an old trail led to the cave. We stopped at a windmill, and I climbed it to get a better look around. Below me, in the direction of the cave, I could see the faint tracks of what looked like an old wagon trail. We had crossed over the trail without noticing it from the ground because it was obscured by vegetation and trampled by the hooves of livestock. Being twenty feet above the ground enabled me to see it. I climbed down, and we drove over to where the trail started. It looked driveable in four-wheel drive, so we entered the lava flow, slowly crawling along over and through the lava. We later found out it actually was a wagon road used by Mexicans at the turn of the century, who traveled to the cave to mine bat guano. The trail had not been used for years and in places was overgrown with vegetation while it wove through and around hills of jagged lava sharp enough to leave cuts in leather boots. I was glad we were driving instead of walking.

After a couple of miles, we came across a diamond-back rattlesnake crossing the trail. The rattlesnake was jet black with pale white diamonds on its back. Animals living on these lava flows are melanistic, including the small mammals, such as mice and pack rats, other snakes, and lizards, enabling them to blend into the surrounding rock. We stopped to let the snake cross the trail and noticed that it had a slight bulge in its middle. Probably one of the mice that lived amongst the lava had become a meal. The rattlesnake slithered into a hole, occasionally rattling its tail to warn us away.

After a two-hour, kidney-bruising ride and one flat tire, we crossed over the top of a ridge and saw a small structure in the distance. The walls were built out of lava rock and covered with a rusted tin roof. We got out to take a look and were immediately overwhelmed by a strong smell of ammonia—bat guano and lots of it. There is no other smell in the world that matches the permeating odor of a large bat roost. Bat guano is deposited on the floor of caves and over years can become many feet thick. We had apparently hit the mother lode; we could smell the guano from a quarter mile away. We followed a trail from the small cabin to the edge of a collapsed lava tube. It was about thirty feet across and twenty feet deep. The tube flowed in a north-south direction with the collapsed portion flowing to the north for about a half a mile toward a small extinct cinder cone. To the south, the tube ended after a couple hundred yards at a dark yawning circular opening—the mouth of a cave. I had spelunked in numerous caves over the years, and it is always exciting to approach the opening of a cave, particularly one new to me.

About fifty yards north of the cave opening along the collapsed section of the lava tube, was a ten-yard-wide area where the roof was still intact, like a bridge crossing over a small river. We walked out on the bridge, and from it we could look down into the opening of the cave. From our vantage, we could see thousands of bats spiraling around just inside the entrance. They were emitting high-pitched clicks easily detected from our location. I had never seen so many bats in one place. We had less than one hour before sunset, so we set up a couple mist nets along the edge of the lava tube and sat down to eat. I figured we would have a busy night catching bats. It was evident from the cabin and the remains of a steel track coming out of the cave that the guano had been mined. At one time it was used to make black gunpowder; it is also a great fertilizer for garden or yard.

Later, in the office I sorted through the records and confirmed that Mexicans had indeed mined the cave at the turn of the century up until 1921. Presumably, this cave had not been touched for fifty-eight years.

Sitting on the lava bridge dangling our feet over the edge, we watched the sun slowly set over a mountain range about fifty miles to the west. There were no sounds other than a slight breeze blowing through the creosote brush and the high-pitched squeaks of a couple million bats. Thrilled with this new discovery, I thought to myself how ironic it was that they are paying me to do this. There are many times over the years that same thought has come to mind. I love working and being in the outdoors.

When I was a kid, my parents took my brother, sisters, and me to Yellowstone National Park. We spent two weeks camping, visiting the geysers, fishing for Yellowstone cutthroat trout and hiking. Those two weeks contain some of my fondest memories from my youth. Yellowstone is what we who work in the Park Service call the "Mother Park," the first preserved large natural park in the world.

One night we attended an evening program to hear a ranger talk about bears. He had built a campfire, and we sat around it near the Madison River as he talked about his adventures with bears in Yellowstone and the natural beauty of the park. I'll never forget looking up at him, his face silhouetted in the light of the fire and partially shaded by his wide-brim felt hat. He seemed tall to me, strong and rugged looking. I remember thinking that I wanted to be that guy. I wanted to experience what he had and work outdoors in a national park. Some kids dream about being firefighters, policemen, or cowboys. I wanted to be a park ranger. Here I was, years later, fulfilling my childhood dream, having the opportunity to view countless sunsets and sunrises and stare into campfires from wild and remote areas throughout the West. I was not yet a permanent park ranger, but I knew it was only a matter of time before I would be working again for the National Park Service.

As the sky grew dark, a mountain range to the east was experiencing a thunderstorm; we could see lightning flashing through the clouds. I suspected that the following day or the next, I would be back out on a fire again.

The sun finally set behind the mountains and the few clouds turned pink, then became blood-red. With the bats flying around in the cave and the red sky, Bela Lugosi in the movie *Dracula* came to mind. Almost on cue, the bats began to exit the cave. Surprisingly, instead of spiraling straight up into the sky, they flew down the lava tube right under our feet and the lava bridge and then spiraled up on the other side of the bridge. With thousands upon thousands of bats flying directly beneath us and then spiraling up so close to us on the other side, it made us feel as though we were right in the middle of the bat flight. At that exact moment, another funnel cloud of bats was emerging from another opening about a quarter mile away from us. This turned out to be the other side of the cave. The bats spiraled up about 100 feet and then leveled off, heading for the Rio Grande River ten miles away.

This bat flight made Carlsbad Cavern's flight look like a few mosquitoes swarming around the nose of a moose. The air was so thick with bats that they touched wings in their attempts to find flying space. Here we were, miles from anywhere, and there were only the three of us to watch it. I have been to Carlsbad many times to explore the cave and watch the bat flight. Though impressive, unfortunately much of the experience is lost when sitting on stone bleachers with several hundred to a thousand visitors and a park ranger or two talking about bat ecology. Carlsbad Caverns has less than a million bats. I was estimating that night at the lava cave that the two flights combined had to be at least three million bats, maybe more. Later, a scientist from New Mexico State University using camera equipment, estimated the population actually closer to five million.

When the spiral of bats was at its peak, two red-tailed hawks appeared from the east. Without hesitation, they flew directly into the bat flight, their talons ready. The bats were so close together that they actually flew into the hawks and each other trying to get out of the way. In just a few seconds, each hawk had caught a bat mid-air. I have observed prairie and peregrine falcons take birds and bats in flight but had never seen or heard of a red-tailed hawk doing it. Buteo hawks do not typically catch prey in flight. The hawks flew off to the west into the sunset, each with a bat still flapping in their talons.

Meanwhile, our nets had caught a couple dozen bats, and we were busy the rest of the night removing, identifying and sexing them. About ninety-eight percent of the bats we caught turned out to be Mexican free-tailed bats, *Tadarida brasiliensis*, which actually means, "withered toad from Brazil." Another common name is guano bat due to its habit of roosting in large colonies. The rest were western pipistrelle and pallid bats. The Mexican free-tailed bat is probably the ugliest bat in North America, with a dull gray to brown coat, short hair and short naked tail not attached to its interfemoral membrane.

The bat also carries a strong ammonia odor from roosting in such large numbers. This bat is famous for its large roosts of millions of bats. The western pipistrelle is smaller and looks like a small bandit with a black facial mask. The pallid bat is a beautiful, longer furred bat, blond in color. All the Mexican free-tailed bats we caught that night were lactating females, so this made it the largest maternity roost in New Mexico.

Once most of the bats had left the cave, we crawled down into it to look around. The cave entrance was as large as a subway tunnel, flat at the bottom with rounded sides and roof. The walls of the cave were smooth but still retained groves engraved by hot lava flowing through it. Parts of the walls were so smooth that the light from our headlamps reflected off the wall.

Just inside the cave entrance, our boots sank into guano over our ankles. The guano had to be several feet deep. Later, we learned that in some places the guano was twenty feet deep. In the light of our headlamps, the surface of the guano appeared to be writhing. Upon closer inspection, we observed thousands of beetles crawling around in the guano. They were feeding on the guano, dead bats, and other organic material. The beetles were dermestid beetles, *Dermestes carnivorous*. Any beetle with a scientific name "carnivorous" does not feed on plants. These beetles feed on flesh and are so thorough that many natural history museums use the dermestid beetle to clean the flesh off of bones for their collections. If they crawl up a pant leg, they can give a pretty nasty bite. While we were wading through the guano, we kept checking our legs for wandering beetles. After that, when I entered the cave, I taped my pant legs closed so nothing could crawl up my legs.

Once when I was a teenager in Texas, I was playing golf at a country club with some buddies. We got stuck behind some little old ladies taking their time, which meant that we hung out a lot waiting for our turn. At the number five hole, I had the misfortune to stand on a fire ant mound without realizing it. Getting bit by a fire ant is no picnic. Some of them had crawled up my leg and started munching on my privates. To my friends' surprise, as well as the little old ladies, I let out a yell and started jumping up and down screaming and slapping at my crotch. It hurt so badly that I unbuckled my pants and dropped them and my underwear right in front of everyone and started yanking ants off, while still jumping up and down screaming. Once my buddies figured out what was happening they starting laughing so hard, they fell to the ground with tears in their eyes. The little old ladies, on the other hand, screamed as loudly as I did. They dropped their clubs, jumped into their golf cart and raced off across the golf course. I pulled my pants back up after I got all the ants off and then lay down on the grass. I was in so much pain I almost passed out. A few minutes later, a country club security guard raced up in a golf cart and jumped out as though prepared to arrest someone. My friends, still red-faced from laughing, told the guard what happened. I lay on the ground moaning. He burst out laughing and my friends broke out laughing all over again. All I could do was moan. The guard gathered up the old ladies' golf clubs and drove off, leaving me in my misery. My privates were swelling, so I headed home, leaving my friends to continue to play. My buddies even had the audacity to thank me for purging the green of the old ladies.

This pleasant memory flashed back to me when I saw the beetles crawling around in the guano. We looked up at the ceiling about twenty feet above us and saw it crawling with bats. Because this cave was a nursery colony, thousand upon thousands of small, young bats with adult bats crawling among them clung to the ceiling. In some places the bats were two or three animals thick. They were in pods of ten thousand or so, scattered across the ceiling of the cave from one side to the other, with most of them squeaking or chirping. The air around us was thick with female bats flying back into the cave to feed their offspring. Occasionally, one of the young bats would fall from the ceiling and land in the guano. If a young bat lost its footing on the ceiling and fell to the floor before it learned to fly, the mother bat did not retrieve it. Once they hit the guano, they had little chance to make it back to the ceiling. The dermestid beetles quickly consumed them. Even adult bats cannot take off directly from the ground, but require a rock or some other object to jump off to get airborne. This meant that an adult bat would also be in trouble if it fell to the cave floor, but most of the skeletons we saw mixed in the guano were those of young bats.

Near the entrance to the cave on a narrow ledge sat a female great horned owl with three fat downy young next to her. The owl ignored our presence and swooped down from the ledge to the floor of the cave, catching a bat that had fallen to the floor. She flew back to her ledge and fed her young, who swallowed them whole with wings and feet sticking out of their beaks before they disappeared. I saw her catch two fallen bats in her talons in a short period of time. The owlets looked fat and happy. In the beam of our headlamps, we also saw a spotted skunk crawling around near the back of the cave in search of the young or old bats fallen from the ceiling. The animals that lived off the bats had a smorgasbord, a never-ending buffet.

The Mexican free-tailed bat is insectivorous and does not hibernate. It migrates to caves in Mexico, Central or South America, and even in the Caribbean for the winter. The lava cave remains active with bats for less than six months of the year. Despite the millions of bats in this one cave, bats around the world, including the Mexican free-tailed bat, are in trouble. Their numbers have been declining over the years, giving scientists concern. The causes are many, including harassment. Like snakes and spiders, these winged creatures are feared and despised. Many people shoot them or kill them with a fly swatter if given the chance. Additionally, in many places, particularly in their wintering habitats, bats are losing their prey base and are being contaminated as a result of widespread use of pesticides.

This bat cave was unique from others in that it was a lava cave and not limestone. Most bat colonies are found in cooler and wetter limestone caves. The guano easily breaks down and decomposes under these kinds of conditions. In contrast, in the lava cave the air is warm and dry and bat guano dries rather than decomposes, causing it to accumulate in layers.

During the summer when the bats use the cave and deposit the guano, the dermestid beetles move constantly through the guano, churning up the surface and breaking it down as they consume any flesh they can find. When the bats leave in the fall, the beetles become inactive, waiting until the following spring for the bats to return. The beetles do not reach their peak numbers until later in the summer when the young bats are born. The result is a layer of undisturbed guano with a layer of disturbed guano on top.

My wife wrote her master's thesis researching DDT residues in the guano. A plastic PVC pipe pounded into the guano gave her a core of six or more layered feet and allowed her to analyze the guano by years. The day she took her samples, young bats were just learning to fly. Bats repeatedly landed on her and crawled up her front and back, onto her head and face. They would get to her head and jump off in their juvenile attempts to get airborne. My wife is squeamish about caterpillars, grasshoppers, and spiders; having a bat crawling over her face was not her idea of a fun time. If she grabbed at the bats crawling on her face, however, they would start biting, which would mean she would need rabies shots, so she let them crawl. We all wore respirators to protect us from airborne rabies, and heavy clothes, gloves, and hard hats while we were in the cave to keep the bats from biting us. The only exposed areas of our bodies were parts of our faces and necks. So when the bats got to our faces we just let them climb up onto our hard hats and jump off. It took a lot of will power to let a bat work its way over my face to the top of my head without tearing it off or running in a panic or screaming at the top of my lungs.

With the guano core back in her lab, she cut it open exposing the layers. She was able to date the guano from 1982 back to 1970 and identified the nice layers of churned up guano followed by a thicker lay of undisturbed guano. She then analyzed the quantify of DDE, which is a DDT metabolite. Remember DDT? Rachel Carson's *Silent Spring*, the endangering of the bald eagle and peregrine falcon? My wife found DDE concentrations in every year of the guano, with the highest concentrations found in 1972, the year DDT was banned in this country, and, surprisingly, in 1982, the year the sample of guano was taken.

DDT adversely affects bats, as it does birds and other animals. In the past, DDT was used in this country to control insect pests. Unfortunately, it is still being used in other countries today. Mexico, where most of the Mexican free-tailed bats winter, remains a user of DDT as do countries in Central and South America. When bats and other animals eat insects exposed to DDT, it is stored in the muscle and fat tissue, and levels of DDT accumulate over time. Apparently the bats in this maternity roost were still being exposed.

The Mexican free-tailed bat can consume up to one-third its total body weight in insects each night. A roost of 500,000 individuals could theoretically consume up to four and one-half tons of insects in one night. A population of three to five million bats significantly reduces the insect population, feeding primarily on mosquitoes, a carrier of more disease than any other insect in the world. Even though

DDT was banned in the United States, free enterprise still allows the pesticide to be produced in this country and shipped to third-world countries. So animals like the Mexican free-tailed bat still occasionally die from DDT poisoning even today over twenty-eight years after the banning of DDT. DDT still impacts North American birds and bats that migrate south into sub-tropical and tropical habitats.

In the spring of 1984, I watched hundreds of violet-green swallows and white-throated swifts die along the Colorado River near Moab, Utah. The birds writhed on the ground for no apparent reason, dying an agonizing death. We collected some and had them analyzed, finding DDE residue in their bodies. The birds had just arrived in Moab after their spring migration. During migration, they had used up most of their body fat, and, in the spring of 1984 shortly after they had arrived, a particularly cold spell with rain used up more of their fat tissue. As the fat was consumed, it released the DDE into their systems, killing them. Park employees working at Zion National Park witnessed a similar event happen several years later.

Bats and migratory birds such as warblers, vireos, and fly-catchers are declining, even more today than in the days of Rachel Carson. The reason is more complicated than in Rachel Carson's day when it could be blamed on DDT. Today the decline includes effects of habitat loss, fragmentation of existing habitat, as well as the continued use of pesticides. With the knowledge of what DDT and other pollutants could do to the environment the United States did something in the 1960s and 1970s. The country is better off for all the environmental acts passed, but now politicians in Washington are listening to lobbyists that represent industry and are trying to deregulate many of the acts we fought so hard to get. Politicians seem more interested in pleasing who the lobbyists represent, than their constituents. Our children are aware of what happened in the 1960s but have lived their lives in a world fairly well protected from harmful pesticides and have somewhat cleaner air and cleaner water. They see animals like the bald eagle and peregrine falcon return from the brink of extinction; things look hopeful to them. Our children did not see what DDT did to bats and birds in the sixties; they see no threat today.

Our children may not care enough or be aware enough to stop the elected officials in Washington from watering down the Clean Air Act, the Clean Water Act and the Endangered Species Act, to name a few. It is crucial that we continue to teach our children about the perils of pesticides and stop the politicians from deregulating those acts that protect us and our environment. I want my children and their children to have the opportunity to see five million bats fly out of a cave in a lava flow in New Mexico.

After a long night of catching bats, we watched them fly back into the cave in the early morning hours just before dawn. They came in sporadic numbers unlike the spectacular flight from the evening before. The sky was turning blue and the sun just beginning to peak over the mountains when the last bat, flying at a high rate of speed, whooshed into the cave. The cave grew silent. Yawning, we took down the nets, ate some breakfast, loaded our gear into the truck and headed for town. What a glorious night it had been. After getting back to the office, we found out the cave was actually on an old Spanish Land Grant and was not on BLM land. We received permission from the owners to access the cave, and during the next couple of years, continued studying the bats and brought in scientists for research, including my wife. The Nature Conservancy became interested and negotiated in purchasing the cave and the land around it to protect it from future disturbances. The bats are now protected at their maternity roost—at least a few months of each year.

4

Physical nature lies at our feet shackled with a hundred chains. What of the control of human nature? Do not point to the triumphs of psychiatry, social service, or the war against crime. Domination of human nature can only mean the domination of every man by himself.
— Johan Huizinga, Dutch Historian

New Mexico 1979

*L*ooking out the window of the school bus, I could see the smoke plume billow into the late afternoon sky. All the talking around me stopped as everyone looked out the window. An occasional tree burst into flames, sending black smoke into the air, and some of the firefighters would "ohh or ahh," like watching a fireworks display. I was part of a Type II hand crew assigned to this fire in western New Mexico. The fire appeared to be several hundred acres in size, burning on the southeast side of a steep mountain near the Continental Divide. As we pulled into fire camp, engines, trucks, and firefighters were busy coming and going. The fire had started earlier in the day, and resources for an extended attack were just arriving. The fire was very active; occasionally another tree exploded like a Roman candle or the fire made a short run through the tree canopy up the mountainside. The vegetation was piñon/juniper, ponderosa pine, and a fairly healthy understory of grass and herbaceous plants. Getting up from his seat, the crew boss told us to hang tight while he checked in and found out what our assignment would be. I figured it was going to be a night shift. When I was in college pulling all-nighters studying for exams, I swore I would never spend another whole night awake, unless it was purely for fun, but here I was during the fire season spending an even greater percentage of time awake at night than I had in college. I guess I must be having fun fighting the fire beast. At least I was getting paid to stay up all night. This assignment was probably going to be another twenty-four-hour time period with no sleep. I had started work at 7:00 A.M. that morning, and I was sure I would not close my eyes until eight or nine the next morning at the earliest.

The crew boss came back and confirmed my thoughts. "Gear up, folks. It's show time," he said. "Our mission for the night is to build line from an anchor point at the southeast corner of the fire across the bottom, hook around the fire's lower southwest flank and start building line uphill, hopefully pinching it into a rocky talus area near the top of the mountain by morning."

He passed around a topographic map showing the fire's location on the side of the mountain. As I looked at the map, what bothered me was the part where we had to build line along the bottom of the fire; it appeared to cross a rocky chute, or chimney. Looking up at the mountain I saw it and found the chute was indeed filled with boulders with scattered ponderosa pine. The fire in this area actively burned trees and clumps of mountain mahogany as well as grasses. Chimneys, or chutes, formed natural chimneys, funneling air. Fires had been known to make incredible runs up chimneys, trapping and killing firefighters inside it. At mid-slope on the mountain, the fire would probably be actively burning after dark because of a potential thermal belt. A thermal belt is commonly located at mid-slope on a mountain and usually has the highest temperatures, the lowest relative humidity and the highest fire danger. This is the result of cold air flowing down into the lower elevations, forcing warmer air uphill. A fire in the thermal belt can stay active throughout the night instead of lying down because of cooler air and a higher relative humidity. I feared that the intense heat from the fire might have cracked and loosened some of the large boulders in the chute, freeing them to come crashing down the mountain unexpectedly. We were going to have to build a fire line across the chute where those boulders would be falling. Working at night, our field of view would be severely limited; smoke and the glare from flames would restrict it even farther, but since we all considered ourselves to be macho firefighters, we did not question the IC's decision to build line through the chute. I had built line under those conditions before and gotten away with it; what was one more time tempting fate? At least when we crossed the chute, the fire would be above us.

One can only tempt fate so many times. By the time we had geared up and made it to the anchor point, it was dark. We started digging a cupped trench to the east, along the bottom of the fire, to catch any debris that might roll down from above us, while another fire crew started working from the same anchor point uphill along the west side. Their goal was also to reach the top of the mountain by morning but on the west side of the fire. We were making a direct attack, building the fire line along the edge of the flames. The fire along our line was a ground fire slowly backing downhill. The fire line was in soft soil and duff, fairly easy digging. The first squad had two chainsaws running and cleared trees and brush out in front of the other two squads. I was in the second squad digging line into mineral soil using a shovel. An inversion had set up, and the smoke was dense, cutting our vision to less than thirty feet. I could not see any of the firefighters in the first squad but could hear their saws.

The piñon/juniper were not large, and, along this part of the fire, the larger ponderosa pine were scattered, which made for relatively easy cutting. The first squad was moving fast, and we were working hard to keep up. We also wanted to reach the east side of the fire so we could hook the fire and start heading uphill. The crew boss scouted ahead of the first squad, checking out the terrain and flagging where the fire line should go. After a couple of hours he came back to our squad and briefed us and the third squad about the terrain ahead. He informed us that we were about fifty yards from the chute. The sawyers were almost there. There was not much to cut across the chute, so they would clear the fire line of trees and shrubs fairly quickly, but for us the going would be slower because of grasses and other plants growing among the rocks. We were going to have to dig the plants out, in some cases by moving large rocks. The work was going to be hard and the footing unstable. The crew boss mentioned that the inversion was about mid-slope, and that indeed the fire was burning in a thermal belt keeping the fire active and causing an occasional rock to break loose and roll down the chute. He said rolling rocks would make crossing the chute extremely hazardous.

Today as a wise old man of fifty-two, I would have told the crew boss or the IC that it was not worth it to work a line through the chute; it was much too dangerous. But when I was young, I didn't question authority? "Dig on," I said, "dig on." It took us less than an hour to make it to the edge of the chute. The chatter among the fire-fighters had been normal as we built line, with someone talking about a movie they had recently seen, someone else about a fire they had been on somewhere, how much overtime they had made so far that summer. But, when we reached the edge of the chute, we all got quiet. Looking up into the smoke and flames, the chute looked formidable, with large boulders silhouetted in the glow of flames. We heard the crackling sound of burning wood coming from above us and the occasional crash of a burning tree falling. The beast was alive and hungry. I think most of us were aware of what could come crashing down that chute and what our chances of dodging a careening boulder might be. We were not afraid of the fire but of what the fire could let loose. By far the biggest fear for me was being unable to see. Visibility remained only about thirty feet because of the dense smoke and glare of the fire. For a long time, no one said anything. Then, like a dumb-ass, I said, "Okay, kids, let's do it."

We all wanted to cross the chute as quickly as possible, but the digging was slow. The two squads spread out to give each other some room in case we had to run. As we dug, we were all sweating and grunting, and no one talked. This was serious work. After about fifteen minutes, we heard a large rock break loose from up above. We all stopped working and looked up, yelling, "Rock!" We could not see a thing. We could hear the rock careen off other rocks as it descended, but, just when we felt we needed to flee, it stopped. I could feel the thumping of my heart in my temples. I looked down and started working again. We reached the midway point, and I began to think we just might get out of the chute unscathed, having tempted fate and won. Just then, another rock broke loose from above. This one did not sound like it was going to stop, and it sounded like it was heading right for us. I yelled, "Rock! Run for it!" The boulder was almost on top of us, but because we could not see it, we did not know where to run. I turned towards the right, but George, the guy next to me, turned to the left. Glancing up, I saw the boulder bouncing down the chute about ten yards above us. It landed on another boulder and bounced into the air, heading right for me. I had no chance to get out of the way in time, so I dove behind another large boulder.

The rock hit that boulder and careened left towards George. I rolled over and watched as it hit him in the middle of his back. The boulder must have weighed at least a hundred pounds. George was a big guy, built like a football player, but the boulder lifted him off the ground as though he was nothing more than a sack of potatoes. He and the boulder sailed through the air. With a bloodcurdling scream, George hit the ground about five yards below and started rolling. The boulder kept going, bouncing off rocks as it rolled down the slope out of sight. George continued screaming at the top of his lungs as he, too, bounced off of rocks, finally coming to rest against a large boulder. Everything seemed to be in slow motion as several of us dropped our tools and ran down the slope to him. He was still screaming, letting us know that at least he was not dead.

He was still conscious when we got to him. Blood flowed across his face and down his shirt. He looked like hell, but his thrashing indicated that he had not severed his spinal cord. We quickly checked him over and found some bleeding from lacerations on his head but nothing that looked life threatening. We worried more about internal injuries and a possible broken back. He lay on his side and was having difficulty breathing. He told us between gasps that he thought he had a couple of broken ribs, and we were afraid to move him. Working carefully we got his fire pack off as well as his blood-stained shirt. Upon close inspection, we found some nasty looking gashes along his back and side.

This was not a good scenario. We were in the middle of a rocky chute, the fire was burning above us and the likelihood of more boulders breaking loose was very good. We had to move George to a safer location. We had no backboard, and the nearest ambulance was about an hour away. We called the IC on the radio, and he immediately dispatched an ambulance. In the meantime, George had stopped screaming and was now quietly moaning. As with many fire crews, we had a couple of emergency medical technicians (EMTs) and a twenty-person medical kit. The EMTs checked him over, making him move his toes and pinching him in various places to determine what sensations he could feel. It appeared that the spine was not severed, but it was likely that he had a broken back. If we moved him, the chance of severing the spine was a possibility. It was about twenty-five yards to the edge of the chute and another 400 or so yards down the steep mountainside to a bench level enough on which to lay him without danger of his rolling off a stretcher or being hit by another falling boulder. From there it was another 400 yards to the nearest road. I remember it was a dark, moonless night and all we had for light was our headlamps. We had no ropes, and the footing was treacherous. We were afraid to move him, but our location was precarious.

Several smaller rocks had already bounced by us since George was hit. As the EMTs bandaged his lacerations and stabilized him, we all discussed what we should do. Suddenly, another rock, almost as big as the one that hit George, broke loose from somewhere up above and came bouncing down, passing us to the left. That clinched it, we had to move him. Either he or someone else was going to die, and we did not have the time to wait for the ambulance, a backboard, stretcher and rope. We cut down two four-inch diameter trees and cut them into eight feet long poles. With our Nomex shirts, sweatshirts, and anything else we could use, we improvised a stretcher, rolled him onto it and strapped him in with cling bandages as best we could. Then, with ten of us carrying the stretcher, we got him out of the chute and down to the level bench. It took us almost an hour. Every time we jostled the stretcher, he cried out in pain, but at least he still had some feeling in his back and legs.

Since there was nothing else we could do for George, one EMT stayed with him and the rest of us went back to work. The crew boss wisely decided to stop work in the chute. We started digging line on the east side leaving about twenty-five yards of undug line in the chute. We posted a lookout at the edge of the chute to monitor the fire and let us know if it got below our fire line. The rest of us kept on building line.

We had a job to do. We did it. While working, I thought, *I'm glad it wasn't me*. At the time, I never really thought about the fact that it could easily have been me with a broken back or even worse, dead. If that rock had landed on me while I lay on the ground, it probably would have crushed me.

The ambulance finally showed up with a backboard, stretcher, and rope, and we went back down to help get George off the mountain.

It was about 1:00 A.M. when we closed the doors of the ambulance and it drove away. We headed back up the mountain to work the rest of the night. When the sun came up, we still had a ways to go to reach the mountain top. Since there was no other crew to relieve us, we just kept working and at around 12:00 noon, we finally reached the ridge at the top of the mountain. The other crew had reached the top earlier in the morning and was building line along the lee side of the mountain in our direction. We ate MREs (meals ready to eat) for lunch and, after a short break, started working in the other crew's direction. The fire was finally lined by about 4:00 P.M. It never made it down to our fire line in the rocky chute, so the piece of undug line never mattered.

We finally headed down off the mountain around 5:00 P.M. I had been working without any sleep, except for short cat naps during breaks, for thirty-four hours. All of us were exhausted. On the way down the mountain, we stopped to pick up George's fire pack. We had left it in the rocky chute. In the daylight, we saw that two canteens in his pack had been crushed and a can of chili dented. He had a sweater and a few other items of clothing in the pack as well. We realized what probably saved him from a worse injury, or even death, was his fire pack and his body size. The pack had absorbed some of the force of the rock when it hit him. His hard hat came off when he hit the ground, but at that first impact he still had it on, which probably saved him from a more severe head injury.

Once we got off the mountain we found a hot meal waiting for us, and we slept in a Forest Service campground next to a river. Most of us were asleep by 7:00 P.M. and slept until 5:30 A.M. the next morning. When we got up, we learned that George had indeed broken his back as well as several ribs, but he was not paralyzed. Still, it took George almost a year of rehabilitation to fully recover. After that ordeal, George decided that he had tempted fate enough. He hung up his hard hat. George, like some people, are quick learners and know when to stop. As for the rest of us on the fire crew, we are dumber than rats who finally learn not to push a lever when all they get is an electrical shock. We keep pushing the lever, "ouch," pushing the lever, "ouch," pushing the lever, "ouch."

The fire line held, and we spent the next two days mopping up hot spots inside the line. This fire was history. I had worked sixty-eight hours in four days.

6

Nature knows no difference between weeds and flowers.
                    – Mason Cooley, American aphorist

New Mexico 1980

*D*riving our Type IV engine down a dusty dirt road towards a mesa ten miles away, Ken and I could see a narrow column of white smoke wafting over the top of the piñon/juniper trees. On a mild August day, in the early afternoon, the two of us had been dispatched to size up and mount an initial attack on a small fire burning on a mesa top twenty miles southeast of Socorro. From ten miles away, the fire looked small, probably only one or two trees and mostly smoldering. The color of the smoke indicated if the fire was active and what type of fuel was burning. White smoke usually means a smoldering fire, black would mean open flames.

The dirt road ended at the bottom of the mesa, leaving us with at least a one-mile walk up an arroyo choked with boulders and thick brush. The fire might be small and easy to suppress, but the walk to it was going to make us sweat. As we unloaded our gear, Ken said, "How come fires always have to be on top of a mountain or most of the way up? We need to put in a request to the fire beast to be a little more considerate and locate these fires closer to roads."

We thought we probably would be on this fire through the night, and, since we had a long walk from the engine to the fire, we geared up for an extended stay out on the line. Besides carrying our tools, we both carried two gallons of water and several MREs. Our packs weighed about fifty pounds. After one hour of back-breaking climbing, we finally topped out on the rim of the mesa. We were several hundred feet higher in elevation from where the road ended. The fire was on the south side of the mesa close to the edge, only a few hundred yards from our location. Walking to the fire, we discovered, as we suspected, that a few trees were burning, but it had also spread into some grass. The fire was about half an acre in size, a little bigger than I thought, but the two of us would be able to handle it. We hoped to have it lined and knocked down by dawn. We would spend the next day mopping up. We called dispatch and let them know we could handle the fire ourselves; no other resources would be needed.

We reached the fire, cached our packs nearby under a tree and started digging line, each of us only carrying a couple canteens of water and a fire shelter. Like dwarfs in *Snow White*, we were whistling and singing while we worked. The physical exertion felt good, and we only took a short break for supper as the sun began to set. We had the fire lined by midnight and an hour later had coals spread out to cool. The digging had been easy, and we only needed to cut down one juniper tree. We did not have a chain saw, so we used a pulaski to down the tree. The fire was contained by two A.M. We decided to knock off for the rest of the night and get some sleep. The night had cooled, and we had no sleeping bags, so we bundled up in whatever clothing we had in our fire packs and stretched out on the ground, our fire packs as our pillows. I thought of the old cowboy near Grants and how cowboys and Native Americans use to do the same. They had no down sleeping bags; they just lay on the ground, sleeping under the stars. The sky was clear and full of stars as it usually is in New Mexico. Being the middle of August, the Perseid meteor shower seemed to be at its peak. Every fifteen minutes or so, a meteorite streaked across the sky with a tail of yellow and green stretching behind it. Ken and I stared up at the heavens and talked about the day, both of us content in the lifestyles we led. As I drifted off to sleep, I remembered a quotation from a friend that brought a smile to my face, "I love the desert, a good beer, and sex, and not necessarily in that order."

We were back to work as night changed to twilight, spreading or burying the remaining coals, and cold trailing the fire perimeter.

We found a few hot spots burning below ground in some roots, some duff smoldering but not putting up any smoke, and rock and soil still hot. We felt other likely spots with our bare hands looking for heat. Any we found, we dug up and spread the material around to let it burn out, or we buried it so it would smother. Since we did not have any water to cool things off, we could only use dirt or let the coals burn out by providing them air.

The fire was basically out by 10:00 A.M., but we needed to monitor it through the rest of the burn period that day. The last thing any firefighter wants to do is call a fire out only to have it reignite and burn up a few thousand acres more. I had heard of employees being fired for having declared a fire out and having it restart. We called dispatch and told them we did not need to be relieved and would have it out by the end of the day, so it was hang-out time for us. We found a shady spot beneath a piñon tree at the edge of the mesa a short distance from the fire. Just below us was a horseshoe-shaped box canyon with an intermittent stream choked with boulders and thick brush. The lower end of the stream opened into the desert a couple miles away and in a different direction from where our engine was parked. Every half-hour or so, we would get up and walk throughout the fire to make sure it was out. While sitting under the tree enjoying the afternoon, we suddenly heard the howling and barking of several dogs from somewhere down in the small drainage. The barking and howling were too deep to be coyotes. We could not see the dogs but wondered what they were doing twenty miles from any house? Just then I noticed some movement in thick brush in the dry streambed below. It turned out to be a mountain lion moving quickly up the drainage. Uh oh, now I realized what the dogs were doing. Some hunters were using the dogs to chase down the lion, and their intention was probably not just to take a photo of it. The dogs could not have been more than five minutes behind the lion, and the hunters were probably not too far behind the dogs.

Ken and I were definitely rooting for the lion, but it was heading into the box canyon with almost vertical cliffs and no way out. It looked like the lion was trapped and would end up with its hide tacked to a shed or spread out in front of a fireplace. We were several hundred feet above the floor of the canyon, so there was nothing we could do. If we yelled at the lion, it would probably turn and run back down into the jaws of death. So, we remained quiet and just watched. At the north end of the box canyon, a wall jutted to a point where a small alcove was located. It appeared not very deep but was large enough to accommodate a standing person. The lion, without hesitating, headed straight for the alcove and, once inside, started running around in circles. It circled the alcove three times. From our vantage, the floor of the alcove appeared to have a fine layer of sand, so the lion was probably leaving some very distinct tracks. It stopped in the middle of the alcove and then slowly backed out. I could not see it, but I swear the lion was stepping into the same tracks it left when it ran in. This would leave tracks that looked like the lion ran into the alcove but did not come out. Once the lion was just outside the entrance, it sat back on its haunches, looked up the almost vertical cliff that was about 200 feet high, and then leaped straight up about eight feet. There hardly seemed to be a place for a foothold, but the lion actually bounded up the cliff for about a 100 feet to a narrow ledge. The ledge was barely big enough for the lion, but it quickly ran to a jumble of rocks and a small drainage that lead the rest of the way up to the mesa top. The lion, without breaking stride, reached the top a short distance from us. It never looked in our direction but bounded off through the piñon/juniper and out of sight.

I could not believe what I had just seen. This lion had just scaled a cliff in less than a minute that any rock climber would have spent a couple of hours climbing. Ken and I looked at each other with our mouths open, and then, with big smiles spreading across our faces, we reached out, high-fiving each other saying, "All right!" From the way the lion had run straight into the alcove, circled, backed out, and then bounded up the cliff, it appeared to us it had done this same trick before. Maybe the lion had raided the hunter's chicken coops or killed a lamb or calf and had acquired a taste for domestic animal as well as repeating a marvelous escape route.

A friend of mine told me about the time a lion had gotten into her chicken coop. She was awakened by the sound of squawking chickens one night and went out to see what was going on, expecting to see a coyote or fox trying to get into the chicken coop. She did not bring a flashlight since a half moon provided enough light. Upon opening the door to the coop and stepping in, a very large mountain lion with a chicken in its mouth jumped right over the top of her and ran off into the darkness. After she cleaned the pee from her pajamas, she checked the condition of the rest of the chickens. Not a single hen or the one rooster in the shed were where they normally roosted. Thinking they were all dead, she walked out into the fenced yard attached to the shed. There she noticed a large pile of chickens in one corner. "Damn," she said, thinking the lion had killed them all. Walking over to the pile, she discovered to her astonishment that every chicken was alive. For some reason they had all jumped into one large pile, and none of them were moving or making any sound, as if they had been hypnotized. Her chickens were paralyzed with fear. She started picking them up and each one ran off to the shed, clucking as it went. At the very bottom of the pile, hidden in a little depression was the rooster. My friend wondered why the rooster was on the bottom. He was the only male in the coop, so maybe the hens thought it important to protect him. Yeah right! As if he thought he was so lucky. Chances were the hens followed the macho rooster, it being the first out of the coop, and he probably fainted in fear. The hens just followed suit and fainted on top of him. There is no chivalry in chickens, no rooster putting himself in front of the hens to protect them from some lion.

Meanwhile the dogs had closed in and finally came into view in a flurry of fur, barking and howling. There were five of them, running as fast as they could. They ran up to the alcove and went right in, running around in circles coming back out and running back in again. The intensity of their barks increased. The dogs never looked up the cliff or tried to follow the lion. Apparently they could not smell were the lion had leaped up on the cliff above the alcove. It would not have mattered anyway, because there was no way the dogs could scale the cliff. The dogs were in a panic, yelping and barking. They had no idea were the lion had gone. We figured the hunters were not too far behind and did not want them to see us, so we hid behind the piñon tree. If they saw us they would want to know if we saw the lion. What was I going to say? "The bad guy went thata way." Shortly thereafter three cowboys on horseback, rode into view carrying rifles with pistols strapped to their hips. Working their way around the brush and rocks, they rode up to the alcove, one of them yelling at the dogs to quiet down. The cowboy dismounted. He kneeled at the entrance to the alcove studying the lion tracks in the shallow layer of sand. The dogs were milling around behind him. We watched him follow the tracks in and walk around in a circle. The dogs must have disturbed most of the tracks, but I am sure some were still visible. He walked back out of the alcove. Taking off his cowboy hat, he scratched his head. Ken and I looked at each other and chuckled. The cowboy looked up the cliff, where the lion had bounded, but of course could not see anything to indicate the lion had scaled a near vertical cliff. He scanned the remaining cliffs to no avail. He remounted, and the three of them spent about thirty minutes looking around the box canyon, but the dogs showed no interest anywhere else except at the alcove. The men kept going back there, and each time they would look up the cliff and scratch their heads in puzzlement. Finally, in disgust, they turned the horses down canyon and started back the way they had come, the dogs trailing behind. The men kept looking over their shoulders expecting to see the lion sitting on a rock. Once they were out of sight, Ken and I laughed, high-fived each other, and said, "All right!" again. We jumped up and started dancing an Irish jig, holding arms and spinning around in a circle sending clouds of dust into the air. Score one for the wily mountain lion.

Ken and I spent the rest of the afternoon checking the fire, thoroughly enjoying the day, reflecting back on the phantom lion who disappeared into a sheer rock wall in a box canyon. I laughed thinking about what stories the three cowboys would tell around the campfire about the big lion that mysteriously got away.

I have crossed paths with other phantom wildlife over the years. In all the time I have spent in the outdoors, wildlife never cease to amaze me. As humans, we tend to get a little arrogant about how smart we are and think the rest of the animal kingdom is so dumb. But most of us have lost the ability to tune into what goes on out in the woods and mountains. When we enter the wilderness, we feel out of our element. We tend to bring everything but the kitchen sink with us. We have our cellular phones and global positioning instruments to tell us where we are at all times or to call for help. After climbing some high mountain peak, it is not uncommon to encounter folks at the summit talking on a phone, instead of just enjoying the moment. Many people are more scared camping in the wilderness where most predators run away from us in fear, than walking down a city street where human predators lurk in dark alleys.

While living in Moab, Utah, in the 1980s, I once witnessed a mule deer buck outwit two hunters. On a beautiful autumn day in late October, I decided to climb Mount Tukuhnikivatz and Mount Peale, the highest peaks in the La Sal Mountains east of Moab. I reached the summit of Tukuhnikivatz in the early afternoon and sat back against a rock to enjoy the view and eat lunch. From the summit, I could see most of the slickrock canyon country around Moab and even the Henry Mountains at least 100 miles to the west. The summit of Tukuhnikivatz is above tree line at about 12,500 feet with the forest stopping at about 11,000 feet. At tree line, spruce and fir forests give way to alpine tundra and rock. At this ecotone grow small patches of spruce trees called Krumholtzs. The trees in some of the Krumholtzs are only a few feet high, dwarfed because of wind, cold temperatures, and snow depth. These trees are as old or sometimes older than the larger trees in the forest below.

While sitting at the summit, I happened to notice a large mule deer buck bound out of the forest and into the smaller Krumholtzs below me. The deer ran through one patch, bolt out the other side and into another. Hot on the deer's heels were two hunters with high-powered rifles. Every time the deer broke out of one Krumholtz, the hunters would stop for a shot, but, before they could shoot, the deer was back into another. The deer was rapidly running out of tree cover and would soon have nowhere else to go but out onto the open tundra. I felt certain once the deer came into the open the hunters would kill it or at least get a lot of lead in the air trying. The last Krumholtz covered a fairly large area, about fifty yards long by twenty maybe thirty yards wide. It was composed of dense spruce that would have been hard for a human to traverse, with the trees only about three to four feet in height. Without any hesitation, the deer ran into the last thicket, but suddenly stopped after fifteen feet. It turned and immediately dropped to its belly facing the hunters. The hunters had not seen the deer drop to the ground, but from my vantage point I could easily see the deer lying on the ground amongst the spruce. The hunters stopped at the downhill end of the Krumholtz no more than ten yards from the deer. I could see them discussing something, constantly looking uphill past where the deer was located. They split up each going on opposite sides. Their plan was an obvious one. They thought the deer was going to continue through the trees and out the other side. When it bounded out of the timber, one of them would then get a shot, depending on which way the deer ran. Unbeknownst to them, the deer remained lying on its belly with its chin on the ground. Its antlers were big enough that, if it had its head up, the antlers would have been above the tops of the trees and probably been seen by the hunters. The hunters moved rapidly past the location of the deer, heading toward the upper end of the Krumholtz. When they were almost to the top, the deer started crawling on its belly back the way it had come. Out in the open, it stayed on its belly, keeping trees between it and the hunters. When it reached the next Krumholtz, it jumped up and bounded back down the mountain and out of sight. The hunters never saw it. They met at the upper end of the Krumholtz and stood there looking around.

Mule deer one, hunters zero! I can imagine those hunters sitting around a campfire talking about the one that got away. Perhaps if they had not been in a hurry and had just sat and waited, the deer would have finally bolted, providing them with a shot.

Patience and staying in tune to surroundings is easy to do if one uses all the senses, not just eyesight, but hearing, touching, and smelling. I like to tell the story about a family having a picnic near a viewpoint at Bryce Canyon National Park. They had walked over to the rim to get a better view and spread their blanket under some ponderosa pines. They sat down and began talking and eating. I was on evening road patrol and parked just a short distance away from them eating my own dinner and enjoying the view. I noticed some movement to the left of where they were sitting. Moving along the edge of the rim no more than twenty feet away from the family was a mountain lion. The lion hesitated when it saw the family but quietly passed behind them and continued up the rim into a thicket of brush and trees.

From my vantage, it looked like the family never saw the lion, so I decided to walk over and talk to them. I said, "Hi, have you ever seen a mountain lion before?"

The dad replied with a confused look on his face, "No?"

I told them a mountain lion had just walked by them no more than twenty feet away. I took them over to where the lion had walked to look for tracks, and we found a couple in soft dirt. They were dumbfounded that a lion had come so close to them and they had not noticed. It scared them a little, but they also seemed disappointed to have missed an opportunity of a lifetime.

We would see a lot more if we stayed tuned into what is going on around us, wherever we are. A mistake hunters sometimes make is looking into the far distance for game first and then focusing closer. Often the game is nearby trying to hide or crawl away as the deer in the La Sal Mountains did. While hiking, I sometimes see more if I occasionally stop and just stand, which mimics the behavior of wild animals. They rarely continually walk, preferring to stop frequently and look around, sniffing the air or listening. For prey species such as a deer or elk, their lives depend on being aware of their surroundings; likewise, predators depend on being able to catch and eat the prey. For many of us visiting wild places, the animals know of our presence long before we know theirs.

Once while working at Rocky Mountain National Park, I was hiking along a trail in the south end of the park, when I stopped to look at a chickaree (red squirrel) eating seeds from a lodgepole pine cone. Glancing to my left on the other side of the trail, I noticed a slight color change or what looked like something out of place beneath a shrub just off the trail. Staring at the shrub and the shadows beneath it, I could not figure out what I was seeing, but I held perfectly still. Finally I saw an eye blink and the ears, nose, and whiskers of a bobcat. The animal blended so well into its surroundings—sunlight and shadows had broken up the pattern of the animal's fur—that, by not moving, the animal was almost invisible. The bobcat waited for an opportunity to pounce on the chickaree. If I had just continued walking along the trail I would have never seen this drama, but, because I stopped to watch the chickaree, I was able to see the bobcat.

Late in the afternoon, Ken and I packed up our gear. We called into dispatch that the fire was out and we were leaving the scene. Just before I dropped off the mesa top, I turned and said a silent prayer to the fire, thanking it for the opportunity I might not otherwise have taken to see an interesting area and witness a mountain lion outsmart three cowboys and a bunch of dogs. Thoughts of that mountain lion still bring a smile to my face.

Returning to town, we dropped off the engine and filled out our time sheet. Ken and I had worked thirty-one hours. Before heading home, we walked across the street to a cafe, ordering two beers and hamburgers. Nearby sat the same three cowboys we saw earlier in the day hunting the lion. They were talking to a waitress and telling her about the lion that had gotten away. Ken and I looked at each other and laughing, clinked our beer bottles together. Later when the waitress stopped by to serve our food, I asked her about the cowboys.

She said they were two ranchers and an Animal Damage Control Officer who worked for the U.S. Fish and Wildlife Service. A rancher who leased BLM land had asked the predator control specialist to kill predators that supposedly posed a threat to his livestock. Apparently it had been the officer's dogs we saw chasing the lion, and he was the one who had dismounted to read the sign. Most of the time when these scenarios are played out the mountain lion, bear, coyote, or bobcat, ends up dead, the skin hanging from someone's shed or the whole animal draped over a barbed wire fence. So it was great to witness one scenario where the predator got away. I have never been in favor of the federal subsidy program of killing predators. This program is a hold over from the earlier part of the twentieth century when government hunters killed off the wolves, grizzly bear, and almost wiped out other predators, throwing the Circle of Life into a cartwheel. I believe there are much better ways to spend taxpayers' money than killing predators, prairie dogs, kangaroo rats, and thousands of animals each year mostly on public land owned collectively by the American people in order to satisfy a small number of ranchers. The ramifications of this kind of unbalancing of Nature can have disastrous effects on the ecology and the environment. Ken and I were glad the one lion had gotten away.

6

A Rose a Flame
At One in Sweet Harmony

— Joanne

New Mexico 1980

*I*t takes someone understanding the simpler things in life to work in a fire lookout. Months of isolation can drive even the toughest of people mad. Shelly and Bob, who worked in a fire lookout and also did wilderness patrol in the Gila Wilderness, would have lived in a fire lookout year round if they had their way. They spent about four months a year in almost total isolation deep in the heart of the first designated wilderness in the country. I liked to hike the five miles to the lookout and visit them on days off, and I knew no happier couple. They enjoyed my company, but I also knew that, when I left, their hearts and souls felt the peaceful return of solitude; even one person was an intrusion to them. One of my fondest memories with Bob and Shelly was spending a night in the fire lookout, during a thunderstorm.

The fire lookout was built on the top of a mountain and offered unsurpassed views of the Gila Wilderness. However, during thunderstorms, it was the highest thing on the peak and lightning sometimes hit it. The tower was well grounded, and the bed and chairs inside were protected with glass insulators on each leg, the same type of insulator used on electrical poles. When a storm moved through, Shelly had to turn off the radio and any other electronic equipment. The only thing anyone could do was lie on the bed or sit in a chair or on a stool not touching any metal for fear of being fried if lightning did hit the tower.

Late one night, a thunderstorm moved over the mountaintop enveloping the tower in clouds, while I had been sleeping out on the catwalk. The sound of thunder woke me up, and, opening my eyes, I saw a bolt of lightning streak across the sky over my head, followed almost instantly by the sound of echoing thunder. I wisely picked up my sleeping bag and went inside, sitting on a chair with my sleeping bag wrapped around me, while Bob and Shelly lay in bed. Bob said, "Get ready for a great fireworks display that will knock your socks off, and I mean literally knock your socks off if you don't keep your feet off the ground." The clouds blocked out any light, and the darkness was like being in a cave. I could not even see my hands in front of my face. Then a lightning bolt burst, changing total darkness to a bright white light with an instantaneous crack of thunder. We stuffed our ears with rubber ear protections to protect our ears drums from the deafening thunder. After a bolt disappeared, total darkness returned, but I would still be seeing after images of white light in front of my eyes for several seconds. Sometimes the lightning streaked horizontal to the tower looking as if it would pass right through us. The tower got hit once while the storm moved overhead, and I could almost feel the power surge through it as it passed down the tower to the ground. Wind and rain came almost simultaneously, with wind blowing large raindrops against the window. The air cooled, and I stayed huddled in my sleeping bag. Eventually the lightning stopped. Shortly thereafter the wind and rain lessened. The clouds parted, revealing stars overhead. When it seemed safe enough, the three of us got up and walked out onto the catwalk to look for any new fires that might have started. The storm had moved to the east, still lighting up the night sky with an occasional bolt of lightning. Everywhere we looked was pitch black, not a single house, glare from a town, or car headlamp broke the darkness. However, looking off to the south we saw a faint yellowish flickering light some unknown miles from our location. Lifting a pair of binoculars to my eyes, the flickering light turned out to be a small fire burning on a ridge top. A tree or snag had been hit by lightning. Shelly got on the radio and called Jill, who was operating the next lookout to the south of us. Shelly gave her the coordinates from our location, and Jill called back shortly that she could also see the fire. Using a compass coordinate, Bob drew a line on a map from our location in the direction of the fire, and Jill did the same from her location. Using the two coordinates, it was simple to pinpoint the approximate location of the fire where the two lines crossed. By radio, Shelly called the Fire Management Officer at his home in Gila Hot Springs and reported the fire.

It is a strange feeling to be so deep into a roadless area with, as far as the eye can see, not seeing a single human-caused light. It felt like Bob, Shelly, and I were the only remaining people on earth. Jill's voice on the radio made me realize that others existed in the small network of people who operate the fire lookouts in the Gila. These people spent their summers in isolation scattered around the wilderness. Each had accepted the post for private reasons. Authors like Jack Keroac and Ed Abbey used to like such work as it gave them solitude to write. Most of the time the only human contact came via radio or the occasional hiker.

Neither Bob, Shelly, nor I were tired, so we sat in chairs out on the catwalk propping our feet on the railing, enjoying a cool breeze and the starlit night. Bob brewed some green tea, and we sipped in silence in the dark, enjoying the peace and quiet as we watched the small glow of the far-off fire. The Milky Way spilled across the sky with the Northern Cross pointing southeast and the constellation Scorpio sitting on the southern horizon. It felt good to be alive. Bob had his arm around Shelly, and I was envious of the peace and love they had for each other. Theirs was a strong bond, and they both loved the wilderness, feeling more at home in the wilds of the Gila than in some town. After finishing our tea, we noticed that the fire looked like it had grown, so it was probably now burning on the ground and beginning to move to other trees and vegetation. It appeared fairly active for that late at night, maybe located in the thermal belt on the side of a mountain. Looking at the topographic map, the fire appeared to along a ridge below the peak of a mountain. The Fire Management Officer called back just as we were going back to bed and said they would be sending in some smokejumpers from Silver City in the morning.

Around eight o'clock that morning, an aircraft showed up from the southwest. Flying by the lookout, the pilot dipped the plane's wings in greeting and also said hello via radio. The plane banked to the south and headed directly towards the smoke column.

The smoke had grown quite visible, and the fire looked to be at least a couple of acres. The smokejumpers had a full day of work ahead of them. The plane, a C-119 Flying Boxcar, had a rear door that dropped open, allowing the smokejumpers to parachute out the back of the plane. It circled the smoke column, scouting out the area. I could envision the pilot and lead smokejumper looking out the window, sizing up the fire and looking for a safe landing zone. After about ten minutes of circling, we saw a couple of long streamers falling from the rear of the plane towards the ground. They had apparently found an adequate landing zone and were testing the wind currents. The plane flew off to the east and turned, heading back to the west in level flight. We saw two jumpers come out the back of the plane as the plane passed over the fire. With their chutes open, they slowly drifted towards the ridge west of the fire. We were monitoring their radio frequency. Once the two were on the ground, one of them (I assumed this was the lead smokejumper) called to the pilot and said the landing zone was fine, and they were okay. The pilot made three more passes with two firefighters jumping each time, a total of eight. The lead smokejumper, now the IC, called the pilot letting him know all had made it safely to the ground. The plane dipped its wings in farewell salute and leveled off on a heading to Silver City.

The firefighters faced a day of hard work lining the fire and putting it out. Bob, Shelly, and I spent the day, naked, kicked back, sitting on chairs out on the catwalk, sun bathing, reading books, taking weather observations and enjoying another gorgeous day in paradise. Watching through binoculars and a spotting scope, we could see the yellow-shirted firefighters working the fire. This was the first fire I had observed without being on it. It felt different to be just an observer and not out there digging line. I wanted a piece of the action. I knew I was not smokejumper material; I had a hard time seeing myself jumping out of an airplane into a fire. Smokejumpers, like the Hot Shots and Helitack crews, earned their keep and are the true glamour folks. Other firefighters, like me, looked up to them.

It was still policy in the early 1980s to put fires out even in the Gila Wilderness. The forest service was just beginning to think about the prescribed natural fire program, now called wildland fires for resource benefit, but had still not implemented anything. I thought the Gila Wilderness would be one of the best places in the West for prescribed natural fires. The Gila is composed of mountains, canyons, and some very inaccessible places. A fire could burn for months in the Gila and never threaten a human being or structure built by humans. Being the first designated wilderness area in the country, what would be a more suitable location for a fire to burn unimpeded than in a two-million-acre roadless area.

Since the trees in the Gila are protected from logging, saving trees was also not a concern. In the Gila, the forest service in the early 1980s had a policy that, during an emergency situation like a fire, a helicopter could be used to transport firefighters and provide support, or a plane could be used to drop smokejumpers, but once the fire was out and the emergency over, the firefighters often had to hike out to the nearest road, carrying all their own gear. Ken, another friend of mine, worked Helitack in Gila Hot Springs and did that all the time. His first fire was twenty-two miles into the back country. A helicopter flew them in, dropping them off a short distance from the fire. The fire was small, so air support was not needed, and the helicopter left them to fend for themselves. They spent a day putting the fire out and then another day hiking out the twenty-two miles to the nearest road. Upon arriving at the trailhead, their supervisor greeted them, but, instead of congratulating them for a job well done, he immediately asked to see everyone's trash. The policy was "pack it in, pack it out." Two of the firefighters did not have their trash and admitted to having buried it back at the fire. The supervisor made those two turn around and walk back the twenty-two miles to the fire, pick up their trash and walk back out, and they didn't get paid for doing it. They even had to account for their gum wrappers. Ken said no one left any trash after that episode.

The forest service has always been strict on wilderness policies, particularly in the Gila. Once someone drove a four-wheel-drive truck along the Gila River, entering the wilderness boundary and traveling a couple of miles up river. The driver got stuck on a sand bar and had to hike out to get help. The forest service found out about the truck. They ticketed the owner and made him hire a team of horses to tow the truck back out of the wilderness. As far as I was concerned, they should have made the owner dismantle the entire vehicle and personally haul each piece out on his back. There should be some places in the world where someone in a $30,000 vehicle has no right to go.

In the 1990s, the U.S. Forest Service and the National Park Service have recognized the value of fire and become more flexible in prescribed natural fires. The small fire I watched from the fire lookout tower being suppressed may now be left to burn. It is not uncommon in favorable conditions today for a fire to burn for a month or more in some wilderness area. This is the way it use to be for thousands of years before people started suppressing fires. The fire burns until inclement weather puts it out; humans only watch from a distance or coach it a little to stay in a certain area.

I like to monitor natural fires. When on site, I walk lightly around or through the fire making sure I do not disturb something that might alter the way the fire burns. I do not add fuel to the fire if it looks like it is going to go out, or take fuel away if the fire looks too hot. If the weather and fuel moisture is within prescription, then I treat the fire the same way I would treat a church or shrine, with reverence and silence. I enjoy just watching the fire move through the vegetation taking notes on its behavior. A naturally unmanipulated fire is almost like a living, breathing creature. At night and into the early morning hours, the fire usually sleeps, but in the middle of the day it wakes up and begins to feed, eating whatever comes within its reach, only to lie back down again after dark. I like to predict ahead of time what I think the fire might do and then see if it happens. Will that downed tree burn, will the fire burn through some rocks, or down a small hill, will that finger of fire stay alive or die out?

I once spent eight days monitoring a fire that only burned about half an acre. For the last four days, the fire struggled to stay alive, but like a dying creature gasping for air, it finally stopped breathing. The last wisp of smoke drifted off, dissipating into the air. What was left behind was a natural mosaic of numerous little fingers of blackened vegetation, a couple of dead trees that had been lying on the ground burned to ashes, some shrubs with only small blackened tendrils sticking out of the ground, and a couple of live trees that had been torched. The wildlife—chipmunks, flycatchers, and jays—already moved around through the blackened vegetation looking for food the fire had exposed; they had begun this even when the fire was still alive. I almost felt like erecting a grave marker and saying a eulogy. "Here lies the Beaver Mountain Prescribed Natural Fire, it was a small fire but lived life to its fullest. May it rest in peace."

After declaring the fire out to dispatch via radio, and just as I was leaving, I turned back to the fire and said a silent prayer, thanking the fire for allowing me the opportunity to spend time with it while it was alive. There were no fire lines, no cut tree stumps, turned over soil, dug out tree stumps or other signs that humans had decided to master the beast. The blackened landscape looked as it should look in a recommended wilderness, untouched and untrampled.

The smokejumpers finished off their fire on the ridge by nightfall and decided to camp out that night and hike out the next day. I spent one last night at the lookout and also left the next morning. Heading down the mountain, just before I entered the trees, I stopped and turned looking back at the fire lookout. Bob and Shelly were standing naked out on the catwalk watching me. On warm days, they hardly wore any clothes, preferring to be as natural as a prescribed natural fire. I waved, and they waved back. Their solitude had returned, and I turned and headed into the forest.

7

The title wise is, for the most part, falsely applied. How can one be a wise man, if he does not know any better how to live than other men? If he is only more cunning and intellectually subtle?
— Henry David Thoreau

Utah 1984

Moonlight from a three-quarter moon bathed the canyon walls and bottom, making walking easy without headlamps. The screech came every minute or so, and shortly Kathy and I found, not just one owl, but two sitting in a dead juniper snag about three feet off the ground. These were juvenile Mexican spotted owls only a few months old. They were food begging, sitting in the snag yelling for mom or dad to come and feed them. Like humans, if they yelled long enough, eventually the parents would show up. The owlets did not fly away as we approached, and I got close enough to see their brown eyes sparkling in the moonlight. One of them did let out a loud squawk, seeming to say, "Are you my mother?" It reminded me of a book I use to read to my kids about a small bird that lost its mother and wandered around asking everyone, "Are you my mother?" I slowly walked closer. The young owls continued to watch me and let me get so close, my face was only about a foot away from theirs. One owl hopped to a branch and crept even closer to me. Bending its head down, rolling it back and forth, only inches from my face it looked me in the eyes. Once again I felt a kinship towards the owl, like the moment with the golden eagle in Bryce Canyon. I whispered to it so only it could hear me, "May you live your life in peace, little one."

Both owls continued to sit in the tree. I was close enough that I could have grabbed them if I had wanted. Temptation finally got the better of me, and I reached up and touched the owl closest to me on the tail feathers. The owl just sat there still looking at me. I gently stroked the soft feathers and, by moonlight, admired the patterns and color. An owl's feathers are much softer than other birds of prey because of small downy filaments interwoven through them. This breaks up air movement, making them silent flyers. I could hear the wind passing through the feathers of the golden eagle at Bryce Canyon and the peregrine falcon in a dive along the Colorado River, but I would not be able to hear any noise from these owls when they flew. Reaching a little higher with my hand, I lightly touched the feathers on the owl's breast and could feel warmth underneath. The two owls stopped looking at us and started looking around. Perhaps they had seen their parents or tired of our presence. With the slightest movement, they lifted off the tree and flew silently away into the darkness. The primary feathers from one wing of the owl closest to me lightly touched my face as it left. Kathy and I looked at each other and smiled. We both walked back to camp in silence, reflecting on the moment.

After getting my permanent status with the Bureau of Land Management, my dream finally came true, and I landed a job as a natural resources specialist with the National Park Service working at Canyonlands and Arches National Park and Natural Bridges National Monument. The job was very diversified. I was the second resource specialist to have ever worked at those parks. The two of us were responsible for wildlife, air quality, water quality, revegetation of disturbed areas, archeology, and visitor management. I was also given the responsibility of fire management, with the distinction of being the first fire management officer for Canyonlands, Arches, and Natural Bridges. However, it did not require a lot of work since it was hard to burn sand or slickrock. Over the next couple of years, we had a couple fires in the Needles District, both started by humans, but the fires never had a chance to do anything because they just burned into box canyons and went out. During the five years I worked in those parks, we did a few prescribed burns and had several fires started by lightning that became prescribed natural fires. On the PNFs, we would spend time monitoring, watching from a distance, collecting fire weather data and fire behavior information, but otherwise let them do their own thing.

In 1984 we had a lightning-started fire in some piñon/ juniper in the Maze District. The Maze is the most remote district in Canyonlands, about a three-hour drive from park headquarters in Moab just to reach the residence area in Han's Flat inside Glen Canyon National Recreation Area. The park boundary was still another two-hour drive from Han's Flat down the Flint Trail and out to the Maze Overlook or into the Doll House. The fire was burning in the Maze in a small canyon below the Maze Overlook. The Maze is actually three narrow canyons that twist and turn and finally meet just below the overlook, forming one canyon that continues for another eleven miles down to the Green River. The canyons are composed of vertical sandstone cliffs several hundred feet high with only a few ways in and out. The fire was estimated to be no more than a couple acres, burning at the upper end of the middle canyon. A pilot flying a small plane en route to the Moab airport from Bull Frog had called in the fire. Since the fire was going to be managed as a PNF, I thought two of us would be sufficient to monitor it. After reaching the Maze Overlook, we parked the Jeep. We could see a small smoke column below us. Since it was going to be a trek to get into the Maze and a hassle to hike back to the Jeep, we decided to set up a spike camp. Carrying backpacks and fire tools, we headed down the trail. Hiking from the top of the overlook into the Maze is like traveling through a jungle gym. We had to take our packs off and push them in front of us or drag them behind us in places. Sometimes we passed them down to each other, slowly working through a jumble of rocks. The most unsettling part of the trail had us stepping over and down a ten-foot rounded bench using ancient Moki steps cut into the sandstone. Stepping down backwards, I could not see the next step below and had to feel with my feet while holding onto other steps. One slip and it would not have been a long fall, but a fall is a fall. We finally made it to the bottom and started hiking down the main canyon, turning into the middle canyon where the Harvest Scene, an exquisite 900-year-old petroglyph panel depicting Indians harvesting maize, is located. Apparently, Indians used to grow corn in these canyon bottoms. The fire was burning beyond the petroglyph panel in the upper end of the canyon. We set up camp near a spring at the mouth of the canyon and spent the next several days monitoring the fire until it burned itself out. During the day, we found a great sandstone bench above the fire and spent the time sitting there watching from afar, occasionally taking weather observations and notes. The fire burned in duff beneath some juniper trees and in sparse grass. Occasionally a juniper tree would torch, sending black smoke into the air.

While sitting back at camp in the early part of the second night, reading *Windsinger* by Gary Smith, I heard the screech from what sounded like an owl calling from somewhere up canyon. Curious about it, Kathy and I decided to find out what it was and discovered the young owls. In camp after our encounter, I was restless and decided to walk up to the Harvest Scene. I found the panel partially bathed in moonlight. The intricate details of the scene seemed to stand out more in the soft whiteness of moonlight than in the harsh light of the sun. The Harvest Scene is a spiritually powerful place, and I could see why the ancient ones from a millennium ago picked that sandstone face on which to carve their story. The rock was smooth, a perfect easel for some artist. I sat cross-legged in the sand across from it and watched the moonlight slowly move across the rock, shifting the shadows made by the etchings, which seemed to slowly dance in the faint moonlight.

My thoughts turned to the songs and stories in the book *Windsinger,* a book about the Maze, among other things, and is meant to be read while camping out there. Gary Smith, a park ranger for a while in the Maze, was in harmony with the world around him, and the book is full of songs and poems he wrote. The Maze and nearby Robber's Roost were two of his favorite places. The story/song "Windsinger" from which the title of his book is named, came to me. It is the story of a young Navajo who sought his name on a mountain, from a wise old man called Naga-Khan. Naga-Khan named the boy Windsinger, which meant, the boy who flew. The name made me think of my spiritual attachment to birds and my encounter with the owls. The photo on the front of Gary's book shows him standing on a lip of rock called the "Diving Board." It is located in the Maze district on the rim of the inner gorge above the Colorado River, just downstream of the confluence of the Green and Colorado rivers. The small lip, no more than a few feet thick at the edge, juts out over the cliff nine hundred feet above the river. I have stood on that rock, and the temptation is almost overwhelming to run and jump and soar off it like a golden eagle, a peregrine falcon, an osprey, or owl. Standing on the rock looking down at the river below, I could imagine how it felt to fly. I have had numerous dreams of flying like a bird or hovering like a hummingbird high above the land. Once, while in college, I had a dream about flying over woods and farmland. I was passing over the roof of a building and remember looking down and seeing the green of a cornfield and the multicolors of someone's flower garden. In real life, I easily get air sick when flying in helicopters or small fixed wing aircraft and fear skydiving, paragliding, hang gliding, or bungee jumping. My spiritual soul wants to fly, but my physical body barfs whenever I do. Ah, the irony of life.

The moonlight finally bathed the entire panel. Looking up to the moon, I saw that it filled the sky above the canyon. The etchings of the Harvest Scene stood out on the rock, making the figures almost three-dimensional. I smiled, stood up and walked back to camp under the moonlit sky.

8

Let no man think lightly of good,
Saying in his heart, it will not come nigh me.
By the falling of raindrops a pot is filled;
the wise man becomes full of good, even if he gathers it little by little.
—Buddha

Utah 1985

*R*iparian areas are probably the most important habitat in the desert, mainly because there is so little of it. Usually, narrow bands of green cottonwood and willow grow adjacent to a stream or river or form a small green dot in a sea of brown at tinajas. Because of their rarity and proximity to water, these areas attract humans as well as livestock, which in turn have abused this important resource. Significant changes have occurred to riparian areas in the West in the past 150 years due in large part to three things: water diversion, salt cedar, and livestock. Impoundments diverting water for irrigation and drinking purposes has forever changed rivers such as the Colorado, Green, and Yampa, the main arteries of five western states. These rivers, once free flowing and meandering through some of the most impressive canyons on earth, have been altered. Places like Glen Canyon and the canyons of Lake Mead are buried beneath hundreds of feet of water. Impoundments changing the water flow and livestock heavily grazing native vegetation have allowed an exotic tree, the salt cedar or tamarisk, to take over riparian habitats. Tamarisk was introduced into the United States from Asia in the early 1900s. People brought the wonder plant into this country to stabilize stream banks in desert environments and also as an ornamental in California, Nevada, and Arizona. Cows and burros in desert country overgrazed riparian habitat, causing erosion and flooding and the loss of native flora and fauna. Tamarisk became the solution to stream bank erosion fifty to sixty years ago. Of the thousands of exotic species brought into this country for one reason or another, about three percent escape cultivation and have caused billions of dollars of economic hardship. Tamarisk solved the stream bank erosion problem — too well — and quickly replaced native cottonwood and willow. Now state and federal agencies are spending millions of dollars annually trying to get rid of tamarisk and bring back the native plants. When humans play God, I am always reminded of a *Far Side* cartoon by Gary Larson where God drops a jar containing Adam and Eve. They escape, running naked across an open meadow. The caption underneath has God saying, "Uh Oh!"

Tamarisk was not planted in Canyonlands or Arches National Parks along the Colorado and Green Rivers and their tributaries, but it moved upstream from Arizona and California, becoming established in Utah in the middle 1920s. One tamarisk tree can produce millions of seeds light enough to be carried by wind. Anyone who floats rivers and has had to row against the wind can attest to the fact that, no matter which direction a river flows, the wind seems to blow upstream. Wind carried the tamarisk seeds upstream; some researchers estimate the tree became established at a rate of about twenty to thirty miles a year. The broken woody parts of the plant can also set root and grow into a tree. A twig or branch falling into the river can float downstream, washing up on a sand bar. It can set root and sprout if given the right conditions.

Tamarisk is well adapted to the arid West and is actually able to excrete salt in alkaline areas. It can get rid of excess salts sometimes in such quantities that humans can actually collect the salt. Tamarisk is also a phreatophyte, a plant capable of reaching the water table. The plants grow in such dense clumps and uses so much water they can actually dry up a spring, tinaja, or lower the water table. This, in turns, kills off native riparian plants that can no longer reach the water, allowing more habitat for tamarisk. Once while walking along Salt Creek in Arches National Park, I actually witnessed water flowing on the surface disappear below ground in the middle of the day because the tamarisk consumes so much water. Later in the day after sunset, the water returned to the surface. Tamarisk, by significantly altering the riparian ecosystem, also can create a barrier impossible to penetrate and overgrow what used to be sandy beaches and islands.

During the 1970s, a researcher studying the Green River in Canyonlands National Park documented the changes along the Green River since tamarisk became established. Earlier expeditions, including John Wesley Powell, had taken photos before tamarisk became established. The researcher in the 1970s relocated the places the earlier photos had been taken and took new photos. Comparing the old and new, and taking measurements of the river channel, a documentation of how much the river had changed could be made. The results showed that what was once a wide, meandering, multi-channeled river flowing around bare sandbars or islands and at one time bordered in willow and cottonwood had become a narrower almost channeled river. Many of the islands and sandbars were densely covered in tamarisk. The tamarisk had stabilized sandbars and islands; instead of washing away each spring during high water, they grew into the bank at the edge of the river and became part of the permanent shoreline. Cottonwood trees that once lined the edge of the river became isolated, sometimes 150 feet from the river. What once had been extensive multi-aged stands of cottonwoods had become decadent stands with dense understories of tamarisk. The water table had lowered so far down that cottonwood seedling roots could not reach it, and they usually died.

Much research and money have gone into studying the effect of tamarisk on riparian areas. The plant chokes out cottonwood and willow, creating mono-stands of one species. Though some wildlife use tamarisk for breeding areas and foraging, it is not as extensively used as cottonwood or willow. Fewer birds will use the plant to build nests; many abandon an area thick with tamarisk in search of more diverse habitats. The results from my work, when I used to conduct bird and mammal transects in Arches and Canyonlands National Parks, showed pure stands of tamarisk to be significantly lacking in diversity and density of animals when compared with cottonwood, willows, or other native plant communities.

The loss of sandbars was the main reason for me wanting to do several prescribed burns of tamarisk while working at Canyonlands National Park. During the winter of 1982-1983, I, along with several other employees, revisited the Back Country Management Plan for Canyonlands National Park. We had a discussion on how the tamarisk had choked out campsites along the river corridors, forcing river parties to bunch up at critical camping areas. Trying to find a camping area during high water flow in the spring was particularly troublesome. There had been times when several groups of forty (the maximum size a river group can be) ended up on the same sand bar. Not what I would call a true wilderness experience when around 100 people are camping in the same place.

On one official work-related river trip, only four of us traveled together. After a hard day of work doing vegetation transects in tamarisk, we camped on a beautiful sand bar on a bend of the Colorado River. We were prepared for a quiet evening, eating grilled steaks cooked over tamarisk wood, and salad chased down with cold beers. As it was a clear night, we did not pitch tents, preferring to camp under the stars. After dark, we sat drinking beers telling fire and river-trip stories while stargazing. With no moon that night, the stars were their most brilliant. Around 10:00 P.M., well after dark, we heard a lot of people talking from somewhere upstream. We could see the beams of several flashlights reflecting off the canyon walls. I was dumbfounded to see lights and hear what sounded like a hoard of people motoring down the river. I thought it was the light show from Moab. Every night during the summer, a boat churned a few miles up the Colorado River out of Moab and floated back down, while a truck pulled a trailer of search lights on the adjacent river road. People watched the lights shining on the slickrock while listening to music. Since it was illegal to be rafting on the river after dark in Canyonlands National Park, the last thing that came to mind was a rafting party, but coming around the bend in the river was not just one motorized raft but eight, all full of tourists. Each raft held about ten people. They all seemed to be talking and laughing with two people in the front of each raft shinning flashlights so the boatman piloting the raft could steer. Our tranquil moment in the wilderness had been shattered by a city of people. They pulled up on our sand bar yelling, "Hi," and without even asking if it was all right, they immediately began unloading gear.

The river ranger with us went ballistic. He wanted to arrest them all. The group was not only breaking a park regulation for rafting after dark, but they were traveling in a group larger than forty people. They were even arrogant enough to set up their porta-potties right next to us and put their tents down at the other end of the sand bar. It was nice of them to be so considerate. Our wilderness experience was annihilated by eighty people while we were deep in the heart of the park and miles from any road or town. Because of the danger of continuing downstream in the dark, the river ranger had no choice but to let them stay. The next morning, he threw the book at them, writing the boatmen a bunch of citations for breaking so many regulations. I wanted to sink their rafts, I was so angry with them.

That group of rafters had picked the wrong sand bar for their camp that night. Unfortunately, one reason they showed up at our sand bar was the lack of other sandbars due to tamarisk. This episode was just one of many that indicated there was a lack of campsites along the rivers. This lack of campsites was a big issue while we worked on the Back Country Management Plan, and a seed was planted in my brain of how to get rid of some of the tamarisk (i.e. burning) and open up more sandbars to camping.

The springs of 1983 and 1984 cured low water flow problems because of heavy snows in the Rocky Mountains. March and April of both years were cold and wet with late snowfalls followed by hot weather in early May when the snow melted incredibly fast. This rapid runoff brought the water flows of the Green River and Colorado River to levels never seen since the Flaming Gorge, Glen Canyon and Hoover Dams had been built. The Colorado River below the confluence of the Green River reached flows above 100,000 cubic feet per second each year for the first time since Canyonlands National Park was established. Water entered Lake Powell below Canyonlands so quickly that the lake began to rapidly rise. In 1983 water engineers who manage the level of water in Lake Powell had not planned for such a rapid rise and were not able to release water rapidly enough from the Glen Canyon dam. Consequently, the lake reached capacity for the first time, and they had to release as much water through the dam as was flowing into the lake. At peak flow, this amounted to 110,000 cfs. River runners in Canyonlands and Grand Canyon were having the time of their lives, getting the shit scared out of them, having never seen whitewater like that. Not since the days of free-flowing rivers, a time before many of them had been born, had flows been so high.

In 1983 because of the misjudgment of Bureau of Reclamation water engineers, the Glen Canyon dam at the head of Lake Powell almost washed away. The only thing that probably saved the dam was three-quarter-inch marine plywood. Glen Canyon dam has two spillways, one on either side of the dam. No one ever thought when the dam was built that 100,000 cfs of water would ever be flowing through those spillways. The spillways were built into sandstone rock. At 100,000 cfs, the water flowed through at such a high rate that it caused the water to cavitate with strong enough force to rip huge chunks of sandstone away. The engineers realized that if the water kept flowing at such a rate, it would destroy the rock on either side of the dam causing the dam to give way. They decided to close one of the damaged spillways while at peak flow. The lake was at capacity and, with only one spillway operating, the water rapidly began to rise to the top of the dam. If water started flowing over the top of the dam, it would probably damage the dam and the hydroelectric plant below it. The only solution the Bureau of Reclamation could come up with was to make the dam higher. They built an eight-foot high plywood wall along the top of the dam. The water kept rising and began to creep up the plywood. Meanwhile the one good spillway was running at capacity, and it too was losing chunks of sandstone. The cliff was vibrating enough that it caused windows in the visitor center above the dam to vibrate, and visitors could feel the ground shaking. There was a real concern that the cliff, along with the visitor center and the dam, was going to break loose and plunge into the canyon. Bureau of Reclamation engineers were shitting concrete bricks that spring thinking of the devastation that would occur downstream. Some even speculated it would take out every dam downstream including the infamous Hoover Dam. Grand Canyon National Park discussed river evacuation procedures if the Lake Powell Dam gave way. The plan was to fly a helicopter down the canyon ahead of a 300-foot wall of water to tell river runners that they had about twenty minutes to kiss their asses good-bye.

Just as the water engineers were losing sleep and using the restrooms a lot, the runoff slowed, and the lake level began to recede. The dam held. Too bad George Hayduke from Edward Abbey's *Monkey Wrench Gang* was not working at the dam. It would have been easy enough to blow the plywood out causing water to start flowing over the dam. The Bureau of Reclamation kept really quiet about what was happening to the dam. The general public never knew how close it came to losing every dam on the Colorado River. The Glen Canyon dam has been cursed by thousands of people for flooding the canyons of Glen Canyon and ruining the ecosystem in Grand Canyon. One eco-freak could have made the history books by sabotaging the plywood and possibly having the dam blow out. Between 1983 and 1984, workers repaired the spillways and the water engineers learned to never allow the lake to fill so fast again. What happened in 1983 will probably never happen again.

Meanwhile in 1983, upstream in Canyonlands National Park, which is just above Lake Powell, the Park Service had their own problems. The river had never been so high since the establishment of the park. Because of safety concerns the superintendent closed the river at Spanish Bottom, which is just above the beginning of the rapids through Cataract Canyon. No one had ever floated the river through Cataract Canyon at such a high level. This was where John Wesley Powell and his famous expedition first encountered rapids. It only has seventeen miles of rapids left before the river enters Lake Powell, but though this stretch of rapids is short in duration, it has some of the largest rapids found along the Colorado River with names like Capsized Rapid, Satan's Gut, Niagara, and Big Drop One, Two, and Three. Many a person has ended up flipping a raft and swimming some of those rapids, including myself, and a few have come out in body bags (not me, so far).

Some acquaintances were on a raft trip when the river went above 100,000 cfs in 1983, and they passed Spanish Bottom before the superintendent made the decision to close the river. They had no idea the river was closed to rafting behind them. They were doing just fine until they got to the last three rapids, Big Drop One, Two, and Three. Rowing their rafts to shore above the rapids, they all got out to scout them out. For some rapids, as a river rises, the rapids wash out and may just become ripples or large standing waves, but when the river rises at the Big Drops they just get bigger. At Big Drop Two is a rock shelve that juts out half way across the river called Satan's Gut. The river, flowing above 100,000 cfs, created an estimated thirty-five-foot standing wave with a death grabbing hole at the bottom. Anyone going into that hole was probably not going to come out breathing unless they had gills. These guys climbed some rocks to look down on the rapids and saw the thirty-five-foot wave. They instantly stopped talking. After a moment of respectful appreciation, they planned their course of action. It came down to two choices, either go to the left or right of a big rock in the middle of the river just above Satan's Gut. If they came close to the rock on the left it should push them to the right of Satan's Gut; too far to the left, and they would be history. On the right side of the rock was another nasty looking hole that might flip the raft. Everyone choose the left path, which brought them closer to Satan's Gut but seemed safer. The path did not leave much room for error. They had three rafts and each was to go through separately while the others watched. My friends were in the second raft. Standing along the shore, they watched the first raft go to the left of the rock and clip a corner of Satan's Gut. The raft immediately folded in two at the top of the thirty-five-foot standing wave dumping everyone. My friends on shore said, "Well, I guess the right side of the rock was the right path, not the left." Meanwhile, the standing wave was spitting out rafters, raft, and gear at the lower end. No one died, so everyone else decided to go for it, but on the right side. They went to the right of the rock screaming, "We are going to die!" They made it through upright. They hold the distinction of being the first to have made it through the Cataract Canyon when the river was flowing above 100,000 cfs. As far as any historic records go, no one had ever tried to run the rapids at that level before.

Meanwhile, with the river closed below Spanish Bottom, groups of river parties were beginning to pile up, stranding a few hundred people. The park had all the visitors motored up the Colorado River to Moab by jet boat. This left the rafts with the boatmen hanging out at Spanish Bottom, drinking beer and getting bored. Some of them wanted to continue into Cataract. The river party that made it through Cataract Canyon, eventually showed up okay at Hite and drove back to Moab, still unaware the superintendent had closed the river. When they got back to Moab and found out the river was closed, they went to talk to the superintendent. Since they were all alive, and river runners are a crazy lot anyway, the Park Service decided if rafting parties wanted to take the risk, they should be allowed to go for it and reopened the river. The word had gotten out about record flows in the canyon, and wild, thrill-seeking river runners were showing up in droves in Moab trying to get on river trips. The Park Service had limits on the number of people allowed through Cataract Canyon, so not everyone could just head down the river. As some visitors cancelled their trip for fear of losing their lives, others where paying double the price to get the opportunity to experience an event that might never happen again. "Die? Who cares," was the battle cry. These people were probably firefighters on vacation.

I ended up at Spanish Bottom a short while after the river reopened, doing some mammal, bird and reptile transects. Of course, I used that as an excuse because I wanted to see first hand the river flowing at such a high rate. One evening I sat on a sandy beach at Spanish Bottom playing my dulcimer and watching the river flow by. An occasional bloated cow floated past with a raven standing on its back, eating and enjoying the trip. I noticed quantities of debris floating down the river, including thousands of uprooted tamarisks. The high water flooded the old sandbars and still existing islands, washing the trees away. Later in the summer after the water receded, I surveyed both rivers and found numerous sandbars and a few islands clean of tamarisk, replaced with fresh sand for the first time in decades.

Other National Parks throughout the West have spent large sums of money on tamarisk control. Big Bend and Zion National Parks, and Death Valley National Monument, to name a few, have removed tamarisk from springs, tinajas, and seeps, restoring water for native plants and animals. In Canyonlands National Park, we spent a considerable amount of time and money removing tamarisk from Horse Canyon in the Maze District. Where once a canyon choked with tamarisk existed, cottonwoods again grow and water flows. The restoration of cottonwoods and the bird life in the canyon is impressive. The tamarisk will never be totally eradicated from the canyon because of a seed source coming from the Green River into which Horse Canyon flows, but it now only takes a few days of work each year by a few people to hand pull tamarisk. In the beginning of the control, it took three years of intensive work and the use of herbicides to get rid of the tamarisk. The last time I visited Horse Canyon, there was no question in my mind that controlling tamarisk in riparian areas is the right thing to do. Sleeping beneath the cottonwoods can almost be deafening in the early morning hours because of singing warblers, wrens, buntings, grosbeaks, and other birds.

I believe the cottonwood trees along the Green and Colorado Rivers in Canyonlands and Arches National Parks are slowly fading away. Most are decadent, and finding a seedling is rare. Most mature stands have a dense understory of tamarisk, making them susceptible to fire. In 1988 a beautiful section of the Green River near Mineral Bottom burned because of an escaped campfire. The fire killed mature cottonwood trees because of the high intensity of the blaze burning in the tamarisk beneath the trees. Most of the burned area regrew only with tamarisk.

Cottonwood trees are the only trees along the rivers suitable for cavity nesting and many cup-nesting birds. Birds such as kestrels, woodpeckers, flycatchers, bluebirds, chickadees, warblers, and yellow-billed cuckoos, to name a few, use the trees. When humans kill cottonwood trees or they are displaced by tamarisk, it is the same as someone killing birds with a shotgun. Since there is a finite number of cottonwood trees along the rivers, birds displaced from one location may not have another place to go.

Loss of breeding bird habitat in North America has always been a concern, and I sincerely believe that tamarisk is a contributing factor in riparian areas in the West. Studies in California show that, when they remove tamarisk and replace it with species such as willow and cottonwood, diversity and density of birds and mammals increase. Also, because of the loss of habitat in Mexico, Central, and South America, neo-tropical bird populations have already been significantly reduced. Breeding bird surveys across North America show a reduction in birds that migrate out of North America for the winter.

My concern while working in Canyonlands was how to get rid of tamarisk and restore cottonwood and willows efficiently and cheaply. If I continued to sit on my haunches, I would be watching a very important component of the desert ecosystem continue to degrade. My biggest fear was waking up some morning while on a river trip to only the sounds of wind and water and not the songs or calls of the yellow-billed cuckoo, yellow-breasted chat, willow flycatcher, or bunting.

Later that night at Spanish Bottom, while staring into a tamarisk campfire thinking about what I could do to eliminate tamarisk along the river, a vision flashed from my sub-conscious mind into my blank conscious mind. What if I burned a section of riverbank covered with tamarisk in early spring before high water flow? If we had another high water flow like 1983, burning the tamarisk first will remove the dense understory, allowing the water to wash the remaining tamarisk away, and a new clean sand bar might return. The barrier of tamarisk would be removed, allowing access to a good high water campsite. Using fire and water to remove tamarisk seemed a viable idea.

I jumped up from the campfire saying, "Yes, I'll do it!" Pat, the park ranger sitting next to me, looked at me with big eyes and raised eyebrows. She picked up her chair and moved a little farther away. She already thought I was crazy; this just put the icing on the cake. During the summer of 1982, she piloted a Zodiac raft with several Resource Management people along the Colorado and Green Rivers while we collected data from vegetation transects. We took canopy cover, density, and height measurements of the tamarisk. We also took measurements of the width of the band of tamarisk from the edge of the river to where the old river channels used to be before tamarisk became established. We found in places that the old river channel was 100 to 150 feet from the present channel.

The survey required crawling under, over, and through the dense tamarisk. Bitten and stung by mosquitoes and wasps, scraped, punctured and cut by tamarisk, we took the measurements. She stayed in the Zodiac the whole time watching the crazy Resource Management people. Yes, I am sure that night around the campfire at Spanish Bottom she thought the sun had finally fried my brain.

During the winter of 1984-1985, when "Resource Management people think of projects to do, since [they] would be out of a job if [they] did not." (That is a quote from a local boatman who criticized me in *High Country News*, a regional newspaper, about the "devastating tamarisk burn" I did on the Green River.) I wrote a prescribed fire burn plan to burn two places, one on the Green River and one on the Colorado. The area along the Green River consisted of a one-mile section of river choked with tamarisk where no campsites existed. The site had about a 100-foot-wide band of tamarisk. The site on the Colorado River was at the mouth of Indian Creek. I sent the plan to the Rocky Mountain Region in Denver Colorado for review, and several copies were circulated through the Canyonlands National Park staff for comments.

From the park staff, I expected comments such as, "What a great idea. What a guy." From the Park Service River Rangers, I expected the comment, "What a 'Righteous Dude!'" Instead, when I talked to the river rangers, they looked at the ceiling or ground and mumbled words under their breath. Apparently they did not think it was such a good idea, but no one actually came out and said so. The river ranger that later wrote the article in *High Country News* made a comment in his article that he thought he was a troublemaker if he said anything, so said nothing. I believe not speaking out cancels the right to criticize later.

The Rocky Mountain Region did not like the idea of burning the mouth of Indian Creek because of some Anasai Indian Ruins located in the area, so I scrapped that burn. Instead I chose an island upstream of Indian Creek at the mouth of Lockhart Basin. The island was about seventy percent covered in tamarisk with the rest being phragmites and a few native willows.

The fire prescription was to burn in March only if high water flow was predicted to reach at least 40,000 cfs on the Green River and 50,000 cfs on the Colorado. These flow rates would flood the areas burned. Snow pack in the Rocky Mountains for the spring of 1985 was similar to 1983-1984. Forecasters expected another high water flow. The stage was set. In late March, two G-men (the mob's word for the FBI, mine for government firefighters) and two G-women, set off to burn the two sites. We put in at Potash and began motoring down the Colorado River in a Zodiac with two fifty-horsepower Mercury outboards and also in a twelve-foot rowboat with a twenty-five-horsepower outboard. A cold front was moving through that day creating some unstable conditions, good for burning but, it turned out, bad for river running. The wind was blowing upstream twenty to thirty miles per hour, gusting to forty, creating whitecaps on the river that caused the Zodiac to bounce so hard I bit my tongue. This made for difficult motoring since we could not read the river. We grounded the Zodiac numerous times on submerged sandbars. The Colorado and Green rivers, when low, have a lot of sandbars just below the surface of the water. While motoring down or up a river, one has to watch how the ripples or water is boiling up to indicate if a sand bar is present, if we read the river wrong, we got stuck. With whitecaps on the river, we could not read the river, so got stuck, requiring us to get out of the boat and push the Zodiac off. The river water was in the forty-degree Fahrenheit range, so after getting out several times into the water, I thought I could become an honorary member of the local Polar Bear Club. My legs were numb and blue from the cold water. The day was overcast, occasionally raining and spitting snow. I was thinking, maybe the fire god does not want us to burn the tamarisk. Maybe the righteous dude river runners have put a curse on us.

We stopped at the downstream end of the island above Indian Creek. I got out the drip torch filled with two parts diesel fuel and one part gasoline and headed into the tamarisk. This fire was a "no brainer" burn, just light the tamarisk and let it burn. The fire had no place to go other than the island. Before I started burning, I decided to check the island for any wildlife. Walking through dense tamarisk, I was almost to the upstream end when I was attacked by a large brown-feathered creature that burst through the tamarisk in front of me. It flew right into my face knocking me down. Using my legs and arms, I crab-walked backwards wondering what the hell had hit me. Looking up, I saw a Canada goose honking at me and flying just above the tamarisk. It landed in the river, continuing to honk. I got up and walked to the upstream point of the island and there amongst the tamarisk was a nest with twelve eggs. If I burn the island, I would destroy the nest. The male and female had landed in the water next to me definitely agitated by my presence. Being a Park Service employee my job was to protect native species, so the guilt piled on. How could I feel right about destroying a nest full of goose eggs? I walked back to the Zodiac, loaded up, and we continued down the river. We left the island alone.

By late afternoon we had made it only as far as the confluence of the Green and Colorado rivers and decided to camp there. We still had to motor up the Green River, but it was getting late in the day, and the confluence had the best campsite. Just as we pulled up to the sand bar, the clouds parted above us and a ray of sunshine shown down on the cliff across the river. I looked up and saw the ray beaming down on a large desert bighorn sheep ram, his horns making a full curl, standing on a rock several hundred feet above us. A few ewes and lambs were below him looking at us. I had seen this guy several times before, it being one of the larger rams in the Island in the Sky District. He looked like he was surveying his domain, standing with his head up towards the sunshine. Just then a bald eagle flew overhead heading downstream. The center of the universe, which to me was the confluence of the Green and Colorado river, was showing us its best. I interpreted the bighorn ram and bald eagle as good signs, good omens. The fire god was giving us the thumbs-up sign. "Burn that tamarisk, you righteous dude!"

However, the ray of sunshine was short lived. The clouds came back together, turning the sky dull and gray again, and a drizzle of light rain began to fall. To make matters worse, the wind increased. Because of the 900-foot vertical canyon walls that jutted out of the river, the wind at the Confluence funneled into a narrow corridor, creating gusts of about fifty miles per hour at river level, but about 500 feet above our heads the wind was screaming around the cliffs probably gusting to 100 mph. The wind screaming along the cliffs at the confluence sounded like a wild banshee flying overhead. This became a bad omen. Perhaps the fire god was trying to tell me after all that by burning tamarisk I would not make the "Righteous Dude" status. To burn or not to burn, that was the question.

Setting up our tents in the sand proved to be difficult; we had to anchor them down with rocks to keep the wind from blowing them into the river. The wind coated everything in sand, including our supper. I was eating so much sand, I thought I was going to break a filling on a tooth. We had sand in our hair, eyes, and ears. After dark, as we huddled around our tamarisk campfire, trying to stay warm, a strong gust of wind slammed into us, almost blowing our lawn chairs over. The wind lifted the fire pan with the fire burning in it off the ground and hurled everything right towards my tent. Jumping out of my chair, I ran after the fire pan as it rolled across the sand sending wood and flaming ash in all directions. Some of the burning wood and ash landed on my tent and started to melt my tent fly. The fire pan and the rest of the fire proceeded down the beach into the river. I stopped the ash from melting my tent fly, but it looked like Swiss cheese. "Great," I said to myself, "the center of the universe is definitely trying to tell me something." Since the fire blew away, I crawled into my tent and went to sleep.

The next morning broke cold and overcast, no tamarisk would burn in this weather, but we decided to motor up the Green River to the burn site anyway, just in case the weather improved. Six miles up the Green River, we came around the bend in the river, and the area we were going to burn came into view. A hole in the clouds opened and a ray of sunshine shown down. Now that seemed to be a good omen. The sky shortly became partly cloudy, and the air warmed considerably. Taking weather observations, we found ourselves within the fire prescription by 10:00 A.M., so we lit the drip torches and fusees and started burning.

There were only four of us, but the fire could only burn about a mile of river bottom because of the cliffs rising from the water at either end; the narrow band of tamarisk abutted vertical cliffs away from the river. There was no need for a holding crew. I could have done the burn myself. The tamarisk at first did not want to start burning, but finally, when we got enough fuel under some trees to get the flames hot enough, the fire quickly burst into fifty-foot flames. The wind for once was blowing downstream and rapidly pushed the fire from north to south. The fire would have made any pyromaniac happy, fifty- to hundred-foot flames, lots of heat and smoke. It only took a few hours to burn a little less than one mile of shore. At the north end of the fire a beautiful, flat sandy area was exposed suitable for a high water campsite.

Now feeling as if I might make "righteous dude" status after all, I stood in the bow of the boat as we surveyed the burn from the river. My chest swelled and I had a big head as we motored along the river looking at the burn. The entire band of tamarisk had burned. Not a single live tree was left. Now all we needed was a high spring runoff. We motored down river to an exposed sand bar free of tamarisk just below the burn and set up camp. I toasted a beer to the fire god in tribute to my success. The river rangers on the trip remained quiet, clearly not happy. At sunset the sky clouded up again, and it began to rain. The rain would put out any smoldering fire left at the prescribed burn. However, it also made for a miserable evening, with us sitting in the rain eating soggy barbecued chicken and salad floating in a nice Italian water sauce. After dark, it started raining even harder, putting out the campfire. The night before wind blew the fire into the river; this night rain put it out. We all retired to our tents to stay dry. My Swiss cheese rain fly let water inside the tent, and I had to lay a tarp over the top to stay dry. I read for a while, but being tired from two days of exhausting work and stress, I fell asleep, dreaming about river babes at the Popular Place, a bar in Moab frequented by river runners.

Sometime in the early morning hours, I was dreaming about a boatman putting a blanket over my head and suffocating me, when I woke up with a start to find the roof of the tent in my face. Jumping up and out of the tent, I found almost a foot of wet snow on it. Snowing in the desert in March! What is this trying to tell me? I shook the snow off the tent fly and crawled back into my sleeping bag. I went back to sleep while listening to the soft sound of falling snow. When we finally got up, it was still lightly snowing, but the clouds were thinning. The storm was breaking up. We ate breakfast sitting in the snow. Cold and wet, we loaded the gear into the boats, deciding to motor down to the confluence and then up the Colorado River to Moab instead of continuing up the Green River to Mineral Bottom. We had endured two days, and faced a third of rain, snow, and wind. We were all very tired. Three of us were in the Zodiac, and Larry was in the smaller row boat. I was sitting next to Pat, who was piloting the boat, and Erica was in the front. Pat put the throttles to full and the two mercury engines began to hum. The Zodiac quickly picked up speed. Pat glanced down to tie the hood of her jacket around her head, and I noticed some gear loose at our feet, so I looked down to stow it away. Suddenly, Erica yelled, "Look out!"

Pat and I both glanced up to see that we were headed straight for a large rock jutting out of the water. "Oh shit!" I yelled as we went up on the rock. The Zodiac shot out of the water up into the air like going off a ski jump, and I found myself floating weightless a couple of feet above the boat. I came down, but, unfortunately, not in the Zodiac but in the river, just missing the rock we had jumped. The boat had managed to stay upright and was downstream of me with Pat and Erica and our gear strewn all over the boat.

Damn! What next? I thought spitting brown ash-filled water out of my mouth. The surface of the river was covered with a fine layer of ash washing into the river from the prescribed burn.

The rowboat had been behind us, and Larry quickly motored over and fished me out of the river. Man, was I cold, already hypothermic. We quickly caught up with the Zodiac, and I stripped down and quickly threw on some warm dry clothes. We floated down river while I tried to warm up. Finally getting some heat back in me, we continued on with me huddled in the bow, shivering. The imagine of me standing in the bow like George Washington crossing the Potomac River, surveying my domain was long gone, replaced with a humbler Jeff, just like the time I stumbled out of the woods at Bryce Canyon. Just before rounding a bend in the river, I looked back at the rock. The only thing that had saved us from dying was that the downstream side of the rock sloped into the water. This had enabled the Zodiac to go up and over it like a ski jump. If it had been a vertical rock, we would have smashed into the side of it. With all of us sitting in silence the rest of the day, we finally made it back to Moab just before dark, cold and tired.

The predicted high water never came that spring. The burn on the Green River never flooded and never washed away any tamarisk. Meanwhile, back at the office, desperate to make my experiment be something of a success, I tried to figure out what else I could do. I came up with the idea of cutting the burned standing tamarisk to open the area up for a high water campsite. I also thought if we kept the area open, maybe next year it would flood. I was a little concerned about using chainsaws along the river since it was in a recommended wilderness area. I justified my decision to use chainsaws because of boat traffic. Almost every day in the summer, raft trips of up to forty people passed by the burn site, most often in large rafts powered by outboard motors. Jet boats also motored up and down the Green and Colorado rivers, power boats, too, sometimes, including the famous Friendship Cruise during the Memorial Weekend, and of course the Park Service's Zodiac with two fifty-horse outboards cruise by on patrols. The noise of chainsaws would be no different. When I proposed the project to the river rangers, eyeballs once again rolled into the back of their heads. There were moans as they walked off muttering under their breaths. I yelled to them, "What? What did I say?" I thought it was a great idea. One of the rangers should have hit me over the head with an oar and knocked some sense into me. Then I would of said, "Oh yeah, that is a dumb idea. What was I thinking."

Four of us in the hottest part of August, armed with chainsaws, motored to the burn site on the Green River. We began cutting in the early afternoon in 100-plus-degree weather. The burned tamarisk was so dry and hard, our chainsaws dulled quickly. One hour of cutting, then two hours went by. We were hot and sweaty and covered with black charcoal. With four chainsaws going full bore, a river party went by. Instead of it being a motorized raft, it was a canoe trip. They stared at us with hate as they floated by. The other three in my party stood off to the side and pointed a finger at me, the guilty one. Everyone in the canoes gave me an evil stare. We turned the saws off, feeling guilty about infringing on the quiet of their trip.

Our tempers began to build. After two hours of cutting, we had only advanced two hundred feet, with another 4,000 or so to go. No way were we going to get this cut in three days. A month didn't even seem hopeful. After two more hours of work, I accidentally cut a tree that almost fell on some of Dan's gear. He let out a string of four-letter words. That was the breaking point. All of us blew up, yelling cuss words at each other. Dan and I squared off with chainsaws running. The other two stood off to the side with sick grins on their faces. They apparently were hoping Dan would take the crazy Resource Management person out. Just as if it looked like we were going to start hacking away at each other, my chain saw sputtered and died. Damn out of gas! I had to start talking fast. "Well guys," I said. "I think this isn't going to work. Maybe this wasn't such a good idea." Looks of relief came across everyone's faces.

We stopped cutting and turned off the chainsaws. Quiet returned to the area. No other work was ever done with the tamarisk, and the site is now covered with tamarisk ten feet tall. However, another part of my experiment was to survey bird and small animals within the burn, and the results were very interesting. There was a significant higher number of birds using the burned area for foraging than unburned tamarisk. Small mammals were also at a higher density than in unburned tamarisk. I even found the tracks of a mountain lion in the burn, the first lion tracks I had ever seen along the river. The data indicated that opening up the tamarisk by burning made the site more desirable for wildlife, probably by creating more edge ecotones of the type heavily used by many wildlife species.

It would be interesting to study wildlife in a large stand of tamarisk for a couple of years and then burn it and monitor the site for five or more years to document the changes. I suspect one would find higher diversities and densities of wildlife using the site until the trees reach a certain density, height, and cover. Then wildlife use would drop off.

After we got back to Moab, the word got around about the crazy Resource Management person who thought burning tamarisk was a good idea. Most river runners think the river corridor is sacred and should be left alone. When I walked into the Popular Place, people shunned me. No one was buying me beers, and I never reached the higher level of righteous dude or boatman status.

Even though river runners did not like me burning the tamarisk, wildfires in tamarisk are nothing new. Every year along the Colorado and Green rivers tamarisk burn; it is usually human caused. The tree is highly flammable. Unfortunately cottonwood trees continue to decrease along the rivers and someday may become extirpated.

I know if I ever have the chance to work in an area with tamarisk again, I will still initiate a program to burn and cut it. I would also take cuttings of willow and cottonwoods from existing trees along the rivers and propagate seedlings to be later transplanted onto the cleared sites. Cottonwoods have been reestablished in California and Nevada along the Colorado River, in what were once pure stands of tamarisk, so I know it can be done. We replaced tamarisk with cottonwoods in Horse Canyon with favorable results. It just takes work. In 2001, experiments are underway in releasing an insect that may significantly reduce tamarisk — biological control may prove to be the best way to reduce this problem plant.

The other important lesson I learned from this one prescribed fire was to make sure one has enough time and resources to adequately carry out a plan and follow up on it. For instance, I would have loved to study the burn for several years to determine its use by birds and mammals.

If the park staff working at Canyonlands and Arches National Parks do not take a more aggressive approach toward tamarisk, cottonwood trees may all but disappear from the river corridor. Clear objectives and priorities should be established. Cottonwood and willow are the most important resources along the rivers and should be protected. Dense stands of tamarisk growing under cottonwood trees should be removed by chainsaws and new seedlings controlled. New cottonwood seedlings should be propagated and planted. Camping should not be allowed near cottonwood stands until the fire danger is reduced. If an escaped campfire burns a cottonwood stand, an aggressive program of ensuring that cottonwood trees are reestablished should be initiated. Research should be devoted to burning tamarisk and monitoring use by wildlife. If more wildlife utilizes a burned stand of tamarisk rather than a mature stand, a program of burning pure stands of tamarisk should be initiated at ten year intervals to enhance the habitat.

Tamarisk is never going to be eliminated; no one will debate that subject, but I know it can be better managed than it is now. Tamarisk burns, and where there are people and tamarisk, there will be fires. The important point is to ensure that cottonwood and hackberry trees and willow are not destroyed. The natural world is in such a chaotic state today that even if I could only get one cottonwood tree established, or enhance the habitat enough so one new pair of songbirds could establish a territory, I would call it a success.

Critics and the press hammered me over this one small, prescribed burn. It is easy to be a critic, harder to be a doer. I like to keep the cauldron stirred. It keeps the good stuff from sticking to the bottom of the pot. Hell, not everything one does is going to be a success, but what a dull life we would live if we only did things that were guaranteed to turn out successfully. The light bulb would never have been invented. I always remember the children's story of the person riding on the back of a donkey and having people criticize him because he was too big, weighing the donkey down. He finally ended up carrying the donkey on his back.

9

Talking about Death
A little while, a moments rest upon the wind,
An another woman shall bear me
— Kahlil Gibran

California 1987

*E*ach year, beginning in late August and extending into October, parts of California, including homes, burn. When combating wildfires, urban interface or "urban in your face," as firefighters like to say, has created major problems throughout the West from the foothills of the Rockies to the Pacific. People, in their desire to flee a city/suburban environment, have moved into the foothills and mountains, building in places where humans should not permanently live. Building homes in forests and shrub lands that evolved with fire over thousands of years can spell only one word, "DISASTER." Northern and Western shrub lands and forests are strongly fire dependent. Fire is the major agent to initiate and terminate vegetation succession; it controls the age, structure, health, and species composition of the vegetation. If fires are prevented (suppressed), plant communities can become decadent and are often replaced with another fuel type or becomes a forest of dead and down fuel ripe for a catastrophic wildfire. Some forests, such as ponderosa pine, can have a fire frequency of ten to thirty years. If fire is not allowed to burn in natural cyclic rhythms but is suppressed over the long term, when a fire finally breaks loose, about the only thing anyone can do is get out of the way. In Western forests it is not a question of *if* a forest fire is going to occur, but *when* and *how big*.

When land is developed, fire suppression is the norm. People just don't seem to want their homes a part of a fire-controlled environment. In those types of settings, every time a fire starts, it is immediately put out. When fire is suppressed year after year—in some places since the late 1800s—the consequence is heavy fuel loading that under the right conditions can become fire storms, burning so quickly and so hot that cars caught in the inferno are melted down to unrecognizable steel heaps. Sometimes a fire burns too quickly, with some people leaving a fire-ravaged area in body bags. Urban interface in fire-prone areas creates extremely hazardous conditions for firefighters. There are many firefighters out there who have seen the ugliest side of the fire beast, and it has scared the shit out of them.

There is no better example of urban interface and no bigger chance of coming out in a body bag than in California near the coast from San Diego north to San Francisco. Large sub-divisions are built on steep ridges, hillsides, and in canyon bottoms choked with dense vegetation. Near the coast, homes can be found on some of the steepest terrain available. Once built, almost everyone immediately puts up their no trespassing signs and manages their landscape so that dense forest or shrub land develops, providing them with privacy. Sometimes dense vegetation grows right up against homes. The roads to these houses are often narrow and winding, sometimes with only one way in and out—a firefighter's nightmare. Fuels such as chaparral, eucalyptus trees, mountain mahogany, and poison oak—all that naturally grow dense—can become volatile when dry.

Weather in California in winter and spring is often cool and wet, but by early summer the skies clear, it gets hot, and it is not uncommon for parts of the state not to see much rain for several months. The combination of lack of rain, dense forest or shrub lands, and homes on steep terrain means dangerous fires. The "pucker" factor is usually rated high for firefighters combating California fires.

The year 1987 was normal in California, wet in the spring and hot and dry during the summer. By late August, the vegetation had dried out, the color of the hillsides had turned yellow and brown. A few days before the Labor Day weekend, a cold front moved onto the coast from the northwest. In 1987 the cold front brought little moisture but did bring wind and dry lightning. As it moved across Oregon and California, dry lightning started a number of fires north of Redding, California, and south of Portland, Oregon. High winds quickly fanned the fires into large acreages and homes burned or became threatened. People evacuated areas, running for their lives ahead of 100-plus-foot flames.

I got the call the day before the Labor Day weekend started. I was needed as squad boss and would also get some crew boss trainee time on a Type II hand crew, destination Northern California, almost on the border of California and Oregon. I was told the crew would be composed of National Park Service employees from Canyonlands, Arches, and Capitol Reef National Parks, Natural Bridges National Monument, and Lake Powell National Recreation Area. We were to rendezvous at the Western Slope Fire Center in Grand Junction, Colorado, where we would be flown onto California.

I have always enjoyed going out on fire assignments with a Park Service crew. Often, we know each other, the Park Service being a small organization in comparison to some other federal agencies. Sometimes, I do not get to see some of my friends until called out on a large fire. About midday, ten of us from Moab loaded our gear into several trucks and headed for Grand Junction, about 120 miles away. When any fire assignment is out of state, it often means a twenty-one-day assignment, so we left expecting not to see home for a while. Arriving in Grand Junction, the other ten firefighters that would make up our crew had already arrived and were milling around, talking and playing Hacky Sack. I knew most of the other people that would form our crew. It was an NPS family reunion.

A charter plane was inbound from Arizona with another fire crew onboard. We had a couple of hours to kill before the plane arrived, so everyone had a chance to catch up on the latest news, get their gear together, continue playing Hacky Sack, read books or sleep. We were staged under a pavilion near the airport terminal. After talking with a few friends, I lay down with my head on my personnel fire bag and tried to get some sleep. I figured sleep was going to be a precious commodity for the next several weeks.

When I got the call in Moab, it was the typical hurry-up call. During the fire season, we kept our fire gear packed and ready and usually had less than two hours before we were on the road. As was usually the case on fire dispatches, we were told to hurry to report to the staging area. We had to get somewhere to catch a bus, plane, or truck, but often when we assembled, we found out that the transportation was late or part of the crew has not yet arrived, forcing us to kick back and wait.

Once I was in the fire bureaucracy, sometimes I felt as if I was in prison. I could no longer go where I wanted, do what I wanted, or dress the way I wanted. My life for the next twenty-one days was owned by the Boise Interagency Fire Center (BIFC). Overhead personnel in the fire organization would tell me when I could sleep, eat, or work. Lying back with my head on my fire pack, I watched people coming and going from the airport terminal. Normal people conducted business, went on vacation, met relatives—did common everyday type of activities. They didn't go to fires. Some of the people glanced over at the yellow-shirted folks sitting or standing around in the shade. I wondered what they thought. Were they seeing us as glamorous firefighters saving the world or just a bunch of slobs looking dirty and hungry?

As usually happened when I just sat around waiting before I got to a fire, I got butterflies in my gut, wondering if the old fickle finger of fate would nail the coffin shut on me this time. I preferred to move quickly into the thick of things. Sitting and waiting, in particular when heading for a large project fire, I worried. I usually had little information on where the fire was, how big it was, what the terrain would be like, how severe the fire behavior might be, what fuels were burning. I want to get there and find out. It was like watching a horror movie and being scared until the monster showed itself. Knowing what the monster was, what it looked like, eased the tension.

Waiting gave me time to start thinking about life outside of firefighting. In 1987 I had already been fighting fires for eleven years, and they were some of the best years of my life. For eleven summers, just about everything I did had firefighting in the background. I would think: Can I go on vacation, or will I miss a fire? For me the greatest fear was missing the big fire that everyone talked about for a year or two afterwards. Not being able to sit around a campfire, drink beer and tell war stories with my firefighting compadres bothered me. I hated it when some fellow firefighter started talking about some big project fire that I wasn't on. Unlike those who fight fires full time,

I have always had the luxury of deciding to not be available. It was usually my decision to stick around all summer waiting for a big fire or head out for a vacation. I found it difficult to make plane reservations a month or two in advance during the fire season, particularly during August and September. For eleven years, my mind had been playing a tug-of-war between taking my chances with the fire season or going on vacation and maybe being bummed when I got back because I missed a good fire assignment with lots of overtime and hazard pay. So, I got excited when the call came in—I had recommitted to the fire season—but the waiting for a bus or a plane set my mind thinking about what could go wrong.

While we waited, our crew boss, a park ranger named Tom from Lake Powell, organized the crew into three squads. My supervisor from Canyonlands was the squad boss for squad one, I the squad boss for squad two, and a friend from Capitol Reef boss for third. Tom was known as a gung-ho ranger who liked to get into the action, whatever it was. He had busted a few heads in law enforcement actions on Lake Powell and loved the excitement—a little too much, especially when the action got hot and heavy. I thought as I drifted off to sleep that this crew assignment was going to be interesting. Little did I know at that time how interesting it was really going to be.

I just woke up from a nap when we heard a prop plane coming in from the east. Glancing up, I saw an unmarked four-engine prop plane drop out of the sky. Looked like our transport plane had arrived. We were not going out on a major airline but on some private contract plane. The plane touched down on the runway, smoke billowing from the wheels. It taxied toward the Western Slope Fire Center, where we gathered up our gear and stood in line. The plane looked old, like something left over from Vietnam.

We loaded our own gear into the belly of the plane and climbed aboard. The plane only had room for about fifty passengers, and another twenty-person fire crew, a Native American crew from the Navajo Reservation in Arizona, was already on board. They stared at us, grunting hellos or nodding when we walked by, but otherwise remained quiet. We settled into the vacant seats and strapped in. After the plane refueled, the pilot started the engines, and, shortly thereafter, we taxied down the airstrip. Once airborne, the plane turned west towards Utah. Sitting in a window seat, I glanced down and watched the desert country of western Colorado and Utah pass by. I could see canyons and mesas in which I had worked or explored, but mostly places I had not yet had the chance to explore. I was sadden to realize I would probably not get a chance to explore every nook and cranny I could see from my window seat. After this fire assignment, I would be heading for a new job at Rocky Mountain National Park, so my new stomping grounds would be Colorado. Exploring the slickrock country of Utah would now be only once or twice a year during my days off. I guessed I would have to wait for my next life to get to all the places I wanted to explore in Utah.

About an hour later, we passed over the Wasatch Mountains, the front range for Salt Lake City and outlying cities. Glancing down, I could see the urban sprawl of the Salt Lake City area, the heartland of the Mormons. I swear cars driving along on Interstate 15 and 80 below us traveled faster than we flew. The plane must be fighting a strong headwind; it might be a long flight to California. Flying over the Great Salt Lake and the salt flats west of Salt Lake City, I saw the first wafts of smoke from the fires in California. We were still 600 air miles or so from our destination and already encountering smoke. The fire or fires were not small. This was definitely going to be a twenty-one-day assignment. By the time we flew over Nevada, the ground was obscured by the smoke.

What seemed like hours later, we finally touched down in Redding, California, under a setting sun shrouded in smoke. The sun was just a red ball in the sky, the smoke was so dense. While unloading our gear, I glanced around. The airport buzzed with activity. Redding was a major fire dispatch center for California. Firefighters were everywhere, and forklifts unloaded planes filled with hoses, pumps, food, and other gear needed to outfit the thousands of firefighters on the front lines. I noticed air tankers lined up in a neat row — several B-26 Type III and PB4Y-2 Type I planes with the capability to dump thousands of gallons of fire retardant on a fire in one flight. I saw helicopters lined up nearby. Even though it was late in the day, they looked as if they had not flown at all as yet. Either there was nothing for them to do, or the heavy smoke had kept them grounded. I suspected the latter. We soon found out that a strong inversion had set up in California, and the smoke was so dense the aircraft could not fly. They had only gotten as far as Redding and were waiting for the inversion to lift. The helicopters waited to fly to helibases nearer the fires. The air tankers would fly out of Redding and support the front lines, returning to Redding for more fire retardant and refueling. So far, none had been able to get to their destinations. The pilots and their support crews must be bummed not being able to fly. Flying meant money and excitement to those guys.

As in war, a crucial part of firefighting is air support. No air support, and the battle might be lost. Those fires in California were being fought with ground support only. That meant hazardous conditions for the firefighters. They didn't have an eye in the sky to keep them informed about what the fire was doing; there would be no retardant drops, bucket work by helicopters, or the possibility for the firefighters to be flown into the fires. It was not uncommon, if the fire was a few miles or so from the fire camp and up a mountain, for firefighters to be flown to a helispot cut into the forest or, more often, to a meadow or clear ridge top. Flying near the fire saved precious time and energy for the firefighters. It looked to me like the fire we were heading for was going to be a hump over the hill.

A bulletin board in the middle of a small meridian was covered with newspaper articles about the wildfires burning in California. The articles said about 10,000 firefighters had been mobilized to a number of fires burning in several states. Smoke conditions were the worst in Northern California. Homes and structures were threatened on one fire called the "Happy Camp Complex." Several communities had been evacuated. Our crew boss and the Navajo crew boss headed off to check in with Operations to find out about our destination and transportation. The rest of us headed for the chow line. The crew bosses returned to tell us we were heading for the "Happy Camp Complex." It sounded like the pucker factor was indeed going to be rated high for this one. After eating, the Navajo crew and ours loaded up in reconditioned school buses.

The buses were gutless wonders with hard seats. Climbing into the mountains outside of Redding, we were in granny gear, moving along at the rapid clip of twenty miles an hour. What would normally take about three hours of driving turned into an eight-hour ordeal. As day turned to night, the dense smoke dropped visibility to just in front of the bus. It was like driving through a dense fog. The driver had a hard time seeing, and the winding mountain road made travel even more treacherous. Vehicles passing us from the other direction could not be seen until almost upon us. I kept waiting for a semi-truck or a car to hit us head on.

Four hours after leaving Redding, we came to a roadblock. The highway beyond had been closed to all traffic except fire-related vehicles. A highway patrol officer manning the road block waved us through. From there to fire camp the smoke thickened. The driver had to put his left wheel on the white stripe in the middle of the road to keep from running off the road. Visibility was almost zero, and the bus driver had reduced speed to about ten miles per hour. I could almost walk as fast as we were driving. Finally, at about 3:00 A.M., we pulled into fire camp. My butt ached from sitting on the hard seats for so long. As the bus made the turn off the highway, the headlights hit a big cardboard sign that read, "Welcome to the Happy Camp Complex," a complex meaning we were not just dealing with one fire, but several. Were we happy campers? I knew at three in the morning after a bone-crushing eight-hour bus ride, I was not. The crew bosses checked in, while we waited in the bus. They came back and said to unload our gear, and bed down for a few hours of sleep. We would be awakened at 6:00 A.M. In the early morning hours, the smoke was thick enough to cut with a knife. It made breathing difficult. *Man*, I thought, *I hope I don't have to spend three weeks under these conditions.*

Unfortunately the conditions never did improve. The Happy Camp Complex turned out to have some of the worst smoke conditions ever recorded for a sustained time. After returning home, I found out that what we breathed at Happy Camp was equivalent to smoking two packs of cigarettes a day. The smoke conditions caused a lot of medical problems. Hardly a firefighter came back from the Happy Camp Complex without a cold, bronchitis, or even some with pneumonia. To this day, I think Happy Camp permanently affected my lungs. When I take a deep breath, I feel numbness in my lungs. I took a physical exam after Happy Camp and found out I was able to only use about eighty percent of my lung capacity. The other twenty percent had been ruined by overexposure to smoke and ash. Eleven years of firefighting most likely also contributed to the problem.

Our crew boss woke us up at 6:00 A.M., and he and the Navajo crew boss headed off to briefing while the rest of us packed our personnel fire bags and readied our day packs for a shift on the fire line. Within a short time, the crew bosses returned, and we gathered around to find out what we were going to be doing. They said the two crews had been pulled together to form a strike team, and Tom, our crew boss, who was strike-team qualified, became strike-team leader. Jim, my supervisor from Canyonlands, became our new crew boss, and I became the crew boss trainee. New squad bosses were picked to replace Tom and Jim. Tom told us we were being moved to a spike camp up the Klamath River, to a placed called T-bar. Moving to a spike camp made me happy. I hated large fire camps—too noisy, too many people. Give me a spike camp any day.

Every time there was a large project fire or a complex of fires, a number of support contractors were hired. They included caterers. These guys showed up in semi trucks with the trailers being full-service kitchens. Other semis had portable showers or laundry services. Semis brought in portable generators that ran twenty-four hours a day. There were water tenders, private fire engines, contractors who had old school buses to transport firefighters, local people who showed up in their own vehicles to contract out to transport people, plus helicopters staged at a nearby helibase. Most of these people were contractors hired to support the firefighters. Wildland fires were big business to many people who relied on project fires for their livelihoods. Many a time, I had been on fires miles from civilization but still got a hot meal for breakfast and supper and good sack lunches. Back in fire camp, I could get my laundry done, take a nice hot shower, and buy toothpaste, shampoo, new fire boots, or clothes. After supper, I could watch a movie or a football game on a large-screen TV hooked up to a satellite disk. Nowadays, the overhead folks who work for operations, demob, or plans all have computers, with GIS, GPS capabilities. So a large fire camp is like a small town with most conveniences. Sounds almost like a vacation resort doesn't it? Great food, good friends, lots of entertainment, good scenery all paid for by the good old United States of America.

On large fires that burn for months, small communities can sprout up much like mining towns of old. The camp can house a thousand or so firefighters and support personnel. Inflatable Quonset huts sometimes were brought in, or the firefighters might be housed in big tents with wood stoves. Fire camps basically had everything but a saloon and brothel. The downside of all this was that large camps had too many people, generators were always running, vehicles moved around, helicopters flew overhead, tools were sharpened. I ended up having to stand in long lines waiting to eat, take a shower, or use a porta-potty. The camps were noisy, and, unfortunately, some fire crews had less than desirable people who stole from other firefighters. There was no way to lock up personal gear when we lived in tents or under tarps, so anyone could just walk in and take what they wanted—cameras, CD players, clothing, and money. In large fire camps, stealing was always worse. About the only thing of value I brought to large fires was my "King radio," which I usually carried with me to keep it from being stolen. At large fire camps, there have been fights and even murders.

As in any community, the camps have law enforcement personnel patroling to keep order. Happy Camp turned out to be one of the worst fire camps for lawlessness. A law enforcement park ranger friend of mine who worked Happy Camp later said there were many fights, things stolen, and one firefighter had his throat slit by someone else. When a bunch of macho firefighters get together from all walks of life, trouble sometimes follows. The saving grace was that firefighters usually worked their butts off for twelve-hour shifts or longer each day, so most just wanted to spend their time off sleeping. Alcohol and drugs were not allowed at any fire camp; anyone caught with any was demobbed or arrested. The clincher was that the rest of that person's crew was also sent home. That put considerable pressure on those who want to break the rules.

For me, I'd take small fires with only a few folks any day, but if I was on a large project fire, I would opt for a spike camp over the large fire camp. Spike camps usually only have a few fire crews, engines, and a few overhead personnel, usually less than a hundred people. The only problem with a spike camp was that sometimes we didn't get supplied on time, and hot meals and showers might not be available. We had no problem in California, but the next year in Yellowstone National Park, while spiked out six or seven miles in the back country, we went a couple of days with no hot food and little water and almost ran out of all food and water.

Back at Happy Camp, we loaded into the buses and drove another hour to T-bar, which turned out to be the name of a guest ranch. The guests had been evacuated due to the fire, so the buildings were empty. We did not get to use the cabins but instead set up camp in a gorgeous meadow along a bend of the Klamath River. We put up a large tarp under sycamore trees and firs along the edge of the meadow. It reminded me of my beloved Gila Wilderness. Large sycamores also grew along the banks of the river, and across from the bend was a vertical cliff that rose straight out of the water. Unfortunately, I could not see how high the cliff was because its top disappeared into a dense layer of smoke. The area had large old-growth fir and pine trees that towered a hundred feet or more. We were in the home of the Northern spotted owl, and Pacific Northwest loggers, where a man is not a man unless they worked in the woods. The smoke layer was about fifty feet above our head, and the air we breathed was smoky but not as bad as it had been at Happy Camp. Everywhere I looked, the terrain went almost straight up, disappearing into the smoke. This fire was not going to be a piece of cake. Dense smoke and steep slopes made for hazardous conditions.

We found out that we were going out on the night shift, so had about seven hours before our shift began. Our crew and the Navajo crew improved our shelters using logs and tarps, and spread out our sleeping bags. I went to sleep, waking in the early afternoon about four hours later. The smoke had lifted a little higher, and the sun had warmed the air. I was stiff from sleeping and from the bus ride. Yawning, I went down to the river to wash up and do a little exploring. The river was fairly shallow, the water clear with a light blue color and rounded rocks lining the bottom. Just downstream from where I stood, I could see a small set of Class II rapids. Since the air was warm, I decided to go for a swim. I went back and got the air mattress I had used for sleeping and headed back to the river. I stripped down to my birthday suit wearing only Tevas and jumped on the air mattress. I floated downstream bouncing through the rapids. Pulling over to shore below the rapids I trotted back up the river to do it again. Several of my fellow firefighters sat along the shore watching as I floated through the rapids. Since I didn't die, with a loud hoot, they ran back to camp for their air mattresses. Before long there was a bunch of us, naked as the day we were born, floating the river. River rats from the desert country always looked for excuses to get naked and go swimming. The Navajo fire crew kept their distance from the crazy Anglos. They were probably wondering what the hell had they gotten into, associating with this crazy crew. The water was cold but refreshing. I was finally wide awake and ready to take on the fire beast. The sun dropped behind a ridge, and the river fell into shadow. The air temperature instantly dropped ten degrees, and I started shivering. Shortly, all of us were coming out of the water and drying off, laughing and ready for a night on the fire line.

During the day, other firefighters arrived — a couple more crews and an engine strike team. While standing in the chow line waiting for supper, I heard someone yell my name and turned to a familiar face. It was Susie, a woman with whom I use to work in New Mexico when I was with the BLM. She ran up and gave me a big hug. I had not seen her in four years, so it surprised me to see her in the woods of California. Susie came with the engine strike team assigned to the same part of the fire as our hand crew strike team. We sat together at supper, and she filled me in about friends in New Mexico.

By 6:00 P.M., two strike teams of Type II hand crews and one engine strike team was geared up for the night shift. All the Type II hand crews were loaded into National Guard duce-and-a-half troop trucks and, along with the engine strike team in caravan, started up a steep logging road towards our assignment.

The trucks slowly worked their way up the logging road. Looking out the back, I watched us pass through old-growth spruce and fir with an occasional redwood grove that towered into the smoke above us. Some of the trunks were four feet or more in diameter. We finally topped out on a ridge and began driving down the other side where we intersected with another logging road. The trucks stopped at an open area where logs were stacked into a huge pile, a log loading area. The area around us showed signs of recent logging — cut stumps and deep skid mark's going up and down the hillside where logs had been dragged. Unlike the other side of the ridge, old-growth timber on this side of the ridge had been logged and was mostly gone. I thought, *We're fighting the fire to save old-growth timber just so it can be logged*?

We unloaded from the truck and started tooling up for the night. Our assignment was to back burn along the logging road on which we had parked. During the day, dozers and other hand crews had improved the road, which ran about one third of the way down a steep ridge and traversed the slope in an east/west direction. The slope above and below the road was steep, making walking anywhere off the road difficult. From where we were standing, I could see that the road went through groves of old-growth timber intermixed with younger, denser pockets of timber and open clear-cut areas of grass and shrubs where the trees had been logged a year or so before. Occasionally a drainage crossed the road with very dense eucalyptus and shrubs, mostly poison oak, in California the shrub most cursed by firefighters. Our strike team was to work a one-mile section in Division B, back burning below the road. We readied drip torches and fusees and started out, most walking along the road in single file. Several engines, including Susie's fell in behind us. They would support our operation. Our only safety zone was the log unloading area where the trucks were parked about a half-mile away from where we were going to start working. That was a long way to be from a safety zone. The identified safety zone, or appropriately called a deployment zone, was not "bomb proof" because of the stacks of timber and its small size. If the stacked logs caught fire and if we had to use the safety zone, we might not survive unless we deployed our fire shelters. A safety zone is supposed to be where a firefighter can go to be out of danger without the use of a fire shelter.

Due to the steep terrain and the lack of a good safety zone, I felt uncomfortable about back burning along the road. Back burning one third of the way down a steep ridge was not the safest plan of attack. All the training I had said that a fire line on an active fire at about mid-slope was asking for trouble. A better plan would be to build a fire line at the top of the ridge and back burn. Our fearless strike team leader and the division boss seemed comfortable with the plan, however, so I remained quiet. Tom informed us of homes on the backside of the ridge and that it was our job to protect them by burning below the fire line and holding it through the night. We tied in with the burnout operations on Division A and started our own burnout in the opposite direction east towards where the trucks were parked. Our objective by setting a fire below the road was to allow a back fire to burn downslope into a ravine, hence creating a black line between the fire line and the main fire. The main fire was not far away. I could see burning trees in the distance and hear an occasional tree falling.

On fires, we sometimes break one of the "watch-out situations." For example, we may not get to size up the fire because it's too big, or not see the fire in daylight, or scout it out—any one of the eighteen situations. However, usually it is only one or two of the "watch-out situations," and, by being aware of it, we can compensate. This time before we even got started, we had broken not just one or two but six. They were: fire not scouted by us, we were in country not seen in the daylight, we had no good safety zones, there was unburned fuel between us and the fire, we could not see the main part of the fire, and the terrain and fuels made escape to safety zones very difficult. Breaking that many can only spell trouble, and we sure found some that night.

We quickly found out that burning below the road was difficult. The road was a typical cut-and-fill logging road. When building roads into the mountainside, dozers cut into the slope and pushed the dirt downhill to form the level area that becomes the road. What that did was create a denuded road shoulder ten feet below the road. We had to get below the fill to light the vegetation, and walking was steep and treacherous. The ground fuel was very dry dense shrub and grasses, and, when lit, it flared up quickly. The terrain made it difficult to get quickly out of the way. In a back burn, we usually have two or three people doing burnout in staggered strips parallel to the fire line, but due to hazardous walking and dense fuels we could not do it this time. Only one of us could burn at a time. I got a twenty-foot piece of nylon webbing out of my pack and tied it around my waist. With several firefighters holding the other end, I climbed down the denuded slope to just above the vegetation and began to light the vegetation while on belay. A new watch-out situation can now be written down: never back burn while on belay. In addition, several firefighters started tossing lit fusees down the slope behind my strip of fire. I lost my footing a number of times, and the three firefighters holding the other end of the line would jerk me up slope so I did not fall into the flames. If any safety officer had seen what we were doing, he or she would have had a heart attack. However, Tom had no problem with our back burning technique. We slowly worked along the road towards the log unloading area where our vehicles were parked. This was the first fire I had ever been on in eleven years where I had to rope up to conduct a back burn.

The burnout actually was going well, with the ground fire backing down the slope towards the drainage below. About three hundred yards along the road from where we had started burning, we came to a small barely flowing creek flowing through a culvert under the road. The vegetation along the creek was dense shrubs and eucalyptus trees with some three-inch-diameter conifers. We burned through the drainage and decided to take a break on the other side to watch how the fire burned downhill. All was going well until the fire reached the bottom of the drainage. We could not actually see the bottom due to darkness, smoke and fire, but when it reached the bottom we heard it. The sound of a small back fire, popping and crackling from consuming wood and leaves, immediately became a roar, and with a loud whoosh, we saw large flames burst into view below us. "Uh oh, I think we screwed the pooch," I said to a friend next to me.

The slow moving back fire was now into the tops of the trees and shrubs and was rapidly burning back up the hill directly towards us. We had a reburn heading straight for the fire line on a steep slope. Tom started screaming, "Get ready to stop the fire at the road."

Instead I was getting ready to make a run for the safety zone. In less than a minute, the fire was bumping the fire line. The road was just wide enough to stop the flames from leaping across, and thank God there was no wind, but large fire brands and ashes rained down all around us. Those of us who did not have our necks covered got burned. Several spot fires immediately started on the uphill side of the road and began to build in size. Tom had worked himself into a fit of rage by now and was screaming at the top of his lungs, "Put the fire out or die!"

"Great," I thought, "just what I want to do, die."

We started lining the spot fires with the engine crews spraying water to cool down the fire in the treetops below the road. Fire was everywhere, and it was getting mighty hot. Just then I heard a loud crack and a crashing sound, followed by a scream. I turned just in time to see a tree come crashing down on one of the firefighters operating a water hose next to Susie. The tree had burned out at the base, and toppled on top of him. The tree was not big and luckily did not crush him. He pushed it off with help from Susie and another firefighter and jumped back up. Susie and I exchanged glances that clearly meant, "What the hell are we doing here?"

The falling tree broke the camel's back, so to speak, and all of us stopped working and started moving towards the road, thinking safety zone. The troops were retreating, deserting the fire line. Tom screamed at us to get back to work. If he had had a gun, he probably would have threatened to shoot us for desertion. He said we had to protect the homes just above us and could not let the fire get away. With flames all around us and burning ash falling on us, I yelled at my squad to get back to work and immediately began throwing dirt on the flames as if my life depended on it, which it probably did.

I heard someone yelling and turned back to look. Tom was yelling at the Navajo crew boss. The crew boss was yelling back that he wanted to move his crew to the safety zone. He wanted to get them out of harm's way. Tom was almost foaming at the mouth, his face a bright shade of red, he was so worked up. With his jugular vein sticking out of his neck and spittle flying from his mouth, he yelled, "Get back to work, you Goddamn asshole!" The crew boss stood there with his mouth open, and all of us stopped working.

It's important to note that a crew boss on a Native American crew can be different than a crew boss on most other crews. These people are held in high regard much like a war chief, an elder, shaman, or even the chief of a tribe. The Native American crews are often made up of brothers, sisters, cousins, aunts, uncles, fathers, and sons or have close ties through a particular clan. The Native American crew boss had a tremendous responsibility to protect his crew and make sure they returned safely. If one of his crew were killed or severely injured, the crew boss could lose face, and perhaps even be shunned by relatives back home. Tom had done the unthinkable by calling the leader of this Navajo crew a "Goddamn asshole."

The Navajo crew boss with all of us watching, looked Tom in the eyes and, without turning his head, said something in Navajo to his crew. They all let out a whoop and started back to work even harder than before. The crew boss also turned and went back to work without saying another word. The look in his eyes was enough. Tom, clearly nervous, turned in our direction looking for support, smiled like it was not a big deal, but in a softer voice said, "Get back to work." I am surprised he did not pee his pants.

Pushing the envelope by working to the point of exhaustion, we caught the spot fires and held the line after several hours. The

Navajo crew kept glancing in Tom's direction. After things calmed down, we took a dinner break, eating from our sack lunches. No one spoke. The tension was so thick, I could have cut it with a knife. We went back to work back burning along the road until we reached the safety zone, where our trucks were parked, at about 3:00 A.M. We stopped burning and spent the rest of our shift holding the line by patroling the mile up the line we had back burned during the night. The Navajo crew spoke quietly the rest of the night and only in Navajo. Tom kept his distance.

At dawn, we loaded into the trucks and drove down the hill towards camp. We passed the day shift crews heading up. Their job would be holding the line we back burned. I was so tired that, when I got back to camp, I grabbed a quick bite to eat, crawled into my sleeping bag and passed out.

I was dreaming about a helicopter flying overhead when I opened my eyes. Instead of hearing the *whop, whop, whop* of rotor blades, I heard several drums and people chanting and singing with an occasional yell that sounded like a war cry. Sitting up, I glanced toward the sound. The Navajo crew had built a fire, and several crew members were beating on drums and singing, while the rest were dancing around the fire bared-chested, singing in Navajo, and occasionally letting out a high-pitched scream. I rubbed my eyes to get the sleep out, not believing what I was seeing. Some of the Navajo had painted designs on their face and chest. They looked as if they were painted for war and ready for battle. Several from my crew were watching, and I walked over and asked what the hell was going on. John said, "They have threatened to scalp Tom. It looks like a war dance to me."

"Cool," I said, "this is just like a John Wayne movie. Where's Tom?"

"He headed off to the ICP at Happy Camp with the division boss," John said.

I watched the Navajos for a while and chuckled. Then I headed down to the river to wash up. The sound of the drums and chanting echoed off the cliffs on the other side of the river. I felt like I had been transported back in time to the days of free-roaming tribes. *God, Tom is in thick soup*, I thought, but at the same time I smiled because it was sort of funny. I saw myself coming back from the fire, and my family and friends at work asking how it went. I would say, "Oh, all right, our strike team leader got scalped by a Navajo crew. Nothing unusual." Newspapers across the country would have headlines about the whole Navajo reservation on the warpath because a strike team leader had called a crew boss an asshole. Wars have been started over less than that.

The Navajo crew kept on drumming, singing and dancing. A little later, a sheriff's patrol car pulled up near them. The sheriff, a deputy, and the division boss got out of the car. Looking nervous, they walked up to the Navajo crew boss. Tom was nowhere to be found. The Navajo crew boss, sweat glistening from his chest and face, yelled something in Navajo. The drumming stopped and everyone turning to face the sheriff. I was too far away to hear what was being said. After a lengthy discussion with the crew boss, with occasional shouting, the sheriff, deputy and division boss turned and went back to the patrol car. The sheriff and deputy got in and drove away. The division boss walked over to us and said that the Navajo crew was being reassigned to another division. Darn, we weren't going to see Tom get scalped. I was thinking *Tom should be reassigned and not the Navajo Crew.* They were a hard-working crew.

The Navajo crew starting packing up. Occasionally one of them looked in our direction, saying something derogatory in Navajo. Probably cursing all of us. Soon, a school bus drove up, and the crew loaded up with some still wearing war paint. As the bus started to pull away, several leaned out the windows and yelled some sort of war cry, shaking their fists in the air. The bus headed down the road. Tom did not show up until later that night on the fire line.

Since we were just one hand crew and not a strike team, Tom took over as crew boss, and Jim and I became squad bosses again. Our assignment for the next shift was to work the fire line from the same safety zone where we stopped burning the night before and continue back burning along the road and then up a dozer line that lead to the top of the ridge. Because of what happened the night before, with us almost getting burned over, the division boss and overhead had decided to move the line to the top of the ridge. The engine strike team that had worked with us the night before took over the burnout operation since they could not use their engines where we were going. Our crew became the holding crew.

We started working up the ridge with everything running smoothly. The dozer line was so steep in places that we had to use our tools as canes to climb. We got to the top within two hours and, with the ground semi-level, began to make better time. We came to another drainage that dropped off the top of the ridge, and just like the night before, the fire backed down the ridge as a ground fire to the bottom and then blew up, reburning back up the hillside to the ridge top. It sounded like a train roaring up the slope, coming right at us. We backed off to the far side of the fire line and hunkered down, waiting for the fire to hit the line. *Here we go again,* I thought. I walked over to the edge of the ravine and looked down to see what the fire was doing. The flames were just a short distance away, hungry to test our line. The night lit up white with sparks and firebrands rising up in front of me. I was silhouetted against it and felt like a spirit rising from the ashes. The fire finally hit the line with fifty-foot flames, but because we were on top of the ridge instead of one-third of the way down it like the night before, the firebrands and burning ash fell back into the fire or onto the line and not into unburned fuel. The line held! We did not get a single spot fire. After that portion of the fire died down, we continued burning along the ridge. Our fire backed down the hill and occasionally torched off a clump of trees or dense shrubs. We had moved only a couple hundred yards when a pocket of dense shrubs below the line burst into flames. I heard a deep-throated *woof.* John, who was working next to me, said, "What was that?"

I was just going to answer, "I don't know," when, bursting out of the brush from below the fire line just in front of the lead firefighter who was carrying a drip torch, came a very large black bear. The bear was panic stricken and started following the dozer line. It headed in our direction, letting out a low throated *woof* as it lumbered in a strange dancing step towards us. Like a bowling ball knocking down pins, the bear scattered the firefighters. The first one leaped off the fire line into burned vegetation, and the rest of us scattered into the brush on the outside of the fire line. The bear, now in an all-out run, headed down the ridge, still following the fire line. As it passed me, I saw smoke coming from its back, and I could smell burned hair. The bear had been burned but how badly I could not tell. It did not injure any of us but disappeared into the smoke and darkness. The fire had almost gotten away from us the night before, the Indians danced a war dance, threatening to scalp our strike team leader, and now a dancing, burning bear running along our fire line. In an uneasy voice, I said, "We sure made that bear dance." I had to slap myself to wake up; I must be dreaming all this. Maybe the Navajo crew had put a curse on us. As the days progressed on this fire, a curse seemed to make more and more sense.

The dancing bear holds a special place in my mind, and I think it was an omen that night in 1987. Perhaps, like some Native Americans who think the barking of a deer or the hoot of an owl are omens of ill luck, the deep-throated *woof* of the bear was a bad omen for our crew. As the days progressed on that fire, things became more and more weird. Perhaps the bear had been a spirit running through the night and had not even been real. In 1998, after fighting fires for twenty-two years, I think back to that night when the fire made the bear dance. If I ever see a smoking bear again on a fire, I will immediately head for home.

We continued burning along the ridge, and eventually the dozer line headed down a steep slope and tied back into the same logging road where we had been before. In the early morning hours, we stopped back burning when we reached the road. With only a couple of hours before our shift ended, we hunkered down with the burnout crew for a rest and spent the last two hours patrolling part of the line. I was farthest up the fire line towards the ridge top and a little away from everyone else. Sitting by myself taking a break, I thought I heard a whistle coming from above. Wondering what that was, I moved a little farther up the slope and, sure enough, heard a distinct whistling sound. I walked back down to my squad and told them I was going to check out the sound and called on my radio to tell the crew boss. My radio battery was dead, and I did not have any spares, so I just told my squad to pass the word down to Tom as I headed upslope. The closer I got to the ridge top, the louder the whistling. Topping out, I walked towards the sound along the fire line. Back where the fire had made the run at the fire line and near where the bear had emerged, I saw a large standing snag spewing flames, ash, and smoke out of a hole in the top of the tree. The top had burned away leaving the hole, and the bottom of the tree also had a large hole in it. Apparently the trunk was hollow, and air was being sucked into the tree through the bottom hole, up the trunk and out the top, creating the whistling. Burning ash and smoke billowed out the top of the tree as from a smokestack, and the ash was blowing over the fire line. I looked down the slope on the unburned side and could see flames.

"Damn," I said. A spot fire had started.

I needed help, but without my radio my only choice was to walk back down the slope and then bring the crew back up. Moving along at a quick pace, I started down the line. When I got to the steep down-slope section I stopped walking, mesmerized by the scene below me. Just below me the fire line disappeared into a grove of conifer trees that hung over each side of the line. Some tree stumps and downed trees were burning inside the fire line, casting an orange, flickering glow onto the conifer trees, creating dark, dancing shadows. The fire line looked like it went into a dark cave. Smoke hung heavy in the air, obscuring the tops of the trees and hovering in patches just above the ground. The darkness, in combination with the orange glow and dense smoke, made me think I was entering the gates of hell of Dante's *Inferno*. In the orange glow, I saw shadows of eerie creatures dancing amongst the trees. I slowly walked towards the opening in the trees, but, just before I entered, I thought I heard someone whisper, "Jeff," making the hairs on my neck stand out.

I said, "Who's there?"

In the left corner of my field of view, I saw the dancing shadow of Pan against a large fir tree. Pan, the god of woods, fields, and flocks, danced in the firelight with his flute.

I was so startled, I stopped dead in my tracks. A huge shot of adrenaline went up my spine, blasting my brain with a hot white flash. Dizzy, I closed my eyes but opened them quickly and shook my head. I spun towards where I thought Pan had been standing, shining my headlamp beam into the trees. Nothing. But just outside my headlight beam, I saw the two-legged silhouette of something quickly running deeper into the woods. I narrowed the beam of my headlamp and looked amongst the trees. My light only showed trees and shrubs. Just barely audible, I heard a laugh and my name being called again, fading away, then only the sound of the whistling tree up on the ridge top.

Man, am I getting tired, I thought. *Here I am entering the gates of hell with Pan playing a whistling tune on his flute to welcome me.* I walked on into the dark opening in the trees, entered hell and continued down to where the crew was waiting. Walking up to Tom, I said, "There is a whistling tree up the line that started a spot fire, Pan played me a tune, and we have to walk through the gates of hell to get to the spot fire."

Tom said, "What?"

"Never mind," I said, "just follow me."

After a hard night of work and getting blasted with a shot of adrenaline, I was exhausted. My legs barely carried me back up the fire line to the ridge top. We reached the spot fire just as the eastern horizon started getting light. The smoke had lifted, so at least it was easier breathing. We spent about two hours putting a line around the spot fire while listening to the whistling tree. Tom had called via his radio, requesting a sawyer to come and cut the tree down. Just as we were finishing mopping up the spot fire, the sawyer showed up to drop the tree. I went over to be his spotter. The tree was big with about a four-foot diameter trunk. Blackened from the fire and with its few remaining branches stark and naked, it stood out in the early morning light. The tree was the tallest in the area, towering above the rest. It was probably the grandparent of all the trees around it. The fire burning through the center of the tree had died down, and the whistling had faded. The tree posed no threat to the fire line anymore.

While working on the spot fire, I kept pondering if I had indeed seen Pan and, if so, what it meant. As the protector of woods, fields, meadows, and gardens, was he trying to tell me something? The logger put on his chaps and started the saw. He lined up the blade and was just about to make his first cut, when it dawned on me that we shouldn't cut this tree down. An overwhelming urge came over me that, at all costs, this tree had to remain standing. Why? I had no idea, but this tree and Pan had some sort of connection.

I tapped the logger on the shoulder and made a slashing motion across my throat, the universal sign for turning off the chain saw. He turned it off, and I then proceeded to tell him my story about Pan and how, somehow, the tree must be important and we needed to leave it standing. The logger, a huge burly guy with a thick red beard, red suspenders, dirty jeans, and logging boots, listened to my story. I expected him to call me a tree hugger or punch my lights out and start cutting the tree down. Instead, after I finished, he just stood there scratching his beard. Finally, he looked me in the eyes and said, "Far out." He picked up his saw and gear and walked over to Tom, who was standing nearby with a puzzled look on his face. The logger said, "The tree stays uncut and standing. If I find out anyone cut this tree down, I will hold *you* personally responsible." With the blade of the saw lying on his shoulder he turned to the whistling tree, bowed, then headed down the fire line and out of sight.

Tom gave me a puzzled look and said, "What was that all about?" He said, "Now I have the loggers pissed off at me, too."

"Never mind, but you heard him," I responded. "The tree stays. It poses no threat to the fire line anymore."

Tom just shrugged. We picked up our gear and, in single file, headed down the fire line towards our trucks. Being the last in line, I stopped and looked back at the tree. Only a little smoke rose from the top. Circling over the top of the tree, a raven called out in a raucous croak. The raven glanced back at me, and I swear I saw a twinkle in one of its black eyes. With a smile, I turned and headed down the line.

Back at the Happy Camp fire, our crew slowly began to shrink in numbers. The first accident happened to someone in my squad during the next night shift. We had to mop up hot spots along the fire line we had back burned over the previous two nights. The inversion that night created the worst smoke conditions I have ever experienced. It was so dense that our headlamps barely shown more than a few feet in front of us. Breathing was difficult, and all of us had to work slowly to keep from passing out. Our breathing came in short gasps, and it was even worse when we were digging in hot coals and ash amongst tree stumps, stirring the hot embers around to cool them off. This put even more smoke and ash into the air. We wore facemasks to help keep us from breathing large particles of ash. Soon our facemasks were brown, and they made breathing even harder. We continued working throughout the night, and conditions seemed to be even worse in the early morning hours. When I reflect back on that night, it seemed as if it was a dream more unreal than seeing Pan, because of the horrible conditions. We should have been smart enough to know that conditions had become too hazardous and backed off, but we heard no one else complaining on the radio, so we refused to be the wimps. Firefighters are stubborn.

Just before dawn, while we were digging up some smoldering tree stumps, I heard a thump and looked over to see Steve face down in the dirt unconscious. I ran over and turned him on his back. He had passed out, and his breathing was shallow. I removed his facemask to give him more air. Grabbing my radio, I called Tom, telling him I had an unconscious firefighter, and we needed medical assistance. The division boss came on the radio, asking for our location and saying medical help would be on the way. Steve regained consciousness in an uncontrollable coughing attack. He began to vomit, then bent over in pain from dry heaves. Brown gobs of dirty mucus spilled onto the ground. We needed to get him down to the logging road and to help. His coughing subsided, and he said he could walk but complained about a horrible headache. Two of us helped him to his feet, and we slowly walked down the hill to the road. Shortly a medic and the division boss drove up, and we got Steve on oxygen. He complained about the headache and still felt nauseous, but the oxygen helped.

Tom and the rest of us gathered on the road and decided the smoke conditions made working too hazardous. We suspected Steve had succumbed to carbon monoxide poisoning. The inversion, dense smoke, and mopping up all night probably had the CO level dangerously high. Several of us, including myself, had headaches. The division boss agreed to talk to the incident commander and safety officer about the hazardous conditions. Since our shift was almost over, we unanimously called it quits and loaded up in the duce and a half and drove back to spike camp. Back at fire camp, I went to wash up. Seeing my face in the mirror, I could see why Steve got sick. My face and hair were black with ash. Opening my mouth and barring my teeth, I saw they were brown and covered with dirt and ash. I spit up a black gob of mucus and blew my nose. The Kleenex tissue was black. "God," I said, "what have I done to myself?"

Many of us on my crew, as well as other firefighters on the line that night, had headaches and also experienced shortness of breath. Because of that shift, I developed a cough that steadily got worse as the days progressed.

Later that day, we found out that Steve had indeed been overwhelmed with carbon monoxide. We all had been exposed to dangerous levels of it that night. We should never have been working in conditions as bad as those. In my twenty-four years of firefighting, that night was probably the worse I have ever experienced; it jeopardized the health of everyone out on the line.

Smoke conditions continued to be hazardous, and after every shift (day or night) firefighters flocked to the medical tent for oxygen. Eventually night shifts were suspended, but it was not until several days later. We were told that we would have one more night shift and then begin day shifts. That night, our crew was placed on a section of fire which we only had to monitor and keep from escaping over the line. No digging in the dirt. I paired up with Hal, and we spent the night watching the fire from the ridge top, keep track as it burned in a ravine below. Hal, a park ranger and one of the nicest, laid-back guys I knew, was big and burly but quiet and gentle, always listened to my bullshit and occasionally laughed at my stories.

When we got back to fire camp that morning, I walked over to the chow line to get something to eat. Carrying my plate to the tables, I saw Susie sitting by herself. I walked over and sat down next to her. Her hands were covering her face, and she was not eating. I asked if she was all right. When she heard my voice, she looked up. Her eyes were red and her ash-blackened cheeks were streaked with tears. I asked, "What was the matter?"

Trying to hold back tears, she started telling me about her night. She had been on the same shift I was but on a different part of the fire. Her area of the division had been very active during the night with the fire bumping the line hard. Her engine strike team had strung a line back into the woods to work on a hot spot, and her fore-man had left her by herself while he went to check on the rest of his crew. Neither she nor her foreman realized she was in a particularly bad area, full of burning trees with a lot of rotten trunks. Being well off the fire line, no one could see her. A wind picked up, and sudden-ly burning trees began to fall all around her. There was no place to run for fear of a tree falling on her. She was also afraid of losing face with her foreman and fellow firefighters if she abandoned her work and retreated to the road, so she stayed put and kept working. Trees kept falling dangerously close, raining burning ash on her. While working, fearing for her life, all she could think about was her kids. She had recently separated from her spouse, who had left her and her children to fend for themselves. That was the biggest reason why she was on the fire, to make extra money to support her family. She had left the kids with her mother. Susie kept wondering what would happen to her kids if she died. There would be no mother or father to take care of them. Her mother was too old to take care of a couple of grandkids. She didn't want to die in some strange place in Northern California. With death so close, all she wanted was to hold her kids in her arms, to love and be loved.

Instead of leaving, Susie fought on, dodging falling trees and praying she would not die. The engine foreman finally returned and, recognizing the danger, yelled for her to get out of there. He told her after they were back out on the fire line that she should have gotten out of there and not waited for him to tell her. She said she was afraid, being a woman, that if she had left he would have thought less of her. When he heard her say that, he laughed and said how impressed he has been with how hard she worked and considered her as good as any man. He told her in the future not to worry about trying to be an equal with a man by putting herself in unnecessary danger. Only an insane person would do that to prove a point.

Susie had faced danger and lived, but she would probably have an emotional scar for years about that night. Facing death and living has a definite effect on one's outlook on life.

Like many women who work in traditionally male jobs, Susie felt she constantly had to prove herself to her male counterparts. If a man had been out there instead of Susie and he had abandoned his post, would the foreman had thought less of him? Susie didn't know. That was what made her hold her ground. One of the firefighting orders is "Fight fire aggressively but provide for safety first." There is a thin line between aggressiveness and safety. Perhaps women feel they sometimes have to push that line to prove they are equal with men. Susie cried afterwards but only when her fellow strike team members were not present. It was important for her to tell someone what she had experienced, and I, being a friend, was lucky enough to be there to listen. I'm sure Susie relives that night. I know I have for some of the times I have been scared on a fire.

Our next shift was during the day, and it ended with two fire-fighters on our crew being injured. We worked with two other hand crews cutting a fire line from the ridge top on which we had been working for several days, down slope to the bottom of a ravine. The slope was too steep for bulldozers, so it had to be done by hand. Working down a slope, we sometimes had to hold onto vegetation. We were breaking several more watch-out situations that day, building a fire line down slope towards the fire. We could not see what the fire was doing, and we had a lot of unburned fuel between it and us.

The slope was covered in dense forest, and our crew had brought along three chainsaws. The saw squad was working in front, with the other two squads clearing slash and digging line to mineral soil. We started cutting and digging about halfway down the slope with another crew working below us and one more above. We were to continue to work downhill until our line tied into that of the crew below us. The crew above us would build line downhill until they tied in with us. When we started building line, we realized we only had two pair of chain saw chaps, so we put one saw aside due to safety concerns. The footing was terrible—steep with heavy brush and hazardous for using a chain saw. It was hard for the sawyers to keep their footing. Our fearless crew boss, who had been below scouting the area, walked back up to us and saw the one chain saw sitting on the ground. Without asking why it was not in use, he picked it up, started it and began to cut timber without any safety gear. He was bucking up a fallen tree when a tree branch buckled on him, causing the saw to kick back. Zip, the chain saw blade went through his left pant leg and cut deeply into his leg just above the knee. Tom screamed and fell to the ground. I had been facing away from him and didn't realize he had picked the saw up. When I heard the scream, I turned. There was our crew boss lying on the ground holding his leg with blood dripping from between his fingers. I thought, *Great, what has he done now?*

Several of us came over to assess the damage. Cutting his pant leg back, we saw a nasty cut down to the bone. He was not going to be able to work with that wound, and we had to figure out how to get him out of there. The only way out was walking up that steep hill. We bandaged the leg and stopped the bleeding. He was lucky he had not cut a vein or artery, so the bleeding was not as bad as it could have been, but he had cut into some ligaments that made walking difficult. After discussing what to do, we decided to send two firefighters from the crew to help him up the hill to the ridge top. Tom started hobbling up the slope with a firefighter on either side of him. The rest of us went back to work. Working our way downhill, we suddenly heard the whine of a bullet overhead, cutting through the leaves of trees, causing some to float down. This followed by the sound of a gunshot.

Someone screamed from the crew below us. *Oh, shit, now what?* I thought.

We all hit the dirt, and the radios began buzzing with traffic, everyone wanting to know what had happened. The crew below us came on the radio and said somebody down in the ravine was shooting at them. The incident command post came on the radio and said that there might be some marijuana patches in the area and apparently, we stumbled onto one.

"Gee, thanks for telling us," I said. I now have nineteen watch-out situations. Number nineteen: "Never build a fire line down slope into a marijuana patch." While trying to figure out if we should continue building line, the inversion began to lift for the first time in days, and the fire became more active. It was starting to rock and roll in the ravine below us, and we could see flames when a tree torched, sending black smoke into the air. The fire threatened to blow up.

A field observer had worked his way down into the ravine. He came on the radio saying that we had better get our butts out of there. Not only had he been shot at, but the fire was starting to torch trees and might make a strong run up the ridge in our direction. If the fire got into the tree tops, our fire line would not hold, and our safety zone was upslope.

The call went out to get up to the ridge top as quickly as possible. We began to climb, but it was so steep we almost needed ropes. We quickly overtook Tom; he could barely walk. Being the macho guy he is, he told us to leave him and save ourselves. We did.

Above me I could see a sawyer carrying his chain saw, and it looked like he was really dragging. It turned out to be the logger with whom we had worked a few nights earlier. He had been cutting timber with the crew above us and was exhausted from running a saw constantly for several weeks without a day off. The steep slope had burned him out. I offered to carry his saw, which he gladly gave to me. He remembered me, grinned and asked, "Seen any more sign of Pan?"

"Nope," I said, "but I think we did the right thing by leaving the tree."

"Right on," he said, "I told some logging buddies, and we're going to mark the tree to make sure no one ever cuts it down."

Hal was just above me, and I caught up to him. He was also dragging, and I asked him if he was all right. He said he had slipped and twisted his back, injuring an old war wound. He could barely walk. He kept saying to leave him, but there was no way I would. The sawyer, Hal, and I helped each other, continuing up the steep slope. Meanwhile, below us, we could hear the fire beginning to boil out of the bottom of the ravine. It sounded like the reburn that had nailed us a few nights before, like a freight train thundering in our direction. We finally made it to the logging road and starting walking out instead of continuing up the fire line up to the ridge top. We called on the radio for a vehicle to get the three of us, Tom, and the two other firefighters helping him. They still had not reached the road. Dispatch said they would send a duce and a half to pick us up.

The fire was really starting to rock and roll, sending up thick black smoke from below us, and we occasionally saw flames bursting above the tree tops. It was going to be close. There was no safety zone anywhere near us. Tom made it to the road about the time the truck showed up. We quickly piled in, and the driver got out of there with the fire billowing up behind us along the road. We never found out what happened to the guy who shot at us, but we did learn his marijuana patch burned. The fire also burned over the line we had been working. Everyone got out without getting burned over, but Hal and Tom had been injured. When we got back to spike camp, Tom was driven off to Happy Camp for medical attention and later was demobbed and flown home. Hal stayed with us that night, thinking he would be all right by morning. But, the next morning he was still in a lot of pain. He could barely stand upright, so he had to stay in camp. When we loaded into the trucks to head out to the fire line, Hal, leaning on a stick, watched us drive away. He could not stand being left behind when his compadres were heading out to the action. I was the last to get in the truck, and he kept apologizing for letting the crew down. I told him he let no one down, and I held him in the highest regards. We hugged and shook hands. I climbed into the truck, and someone up front beat on the roof of the cab to let the driver know we could go. The truck started moving, sending up a cloud of dust. Hal, bent over from the pain in his back, waved good-bye to us. The wounded soldier who had given so much to his country was devastated that he could not give more. Waving to him, I fought back tears. "Take care buddy. May the force be with you," I yelled back. When we got back to camp that night, Hal was gone. They had sent him home.

Like most twenty-one-day fire assignments, the days start blending together, and I lost track of what day of the week it was. All I could do was get up in the morning, eat, get the shift assignment, gear up, load up, drive to the fire line, work at least ten hours, hike back to the tracks, drive back to fire camp, eat, and go to sleep. I went days without a shower or shave. My underwear and socks, in particular, began to have a pretty interesting odor, and I could swear that a swarm of flies followed me wherever I went. Even rinsing my clothes in cold water, after a while didn't seem to help. Because of sleep deprivation, hard work, and poor air, the old body began to not recharge itself as fast as it did in the beginning. My cough got worse, and the whole crew began to sound like some prisoners in a POW camp. The smoke conditions were so bad at the Happy Camp Complex that, after twelve days of work, everyone working the fire lines looked sick and had a persistent cough.

We lost two more people from our crew a couple of days later after a shift had ended. We loaded up into a duce and a half to drive back to spike camp. Some time during the day, unbeknownst to us, a tree had fallen along the edge of the road. The tree was on top of a small knoll through which the road cut. Just a portion of the top of the tree hung over the road.

The truck driver, a young guy in the National Guard, only had to drive us back and forth from fire camp. The rest of the day he hung out at the truck in case he got a call to move. Doing this day after day, he was probably so bored he knew how many stitches there were on the canvas cover over the back of the truck. At the end of the shift every day, he was always in a hurry to get back to camp. He always drove too fast, and we had to keep reminding him to slow down.

The day the tree fell, the top of it was just high enough to miss the top of the truck cab but not high enough to clear the back of the truck where we were sitting. The weather had been nice that day, so the driver had taken off the canvas top leaving the back open. It was more pleasant to drive in the open air. As was my custom, I got in last, securing the gate. Someone up front banged on the roof of the cab, and the truck started down the mountain.

We had not been driving for more than five minutes, and I was beginning to doze off, when I heard a sickening *whack*, followed by a scream. Glancing up, I saw that everyone in the front of the truck who had been sitting up was falling over like bowling pins. The tree hanging over the road was hitting everyone in the head or shoulder. When those of us in the back realized what was happening, we ducked just in time, and the tree passed over us, but about half the crew had been hit. Several lay in the bottom of the truck writhing in pain. One of the firefighters named Joan had been sitting closest to the cab on the side with the tree. It had hit her in the side of the face, leaving a gash on her cheek and a partially torn ear. She lay in the bottom of the truck holding her face, blood dripping onto the floorboards. Another firefighter, Tim, had been directly across from Joan, and the tree had hit him in the shoulder dislocating it. He lay next to Joan holding his right shoulder and groaning in pain. Several others were hurt, but Joan and Tim were the worst.

The driver didn't even know what had happened and was still blazing down the road. We yelled and banged on the cab to make him stop. He finally pulled over. With supplies from our medical kit, we bandaged up Joan and Tim and checked everyone else who had been hit. We had the driver back up, and we cut down the tree so it didn't hang over the road and endanger anyone else.

When we got back to camp, Joan and Tim were driven off to Happy Camp where a medical staff was on hand. They got back late that night all bandaged up, and the next day when we headed out they stayed in camp. That night, they were gone. Now we were down to fifteen people from the original twenty.

Usually when fire crews drop below seventeen, overhead considers it too risky to send the crew to the front lines. Often the crew is demobbed. However, resources were in such demand, they kept us. We struggled on, our crew looking more bedraggled every day, but we were getting closer to the end of our twenty-one days when we would be demobbed. I wasn't sure if we were even going to make the full twenty-one days. I felt as if we were coming apart at the seams. We needed some rolls of duck tape and baling wire to keep the rest of us from falling apart.

To make matters worse, on day sixteen, when I made my morning pilgrimage to the porta-potty, I felt a burning itch between my legs. Dropping my trousers to sit on the toilet seat, I saw that my crotch was bright red. The inner part of my thighs had a red rash and my rear was on fire. The rash had festered, with little pimples starting to ooze a clear liquid. "Oh, oh!" I whispered. "Poison oak. How did I get that?" Then I remembered that during the last night shift, I had wandered off into the woods to relieve myself. Squatting down in the dark, I remembered some woody twigs sticking me in the rear. The twigs did not have any leaves so I didn't pay any attention. I began to realize I must have been squatting in poison oak.

I was too embarrassed to mention anything to my fellow fire-fighters. I decided to keep the situation to myself. The itch was overwhelming. Every chance I got, I had my hands in my pocket scratching away. My privates sure itched, and scratching was irresistible. Back in fire camp that night, I took a shower. I got the water as hot as I could stand and just spread my legs and let the water flow. That scalding water felt good.

On day seventeen, the overhead folks decided to do a big back burn. The fire had been burning in a drainage for several days and was making a run for a ridge top one ridge over from where we were. We were still working off the same logging road, but now a couple of miles away from where we started. Late in the afternoon as the sun began to set, several Type II crews, including our bedraggled crew, and a large number of California Department of Forestry engines lined the logging road. One hotshot crew outfitted with flare guns, fired flares onto the ridge across from the road. The head of the fire was on the back side of the ridge throwing up 100- to 150-foot flames. For sixteen days, the inversion had been so bad that we never got any air support. There had not been the opportunity for bucket drops of water or fire retardant or a helicopter sling loading supplies or any of the other countless job's air support could do. But, it was do or die time for the ground troops. The wildfire threatened to jump our lines and burn into some homes. The decision had been made to light up several thousand acres and stop the fire in its tracks.

The flares ignited the dry fuel easily. With a deafening roar, sounding like a freight train, the ignited fire raced up one side of the ridge towards the main fire that burned on the other side. Both fires met on the ridge top in a loud *whoosh,* and an incredible fireworks display commenced with flame heights reaching a couple hundred feet. Ash and firebrands rained down on us again, and we worked on into the night putting out spot fires. By midnight, everything had cooled down, and the main head of the fire had burned itself out. We had back burned about 5,000 acres that day, but it looked like the beast had been slain or at least mortality wounded.

We got back to fire camp in the early morning hours. I was too tired to clean up or eat, having spent eighteen hours on the fire line. I fell on my sleeping bag, with hardly any energy left. I unlaced my boots and started taking off my clothes. Before I snuggled into the sleeping bag, I noticed my legs and arms were black with ash, the rest of my body looked ghostly white in the dark. Smiling to myself, I realized my sleeping bag was going to have a ripe odor from my body, but I was too tired to care. Using my coat and sweater for a pillow I fell instantly asleep.

I assumed we were going to head out again in a few hours, but no one woke us up. We slept until midmorning. When we got up and ate, we found out they were sending us for two days of rest and relaxation (R&R) in Eureka. We loaded our gear onto a bus and started the long drive out of the mountains towards the coast. It had been a hellish eighteen days. I had never worked under conditions as bad as that fire and never saw so many people get hurt on my crew. It was like the "Fickle Finger of Fate" kept dealing us a losing hand. Perhaps the Navajo Crew had indeed put a curse on us. Tom certainly got nailed, maybe because he yelled at the Navajo crew boss.

Eureka, on the coast, turned out to be smoke free. For the first time in eighteen days, I could breathe clean air. The smell of clean salty air was as precious to me as a glass of cold water on a hot summer day in the desert. The bus brought us to the county fairgrounds, and we were told to bed down in a big building with a bunch of other crews, sleeping on a concrete floor. Almost everyone was coughing, and the air was stagnant with sweat and the smell of smoke from soiled clothing. *Oh boy, this is going to be a fun R & R*, I thought. Our new crew boss, George, was thinking the same thing. He said, "Lets head into town and check into a hotel, our *per diem* will pay for it."

We loaded back onto the bus and left "Hell Central," moving into some rooms at a nearby hotel. After eighteen days of sleeping on the ground, I had a private bathroom and a soft bed all to myself. I got some medicine to treat the poison oak, soaked my infected crotch in scalding water and slept for twelve hours.

One night later, we were on our way back to T-bar spike camp, but in greater spirits. I had some medicine for the poison oak, felt refreshed and my lungs semi-cleared. All of us were ready to take on the fire beast again. We only had two more days on the fire line before our twenty-one days would be up. Time to start thinking about heading home. However, getting back to spike camp, we found out that we were already done. The beast had indeed been slain, and, since our crew was below the minimum number, we were one of the first to be demobbed. We were going to be bused back to Redding and flown home. We spent one more night at T-bar. Loading up the next morning on a bus, we drove back to Happy Camp to go through check out. Happy Camp looked even more miserable than the first day I saw it. Everyone there was coughing and hacking; dense smoke still hung in the air. The sooner I could get out of there, the better, as far as I was concerned. I found out that several other firefighters had gotten poison oak worse than I. One person had inhaled smoke as the fire burned through a big patch of the stuff and gotten poison oak in his throat and down his esophagus. He had to be hospitalized. I still had not told anyone about my flaming crotch. I thought the safety officer, in his briefing statements, should have mentioned poison oak and to look out for it. I knew it existed in California, but thought it was more a coastal shrub than an inland plant. Live and learn. Now every time I'm in the woods in California, poison oak is on my mind, and I always warn others.

In Redding, while going through demob, I ran into Susie. She was also heading home and had a smile from ear to ear. She figured she had made enough extra money to give her kids a great Christmas and pay her bills. Most important, she had lived through it.

We were stuck in Redding for two days trying to get through the demobilization process. Often on big fires with many personnel, it takes days to make arrangements to get everyone back home. However, it was nice where they had us staged. We had showers, a big screen TV, and constant movies playing, as well as all the food we could eat. Firefighters were playing cards, Hacky Sack, and football games, and folks caught up on the news. We finally were loaded up in another contract plane heading for Grand Junction. There were two flight attendants on the flight, and they seemed to be holding their breath when near us. I think they thought we stunk. I thought we smelled pretty good. At least, I didn't have my hand in my pants scratching away anymore.

So, Happy Camp came to a close, just memories, war stories to tell around the old campfire with a cold beer. For smoke conditions, it was the worst fire assignment I had over twenty-four years of fire-fighting. I guess I inhaled the equivalent of thirty-six packs of cigarettes during the time I was on the fire. I don't think my lungs have ever recovered. I still feel a little numbness when I inhale deeply, and physicals indicate I do not have the full use of my lungs anymore. It is a cumulative thing, so it's built up over twenty years of firefighting, but Happy Camp was indeed the worst.

Back in Moab, I loaded my personal stuff from the office into my Jeep. My life at Canyonlands had come to an end. I was heading for Rocky Mountain National Park. My new job had actually started while I was in California. I had called my new supervisor from the T-bar spike camp and told him I would be a little late.

There was nothing more depressing than cleaning out my office after spending five years in a job I loved. I missed my going-away party by being in California, and did not get to say good-bye to all my friends. The ranger districts in Canyonlands, Arches, and Natural Bridges are isolated from each other, and the radio was usually the best means of communication. After my Jeep was loaded, I picked up the radio and said adios to my desert rat compadres. Friends from the Island-in-the-Sky District, the Needles, the Maze, Natural Bridges National Monument, and Arches came on the radio and said good-bye. I felt sad not seeing everyone in person. It had been a great five years, some of the best in my career.

I was going to miss the red-rock country. My spouse and kids had already moved to Colorado with all our household goods, so there was nothing but the stuff from the office. I headed out of town, following the river road along the Colorado River, which wound through Professor Valley, passing Fisher Towers and on out to Cisco. I put on a Mannheim Steamroller tape and reminisced about all the good times. I lived in Moab when it was still quiet, before mountain bikes and rock climbing became the fad. I had no idea then, driving east towards Colorado that the canyon country was going to change so drastically. Canyon country today is crowded with hoards of four-wheel-drive vehicles, mountain bikes, expensive climbing gear, and kayaks. Moab will never be the same. It is now *the* "in" place to be. One of my kids was born in Moab, and kids at his school in Boulder who have been to Moab think he's cool when he tells them where he was born.

Driving along I-70, a smile came to my face when I started thinking about how I was going to spend some of the overtime money. I decided we were going to have a great Christmas. We would go to Disney World and the Florida Keys. I was going to kick back on a sandy beach and do some diving amongst coral and colorful fish. It turned out to be one of our best family vacations. I forgot about the thirty-six packs of cigarettes I had inhaled during the three weeks on the Happy Camp Complex. Sitting on a beach in the Florida Keys, I wondered what the next summer was going to be like—a busy fire season or quiet?

10

Look how Quiet it is. All the Earth is Silent.
Night has Embraced the Sky with a Gift of Stars.
Now a Man can Stand, Speak his words echoing through the Ages,
History and all Creation.

— Forbush & Penguins, Graham Billing

Yellowstone National Park 1988

S pring in the Rocky Mountains began wet and cold, with below-normal temperatures and above-normal precipitation. Yellowstone had a late spring snowstorm over the Memorial Day holiday that closed park roads. I had been camping in Yellowstone at Lewis Lake with my family and woke up Memorial Day morning to heavy wet snow that blanketed our tent. We left the park just as they closed the road. Little did anyone know that the snowstorm dropped the last decent precipitation the greater Yellowstone area would receive until September 10, three and one- half months later.

From the time the park was established in 1872 until 1970, a span of almost 100 years, the National Park Service, like everyone else, saw fire as evil and made every effort to extinguish it. By 1988, the lodgepole pine forests that cover a large percentage of Yellowstone had built to dangerous levels, and, with the drought, the stage was set for fires not seen since the park was established.

By 1988 Yellowstone National Park had a well-established fire program, managing prescribed natural fires (PNF) started by lightning. They were one of the few areas in the lower forty-eight states that had a land mass big enough to consider PNFs a viable option. In early June 1988, they had their first PNF of the year. It burned for a short time but eventually fizzled and died. At the beginning of June, fire management folks thought the summer would be normal and were not worried about letting a PNF burn. However, the weather remained warm and dry, and, in July, Yellowstone experienced episodes of dry lightning which ignited several more PNFs. By July, twenty-one fires had consumed about 16,500 acres. With no precipitation in site, the fire-management folks began to worry. The long-term forecast looked bleak, with continued warm and dry conditions. At that time, fire management decided to declare all PNFs wildfires, and gave the order to suppress them. As fate would have it, the very next day, on July 22, a careless woodcutter outside the park started a fire that became the infamous North Fork Fire, the worst fire recorded in the greater Yellowstone ecosystem in the history of the park. This fire burned through the heart of Yellowstone National Park for the next three months until the snows of winter finally put it to sleep. It almost burned the Old Faithful Inn and the complex of other buildings on September 7 and threatened the communities of West Yellowstone, Mammoth Hot Springs, and Gardiner, Montana, as it burned north. Other fires—the Huck, Hellroaring, and Clover Mist fires—sprang to life and began to consume hundreds of thousands of acres of forest. By early August, thousands of firefighters were called into action to battle the beast, flowing into the Yellowstone area from all over the country. At the same time, other fires were burning in Idaho and other western states. Fuel moistures in Yellowstone were incredibly low, and the stage was set for Murphy's Law: What can go wrong will go wrong.

It did not seem to matter what types of suppression tactics were used on the fires by the Boise Interagency Fire Center. The fires continued to burn steadily, consuming thousands of acres everyday. The news media began to circle Yellowstone like vultures looking for carrion. They fed on people in tears over the loss of a home, or people mad at the National Park Service for letting the fires burn out of control. Sensationalism reigned. The public loved a good disaster. When fires such as the North Fork and Clover Mist burned some homes and threatened some communities, the press was ready and waiting with cameras. People all over the world thought the fires were destroying Yellowstone National Park. They called or sent letters by the thousands, and many offered to send trees or come and plant trees thinking that was the right thing to do.

The straw that broke the camel's back and enraged the public, particularly local communities, occurred when a reporter took a statement out of context and flashed it across the associated press. The reporter had tagged along one day with one of the Yellowstone National Park scientists establishing vegetation plots out in front of the advancing fires. His plan was to monitor the fire as it moved through the plots, documenting fire behavior and gathering information afterwards on how much of the plots burned and how hot the vegetation burned. At one vegetation plot, the fire was slowly approaching. Without thinking what he was saying the scientist said, "Burn, baby, burn." He was only referring to the vegetation plot and nothing else, but the reporter wrote those famous words down. The next day in papers and on television reports all over the country the headlines read, "National Park Service says, 'Burn, Baby, Burn.'" The press led the public to believe that the National Park Service was advocating a let-burn policy. Even the fire dogs from BIFC started bad-mouthing the National Park Service for this supposed policy. Everyone needed a scapegoat, and the National Park Service made a likely target.

By this time, however, "let burn" was the farthest thought from Yellowstone National Park's superintendent's mind, and the Rocky Mountain Region regional director's mind. They were both being hammered by the news media, congressmen and senators, and anyone else with a mouth to voice an opinion. The staff at Yellowstone acted very professionally throughout the ordeal, but "Burn, baby, burn" will probably go down in history as a quotation used completely out of context.

By early August, the director of the National Park Service sent out a memorandum requesting that all National Park Service fire-qualified personnel be made available for firefighting and to train those not qualified but physically fit enough to fight fires. My supervisor at Rocky Mountain National Park was dispatched to a fire in Idaho, and I was left as the acting-fire-management officer. I was given the assignment of pulling together a National Park Service hand crew. I got on the phone and started calling neighboring parks, asking about availability. Great Sand Dunes National Monument came up with one person, Bent's Old Fort with two, and Florrisant

Fossil Beds with two. I received permission from the park superintendent to get together an additional fourteen people from Rocky
Mountain National Park with myself as crew boss. Within two hours,
we had a twenty-person Type II crew. I called Northern Dispatch out
of Fort Collins, and they put us on the board as available.

The first night on the board, we received a call-out to a small
fire on the front range near Loveland, Colorado. We met at the fire
management office at 4:00 A.M. the next morning and, by 8:00 A.M.,
were on a twenty-acre fire, digging line. Like Wyoming, Colorado
was also experiencing dry conditions, and by mid-morning the fire
became fairly active. Trees were torching, and we were digging a hot
line with flames bumping the line fairly hard. The predicted weather
called for a cold front to move through with wind but no precipitation. The outlook spelled blow-up conditions. I was the IC for the day
and called into Northern Dispatch for reinforcements, asking for
another Type II hand crew and some Type VIII engines that could
move around in the tough terrain. They called back later in the day,
reporting that a crew had been dispatched and estimating the time of
arrival to be late that night. We would also have some small Type VIII
engines available the next day.

We worked until sunset getting a line around the fire. I had
been feeling crummy the entire day, and later that evening, when I sat
down to eat, I was hit with waves of hot and cold. Shivering and feeling sick, I spread my sleeping bag under a tree, crawled into it and fell
asleep without finishing my dinner. Sometime during the night, the
other crew arrived. I woke up when I heard them unloading. Coughing and a sore throat made me realize I had caught a cold. Without
getting up to see who showed up, I went back to sleep. We got up at
5:30 A.M., and I felt horrible, but, being a crew boss, I got ready for
another busy day. To my amazement, the other crew was another
Park Service crew from Utah. Most of them were compadres from
Canyonlands National Park, Arches National Park, and Natural
Bridges National Monument, plus a few from Capitol Reef National
Park and Lake Powell National Recreation Area. Some had been on
my Happy Camp crew the year before — family reunion time while
eating breakfast — I caught up on news from Moab.

With some food and coffee in my belly, I began to feel a little
better. Rumor had it that we would be heading to Yellowstone after

we finished with this fire assignment. Everyone wanted to be in Yellowstone in the middle of the action and worked hard to get the Colorado fire mopped up in one day. By that evening, there was not a whiff of smoke or hot coals left. We were demobbed from the fire, and both crews headed back to Estes Park. I sent everyone from my crew home but warned them to be ready to head out for three weeks the next day. The other crew stayed the night in Estes Park.

The next morning, not long after I had walked into my office, the phone rang. It was Northern Dispatch announcing that the two Park Service crews were to form a strike team, destination Yellowstone National Park. By the middle of August, fire overhead folk in Yellowstone were grabbing all available firefighters. I called my crew together, and the excitement about working on history-making fires began to build.

Since its establishment in 1872, Yellowstone had never had fires like the ones burning out of control in and outside the park. No firefighter wanted to miss the action. As for me, as soon as I got the phone call, the old python began to coil and tighten in my gut, and I began to worry about being responsible for nineteen people who would have to face unbelievable fire conditions. This was my first assignment as a crew boss, and I realized it would be a challenge to stay relaxed with so many relying on me to make good decisions. I wondered if I would be able to hold up to the test. I had to keep my crew healthy and try to prevent the events of the previous year in northern California.

It took most of the day to get transportation arranged for us, resulting in a typical hurry up and wait. Finally, just after sunset, a bus drove up, and we got our marching papers. Our destination was the Huck Fire, burning in the southern part of Yellowstone National Park and in the Teton Wilderness next to the park. We were on the road by 8:30 P.M. and drove through the night. As night began to give way to twilight, the bus pulled into a small town east of Grand Teton National Park, and we stopped for breakfast at a local café. Unloading from the bus, I noticed the overcast sky, and my nostrils filled with the familiar smell of wood smoke. What I first thought was clouds and low-lying, early-morning fog turned out to be smoke. It hung heavy in the air due to an inversion. We were still fifty miles from the fires, but the smoke was as dense as on a fire line. The fire beast was alive and well and consuming its breakfast as we ate ours.

The café was empty until forty hungry firefighters filled the tables. The one cook and two waitresses—slightly overwhelmed— managed to feed us plates piled high with stacks of pancakes, eggs, bacon, sausage, and toast. Firefighters love a good breakfast. We went through a few gallons of coffee while the waitresses asked about our quest and provided us with the latest news. She had no idea we were a National Park Service strike team and bad-mouthed the National Park Service for letting the fires burn out of control when they should have been putting them out. After we paid the bill, the cook and wait- resses stood next to the door and wished us well. I felt as if I was my dad in World War II, heading off to war and being cheered on by those who stayed behind. The folks in the café wanted the fires out and the blue skies back.

We arrived at the Incident Command Post for the Huck Fire a little before 11:00 A.M. The ICP was located at the Flagg Ranch where my family and I had stopped for breakfast in a snow storm back in May. Little did I know then that I would be back several months later wearing Nomex. The ranch was empty of visitors, having been evac- uated because of the fire. Unloading from the bus, I looked up at the ridge to the east of the ranch. Lodgepole pines burned and torched as the fire made short runs through the tree tops. Engines were lined up along the road, and several fire crews were spread out along the west side of the road looking for spot fires. The air was thick with smoke, which did not help my cold at all. My throat was irritated, and I already had a deep cough. I had only been on a twenty-one-day fire assignment three days and already had a cough. I was worried the next nineteen days were going to make it worse.

We checked in and were surprised to see the that fire camp was devoid of tents and gear normally at an ICP. Usually a fire camp on a big fire was full of tents, tarps, and other gear, but the Flagg Ranch hardly had any hand crews. I asked where everyone was and the response was "spiked out." All right, spike camps. That's what I wanted to hear. The Yellowstone fires turned out to be unique because many of the thousands of firefighters, spent most of their twenty-one days somewhere in the back country, miles from any road. They were usually flown in by helicopters and supplied by helicopters or pack animals. Having so many people in back-country areas created a logistical nightmare in trying to keep everyone supplied. Some days during the height of the fires, the smoke was so dense that helicopters could not fly. The spike camps had to rely on horse and mule pack strings bringing in food, water, and other supplies. The packers and their animals got so strung out and tired that they could not keep up with the demand for supplies. Some spike camps ended up without food and water for a day or two at a time.

Operations was trying to figure out the best place to send us, so they staged us at the ICP. The word was, when the smoke lifted, we were going to be flown into a spike camp in the Teton Wilderness. We spent the afternoon bedded down beneath some trees and were told to not wander off. Late in the afternoon, the inversion lifted, and we were driven to the helibase. Chinook CH-47 military helicopters were lined up, and all of them were starting their engines. Smaller Llamas and Jet Rangers already lifted off with sling loads of supplies or long lines carrying water buckets. There were only a few hours of daylight for air missions, and air operations was making the best of it. The Chinooks were military aircraft brought in to assist the firefighting efforts. One firefighter on my crew got apprehensive when he saw the dark green ships. He was a Vietnam vet and began to have a flashback by just seeing the helicopters. Memories suppressed for years began to well up. I could see beads of sweat on his forehead, and he looked pale. I asked him if he was all right. He just gritted his teeth and smiled. The Chinooks could hold forty firefighters at a time, so our strike team loaded through the back with all our gear and tools. I was one of the last on board and sat near the back ramp, which they kept half open to allow us to see out. The rpms of the rotor blades increased, and shortly we were airborne.

Once above trees, I got a good look at the countryside through the back door. Everywhere, smoke columns plumed. It looked as if the entire world below us was on fire. Thousands of acres were burning. I was awe struck by the immensity of the fires. I had been on hundred-thousand-acre fires before, but nothing of this magnitude. As far as I could see to the north flames or smoke filled the landscape. Several giant smoke columns rose thousands of feet into the air. That old familiar knot in my gut showed up.

The Chinook landed in the middle of a long, narrow meadow surrounded by forests of lodgepole pine. The back ramp descended, and we unloaded. It was like being dropped off in the middle of battle. The hill east of the meadow was in flames with trees constantly torching. Smaller Llama and Hughes 500 helicopters flew overhead with buckets slung beneath them to drop water on hot spots. Firefighters worked the edge of the meadow, back burning and putting out spot fires trying to burn into the meadow and towards the spike camp. Looking over the hill on the east side of the meadow, I watched a strange thundercloud forming. A gigantic cloud was billowing up probably 30,000 feet in elevation, and I even thought I saw a lightning bolt or two. The sides of the cloud kept bulging out and taking on new shapes. Heads of demons seemed to form for an instant, opening their mouths to scream out, only to be consumed back into the womb of the cloud. What intrigued me the most was how fast it was building. This was the main smoke column of the Huck Fire. I was watching a blow up of Biblical proportions. The head of the fire was so hot that the main smoke column had created its own weather cloud, with lightning in its interior.

We tossed our gear along the edge of the west side of the meadow, beneath some lodgepole pines and checked in with the IC. We were ready for action. The IC for this spike camp was actually the division boss. As we formed a half circle around him, He said, "Welcome to hell, ladies and gentlemen. Don't mind the torching trees and small crown fire on the other side of the meadow. It's a common occurrence around here, and you will get use to it." He gave us our assignment for the evening—to look for spot fires on the west side of the meadow and secure the fire camp from any fire outside the fire line.

We were the strike team for the night shift. We grabbed a quick bite to eat and headed out to our assignment, spending that night gridding out the hill around the spike camp and to the north, lining and putting out all the spot fires we found. For most of the night, we stayed in a line—all forty of us—strung out through the woods. The smoke was bad, and visibility in the woods especially poor. We kept saying to each other, "Keep the person next to you in sight." By dawn, we had secured the area, lined all the fires and flagged a path to them with brightly colored plastic flags that led away from the fire line, so other firefighters during the day shift could relocate them and check their status. We got back to camp, at 7:00 A.M., ate and went to sleep.

Sometime later, I woke to the sound of a 206B helicopter flying overhead. The smoke inversion had lifted, and the ships were in the air, supporting the ground troops. Almost every day through the twenty-one-day assignment, the morning hours were socked in with smoke. Around 3:00 P.M., it lifted enough for helicopters to fly. When the inversion lifted, the fires all across the park would blow up and consume a few more thousand acres before lying back down after dark. At that same time, the air show would be hot and heavy. Ships flew in food and supplies, with others carrying buckets of water slung beneath them to drop water on the hot spots. For every night shift, we had the sound of helicopters in mid-afternoon as our wake up. Getting up the second morning on the Huck Fire, I noticed that at the north end of the meadow the fire was rocking and rolling, bumping the line. I switched on my radio and listened to the constant chatter of ground crews and air support. The fire had burned over a section of the line, and ground crews were working their butts off, trying to stop it. Two-oh-sixes were flying nonstop, dropping water.

Many of those days in August, the fires would burn actively during the afternoon, making some incredible runs through thousands of acres in a few hours. Firefighters had to scramble to get out of the way. Then, with the dark, the fires would often lay down, spending the night cooking but not boiling, with firefighters building new line, mopping up spot fires and back burning, only to see the fire blow up again the next day, burning over the newly constructed fire lines. Because of low relative humidities, some fires would occasionally stay active through the night, particularly if the wind blew. Cold front after cold front rolled through Yellowstone during August, bringing winds but no precipitation. Fire behavior specialists—some of the top dogs in the country—were amazed that during the Yellowstone fires with cold temperatures at night the fuel moisture never really rose. There was hardly any moisture in the air. The smoke would sock in at about dark and stay dense through the night. The next morning, the same scene would start all over again. This went on day after day. On August 20, fires in the greater Yellowstone area burned 160,000 acres in one day alone.

The second night on the line, we back burned along a fire line that hand crews had dug during the day and where the fire had bumped the line. The air temperature was warm and the relative humidity low enough that trees torched throughout the night. The live fuel moisture was so low that I torched off one lodgepole pine with a cigarette lighter at three in the morning. I held the flame of the lighter against a twig until it started to burn. With a *whoosh* the whole tree lit up like a Roman candle. By dawn we had back burned about a half mile of line, back out into the meadow where the spike camp was located.

During the early morning hours, just before dawn, I listened to a radio transmission from another spike camp somewhere else on the Huck Fire. The division boss was talking to the ICP. His spike camp had not been supplied in a couple of days, and the firefighters were out of food and water, having to drink boiled water from a near-by stream. The division boss was clearly agitated. He had been at the spike camp for sixteen days with no end in site. The smoke inversion had prevented helicopters from bringing in supplies to his camp the day before, and the horse packers were so overworked they could not keep up with the demand. The division boss said that his division was shut down until food and water arrived. They had worked for a couple of days on nothing but fumes, as it was.

The problem with keeping firefighters supplied occurred all over the Yellowstone area. A buddy of mine working air operations out of West Yellowstone said folks were losing hair trying to keep order. Even though our spike camp on the Huck Fire was being sup-plied, later on during our twenty-one days at Yellowstone, we were going to find out first hand how the division boss who shut down his division felt because we went a couple of days without any food sup-plies.

Once again, in the early afternoon of the next day, we woke to the sound of helicopters. The fire had blown up and again pushed the line we had back burned during the previous night's shift. The day shift crews had to back off because of safety concerns, and the fire again burned over the line. That night we were back burning again and building fire lines around several places where the fire had slopped over. Again and again, day after day, fire crews all over Yellowstone played out the same scene—build line, back burn, fire burns over, back off, build another line, back burn, fire burns over, build new line. A friend of mine working the North Fork Fire was flown in every morning by helicopter to some part of the fire and had to be evacuated almost every afternoon, as the fire roared over the hill. The stress of being put in danger every day took a heavy toll on crews.

On most fires there might be a few days during a twenty-one-day assignment that the fire made everyone run with their tails between their legs, but at Yellowstone that had become almost a daily event, day after day, from late July until September 10, when it finally snowed. Snow and the onslaught of winter were the only things that stopped the Yellowstone fires. Looking back, they should of just staged firefighters around buildings throughout the area and let the fire do its thing in the back country. A lot of money was spent building fire lines that the fires burned over or around, but by this time the media had created such a news event that the National Park Service had no choice but to continue an all-out war to suppress the fires. Washington had taken an interest, and politicians had become involved. Boise Interagency Fire Center took over the driver's seat, the Park Service was riding in the back seat; by the end of the fires, the National Park Service was almost locked in the trunk.

Just about everyone recognized that fighting the Yellowstone fires was different than in most other parts of the country. Our division boss on the Huck Fire was from the forest service where timber was supposed to be logged. Unburned trees meant money. He kept telling us in the briefings not to worry about trying to save trees. He told us we were in a wilderness area; saving timber for logging was not an issue. I thought there really was no reason for us to be in the Teton Wilderness at all, digging so many fire lines, disturbing vegetation, cutting down old growth timber. I tried to keep chain saw work to a minimum on my crew, but huge old-growth trees did fall victim to chainsaws in forest service wilderness and in Yellowstone National Park. The U.S. Forest Service, who guarded their wilderness areas with strict guidelines, considered the fires a national emergency; as such, most wilderness ethics had been abandoned. The sound of chainsaws could be heard for miles in the back country. I saw stacks of timber that looked like a logging operation cut and lying along fire lines in Yellowstone and inside Forest Service wilderness areas. It was too easy to use saws when we had them, and most firefighters slept better knowing they had a couple of saws working, dropping hazard trees that could cause the fire to burn over and endanger them.

After several night shifts, they switched us to days. On our first day shift, we dug an indirect line until we saw the "whites of the eyes" of the firefighters on the next division to the South, who were digging line in our direction. Our strike team humped all day long. Several firefighters on my crew worked on trails back at Rocky Mountain National Park and spent all their time working with shovels and pulaskis, so I put them on point. They almost dug the line by themselves with the rest of us cleaning up after them. We leapfrogged throughout the day with several other crews, digging line until we tied our line into that of the crew in front of us. Then we would move out in front of that crew a hundred yards and started digging until the crew behind us hit the end of our line, then they would move ahead.

We dug one mile of line that day, working through stands of timber interlaced with open meadows. By early afternoon we were building line up a steep hill closing in on the next division. Stopping to wipe sweat from my brow I thought, *Man, how many times over the years have I been on the side of a steep hill fighting fires?* I did not even want to think about it. A field observer had flagged the line ahead of us, so we just followed the blue flagging tied to the branches of trees. Occasionally a long strip of flagging would have writing on it, identifying a meadow nearby that could be used as a safety zone or pointing out a spot fire that I would send a squad off the line to mop up. My saw squad had slowed down to cut down some large trees, and the other two squads and myself moved on, leaving them to catch up.

The smoke had been dense during the morning, and the fire inactive. In the early afternoon just as we were tying in with the other division, the inversion lifted. When the smoke began to clear, the fire started to rock and roll, bumping the fire line within a short time. Trees along the line began torching, and fire made short runs through the tree tops. At several places, the fire threatened to slop over the line we had spent all day digging. We found ourselves in a small clearing near the top of the hill with the fire burning hot below us. It made a run through a stand of timber below us and threatened the other crew of our strike team. Below us, they had not yet started up the hill. From my vantage, I could see one squad from the other crew move out into a small clearing. They immediately began to dig line around themselves, clearing vegetation to dirt. It looked as if they prepared to make a stand, possibly think about deploying their fire shelters. The fire was coming their way having jumped the fire line nearby. The radio traffic was busy, and all along the line, crews were having a hard time. Air operations came on and said support was on the way.

A couple 206s showed up with buckets and began dumping water on hot spots. Just below us a hundred yards away and about a 200-foot difference in elevation, a stand of timber ignited, and thick black smoke started billowing up into the sky.

The fire was now heading our way. Suddenly, the squad boss from my saw crew burst out of the woods below me near the hot spot and saw the rest of us. His radio battery had gone dead, and he didn't have a spare. With his hands he made digging motions, as if working with a shovel. It was pretty clear what he was trying to say. "Get our butts down there, ASAP!"

We headed down the hill and found that the saw crew had tied in with the San Juan Hotshots working a raging fire that did not want to stop at a puny fire line. I put the other two squads to work, and placed two firefighters out in a small clearing away from the line looking for hot spots. Everyone butted heads with the fire beast. At times the flames would flare up over our heads, and it was hot enough to singe my eyebrows and redden my face, giving me first degree burns. The hotshot crew was kicking butt and showed no fear.

The San Juan Hotshots, a Native American crew, showed no sign of breaking ranks or retreating. Even though my gut told me to back off, the hotshots had things under control. We stayed with them. Just about the time we all recognized that we were getting the upper hand, the fire lay back down again. Almost as quickly as the threat had started, it was over for the day. The air temperature cooled. The rh rose as the sun moved closer to the western horizon. After showings its face for only a few hours, the beast went back to sleep for the night. The inversion began to set up again.

We took a break, sitting on the side of the hill looking over the area that had burned. Jim, the Vietnam veteran experiencing flashbacks, had had a hard day. I noticed he was sitting off by himself. He had his head between his legs, and I could see him shaking. I went over, sat down next to him and asked if I could do anything. He told me he was not sure if he could handle the stress. The combination of lack of sleep, eating poorly, and the hard work that day had overwhelmed him. I had to admit it had been one hell of a day, building a mile of line and then battling the beast head to head for a couple hours. Jim and I were sitting quietly, enjoying the peace and quiet, when the division boss called our strike team by radio. He said we had been reassigned to another fire and were to report back to spike camp.

When we got back to spike camp, the division boss told us to pack our personal fire bags and stack them in the middle of the meadow in a giant sling net. We were told our bags would be flown out, but we had to walk a few miles to a trailhead to be picked up by buses. After stacking the bags in the net, we ate a hot meal of turkey, mashed potatoes, and corn that had been flown to spike camp by helicopter. While we ate our dinner, a Chinook flew in and dropped off two military fire crews and picked up our gear, flying off into the sunset. Because of a lack of firefighters, the military had been mobilized and a division trained for firefighting. They had all been dispatched to Yellowstone. The soldiers dropped off in the meadow looked gung-ho and ready for action. I kept expecting them to pull out their M-16s or a grenade launcher and try to kill the fire beast with weapons instead of shovels. Their shirts were clean, boots polished, and even their Nomex pants looked pressed and creased. On the other hand, our strike team smelled, we wore dirty clothes, and the men had unshaven faces.

As in any war, the front-line troops were being replaced with fresh ones. We kept hoping the Chinook would come back and get us, but the sun had set, and air support had retired for the day. It was time to start walking. We loaded our fire packs with what gear remained and left spike camp in single file along a nearby trail. For the first mile we hiked through dense smoke, but the air cleared the further we got away from the fire. By the time we got to the trailhead, even the sky overhead had cleared. I looked up and could see a million twinkling stars overhead. I had not seen the heavens for five days. It was like seeing an old friend again, and I smiled.

While hiking out of the Teton Wilderness, I walked with Jim at the end of the line. He talked about his Vietnam flashbacks and the hard time he had since his return. Talking was like a verbal massage.

As with Hal in Northern California the year before, as Jim talked, I could see the tension in his face began to dissipate and his muscles begin to relax. By the time we reached the trailhead, he had settled down and was feeling better. A bus was waiting for us when we stepped out on the road. As we loaded up, Jim told me he thought he could hang in there.

It was almost midnight by the time we stepped off the bus at the ICP. We had been in the wilderness for five days. None of us had showered in six days, and we were pretty odoriferous, but no one seemed to notice; we all smelled the same. The air temperature had dropped into the high teens. Because we could only carry a limited amount of gear in our fire packs, few of us had the clothing to be comfortable in temperatures way below freezing. The days were still warm, but the nights were already getting very cold. Winter knocked on the door of the Yellowstone area. We bedded down amongst willows just across the river from the Flagg Ranch and slept till dawn.

The next morning we were told our new assignment was the Hellroaring Fire in the northern part of the park. There was no bus available to drive us, so we spent most of the day waiting at the ICP for transportation. In the middle of the afternoon, some overhead personnel ask if we would be willing to patrol the area and pick up trash, so we spent two hours working through the camp, along the park road and helibase picking up cigarette butts. It was a little degrading to be picking up trash along a road after five days of building hot line, lining spot fires and back burning. However, that is often the way it is for Type II crews. One day a crew might be kicking butt building a hot line and fighting the beast head to head, and the next day picking up trash. Type II crews are the true grunts of firefighting. A hotshot crew, smokejumpers, or helitack personnel would not be asked to pick up trash.

Late that afternoon, a bus finally arrived. The North Fork Fire had closed several roads through the park so we had to drive south through Grand Teton National Park, on into Jackson Hole and then north into Idaho, and east to West Yellowstone. Before we left Jackson Hole, we made a stop at a department store so we could buy gloves, wool caps, long underwear, and other essentials. The nights were becoming bitterly cold, and we needed long underwear, gloves, wool caps. While waiting, I sat outside the department store watching the tourists and residents carry on their everyday lives. The residents had been living in smoke and flames since July. Everyone looked tired and haggard. Even the tourists appeared to have had enough. I did not see a smile on anyone's face. I bought a copy of the local newspaper. The headlines on the front page were about the fires, which the media blamed on the Park Service. Everyone seemed to be saying it was their fault. As for me, after seeing one of the fires up close and personal, I knew that the reporters did not understand the ecology of lodgepole pine forests. These forests evolved with fire, and sometimes they were going to burn in the magnitude Yellowstone experienced in 1988. When the conditions were just right, all one could do was stand back and watch. It wasn't as if the fires of 1988 were anything new. Similar fires had previously burned in the Yellowstone area, but the last time they occurred, some 200 years before, no towns or businesses relying on tourists had been threatened. The only humans in the area then were Native Americans.

Under some conditions, a fire can burn thousands of acres, and only a change in the weather can put it out. Once every few hundred years, the greater Yellowstone area had experienced fires as in 1988, but, for the first time since the ice age, the cycle of fire ran into a road block—humans who had it in their heads that fire destroyed things. For seventy-five years they had suppressed fire, thus actually helping create some of the very conditions needed to support a really big fire.

When the inevitable happened, local residents were upset because the fires were ruining their livelihood, scaring away the tourists. The park concessionaires and nearby communities that relied on tourism thought the tourists would not come back for years, because the fires had destroyed the park. The loss of tourists never became a problem; by 1989 all the critics had quieted. The tourists came in droves in 1989 to experience first hand the awesome power of the 1988 fires. The park was not destroyed, in fact quite the contrary. It rebounded in awesome beauty after the fires. The burned forest turned into acres of wildflowers and grasses, and the wildlife seemed to rejoice in the abundance of food. What had once been thousands of acres of monotonous lodgepole pine that had little value for most species of wildlife, became a smorgasbord of food. Not one business collapsed into financial ruin due to the fires.

   We arrived at the West Yellowstone airport in the early morning hours and bedded down in nearby large military tents. The airport looked like a battle zone with military helicopters, private helicopters, and air tankers neatly lined up in rows. Supplies were
stacked in various piles. Almost everyone lay asleep, except some
overhead personnel who worked through the night making sure the
crews would be supplied during the day.

   We got up at dawn and, after breakfast, loaded onto another
bus, heading into Yellowstone National Park through the west
entrance. The road followed the Madison River, weaving in and out
of woods and meadows. Smoke and fog hung low over the water as
the sun, a yellow ball enshrouded in smoke, slowly rose in the east.
Its rays filtered down through the trees as through water. The hills on
the south side of the river had burned or were burning, and everywhere we saw smoldering tree stumps with small flames. It looked as
if there had been a major battle the day before.

   Most of the drive from the west entrance to Mammoth Hot
Springs passed through such burned or burning forest. Looking out the
window, I noticed that the wildlife seemed totally unaffected from the
fires. Buffalo and elk fed or bedded down in the meadows while fires
burned around them. The fires were just another part of their landscape. Trumpeter swans, white pelicans, and water fowl floated in back
waters along the river. As the sun rose through the smoke and mist, the
whole setting began to look surreal; I felt as if I were in a dream.

   I imagined myself as a Native American or mountain man riding horseback or walking through the wilderness while a forest fire
burned nearby. They probably kept a wary eye on the fire but otherwise carried on as if no fire existed. During the summer months, there
must always have been forest fires burning somewhere in the West.
Any people passing through the area, like the wildlife, just avoided
the flames. Also like wildlife, they probably visited burn sites for
years afterwards because of the abundance of game and edible vegetation that followed in the wake of fire. No yellow-shirted firefighters
tried to stop what was natural.

   Seeing the wildlife carry on as if the fire was just another part
of the scenery seemed natural. Firefighters were unnatural. We did
not belong in the scene. Observing wildlife feeding undisturbed in a
meadow while trees torched nearby is not the way fire is portrayed in

Bambi, with all the wildlife fleeing the raging fire, the coyote and bear running side by side with the rabbit and deer. In real life, the coyote (now the wolf in some parts of Yellowstone) would take advantage of the situation and eat the rabbit while watching the fire.

Of course some wildlife did die because of the fires but not in disastrous numbers. On the Clover Mist Fire, I saw a few elk carcasses, but these formed only a miniscule part of the population. More wildlife probably die on park roads each year than in fires. At least the fires kept the tourist off the roads in 1988, saving some wildlife from being run over by cars.

The roads were empty of tourists as we passed Madison Junction, the campground where I had stayed as a child that convinced me I wanted to be a park ranger. The area had been turned into a fire camp with tents and tarps scattered through the woods. Other campgrounds we passed stood empty. Yellowstone, for all intensive purposes, had been closed to tourists for the first time since its establishment in 1872. The park staff tried their damnedest to keep it open, but, at the peak of the fires, so much was burning that no part of the park went unaffected. A large part of the west, north, northeast, and south sides of the park were burning. Only the central portion of the park remained unaffected, but most of the roads into the park passed through the hottest parts of the fires. Only the road in the southeastern part east of Yellowstone Lake remained unburned, and the Clover Mist Fire came within a few miles of that road.

We drove through Mammoth Hotsprings and on into Gardiner, Montana. The forest service office in Gardiner had become the ICP for the Hellroaring Fire. Once again hardly any fire crews camped around the ICP; everyone was spiked out. We were staged with a few other crews at a caterer's tent set up along the Yellowstone River just south of Gardiner. The caterer running the food services said they were feeding a thousand firefighters, all out on spike camps. They would cook up hot meals and put the food into metal cans and cardboard boxes. The food was then flown into the spike camps by helicopter or carried in by horseback.

In the afternoon, the inversion lifted, and we were driven to a nearby airstrip where Chinooks were picking up firefighters. I made the mistake of being last in the line of my crew, and four of us missed getting on the helicopter because it was full. As the helicopter took off, I had a sick feeling that I had missed the boat. Four of us from my crew and one other full crew of twenty were to take the last flight, but shortly we were told there was not going to be another flight that day. We were stranded! My crew was in the back country fighting fire, and I was stuck at an airstrip. We were forced to spend the rest of the day at the caterers, sipping coffee and staring at the sagebrush. I kept thinking, I hope the shit doesn't hit the fan with the rest of the crew. The squad bosses were competent, and I had faith in their ability to keep the crew out of trouble. They were with the other Park Service crew, who had a competent crew boss and assistant crew boss.

The four of us bedded down along the river. In the early morning before dawn, I was awakened by a forest service employee. She said that a member of my crew's brother had passed away back home. The parents requested that their son come home for the funeral. I drove with her into Gardiner to use the radio to get hold of Al, one of the squad bosses who was a good friend of John, the crew member whose brother had died. He said he would tell him. We arranged to get John out of the back country. He was to hike out to a trailhead and be driven to Bozeman, Montana, where he could get a flight home.

The next morning, we learned a helicopter would not be available, and the four of us were loaded into a truck and driven to the same trailhead, from where we were going to hike to the spike camp. Before we got started, John showed up at the trailhead. We talked for a while about his brother. The brother had been sick for quite some time, and his death was expected, but it was still a shock to learn he had passed away. We shook hands, and John headed towards civilization, while the rest of us readied to go into the wilderness. We were hiking to a place called Coyote Creek, on the north boundary of the park. The fire was burning inside, as well as outside Yellowstone in the Gallatin National Forest. At the trailhead just before we left, we met a park ranger checking out a pack string bringing hay into the back country to feed stock at our spike camp. Yellowstone has a policy about only using certified weed-free hay, and each bale was supposed to be tagged. He was making sure the packers were being responsible. Uncertified hay could introduce some noxious weed into the back country. We talked with the ranger for a few minutes about the fires. He had been working almost nonstop since July. He said everyone living in the park was coping fairly well, but all were looking forward to the quiet of winter. "At least I can afford a good vacation this winter," he said.

It was about a seven-mile walk to the spike camp. The landscape was beautiful with sagebrush meadows and patches of forest composed of aspen and pine. The trail passed over a spectacular gorge, with a river cascading over boulders a hundred feet below. I admired the suspension bridge's craftsmanship. Some of the best Park Service employees build structures like that bridge, often only with hand tools. After we crossed the bridge, we followed the trail to the top of a hill, and from the summit we had a panoramic view of northern Yellowstone. Again we could see smoke columns everywhere we looked. Our destination was a fire so big I couldn't figure out what was the main part of the fire. I knew then that the only thing going to put that fire out would be weather.

After several hours walking, we came across several large footprints in the dusty trail. The tracks looked like a barefooted human track, but I then realized we were looking at the hind footprint of a bear. I had not really thought about being in bear country while on the Huck Fire, but suddenly it came to the forefront of my mind — grizzly country! I had been camping in grizzly country for over a week. I became paranoid and starting looking around, expecting to see a big lumbering beast break out of the woods in a full charge. I wondered how the bears were handling the fires. Were the fires making these bears dance as happened in northern California the year before? I reached down and placed my hand in the print. There was plenty of room to spare. This bear was not small. I was not sure if the track was from a black bear or grizzly, but in one track of a front paw I noticed long claw marks. Grizzlies were supposed to have long claws used for digging, but sometimes the claws wore down during the summer, and sometimes black bears had long claws. Just seeing claws didn't necessarily mean it was a grizzly. Whatever it was, I did not want to shake hands with it.

I thought about all the food being flown into the back country to spike camps. What effect might it be having on the bears? The Park Service in Yellowstone had for years diligently educated visitors not to feed the bears. The first time I visited Yellowstone with my parents, it was common in those days to see bears, both black and grizzly, begging for food along the park roads. Now it's rare to see a bear from a road. The bears are all in the back country carrying on a natural life with little human contact.

In 1988 thousands of firefighters had been put out in spike camps all over the greater Yellowstone area, but the firefighters' primary concern was fire not keeping food away from bears. By August, the fires were out of the hands of the National Park Service and being managed by interagency overhead. Concerns about feeding bears were not as important as putting out the fires. Speaking from personal experience, some firefighters are notoriously messy. It was common to find opened MREs (Meals Ready to Eat), cans of food, soda cans, uneaten sandwiches, gum wrappers, and even turds and dirty toilet paper lying around fire lines. Bears stumbling across a fire line or spike camp might think they'd found heaven because of all the readily available food. While on the fires in Yellowstone, I found opened MREs and other food on the fire lines. Our strike team cleans up its messes, but other crews were not as diligent. During the height of the fires thirty to fifty spike camps had been placed throughout the park with upwards of 200 people per camp. Obviously a lot of food was being flown into the back country. On the Hellroaring fire, I found boxes of opened MREs and juice cans a mile from spike camp. Maybe the combination of the fires and the presence of so many people had pushed the bears far away from the fire lines and spike camps. The sound of chainsaws, helicopters, and so many firefighters in so many places might have driven the bears to Canada for all I knew. While spiked out along Coyote Creek in Yellowstone National Park, we had a liaison National Park Service person stationed at the camp, to assure that the camp stayed clean; nevertheless, food was there in great amounts.

In the early afternoon, the four of us finally reached the rest of the strike team. They were working on improving a hiking trail that followed Coyote Creek, using it as a fire line. The assignment was to cut timber and other vegetation away from the trail to make a fire line that would hold. I worked with my crew for the rest of the day, cutting trees with chainsaws in the wilderness of Yellowstone National Park. I never thought I would see the day when so many trees were cut inside a national park. We had logs stacked four or five deep along the trail on the outside of the fire line. It looked like a logging operation.

Our spike camp was actually a designated back-country camp-site. Five crews including our strike team worked out of the camp. With a few overhead folks, over 100 people camped in a back-country camp-site designated for probably no more than seven to ten people. In a few days, we had social trails winding throughout the area, and the vegetation looked hammered. The packers supplying our camp hobbled their horses at night and allowed them to graze in a nearby open mead-ow. I think we had a bigger impact on the ecosystem than the fires.

This spike camp, like others, formed a division on the large project fire. Working in conjunction with the adjacent division to the north, we planned to build a six-mile indirect fire line along the west side of the fire, string out a hose lay and back burn along the entire line. We spent the next five days improving the line, constructing holding tanks out of logs lined with plastic, laying out one-and-one-half-inch hose with a gated Y every three hundred feet with one hundred feet of one-inch hose running to nozzles off the main line. Each holding tank had two or three Mark III pumps rigged, so we could pump water in either direction. The overhead folks flew in a hose and pump specialist just to design the hose line. We referred to him as the "Plumber." Every one-quarter mile or so, he had us put in a line running from Coyote Creek to the main hose line or to a holding tank. It was going to take an army just to run all the pumps once we had fire to fight. This six-mile hose line must have used up every available hose in the country. Helicopters every day kept flying in more hose that we diligently laid out along the line.

Meanwhile, the fire burned unimpeded a mile or so away, every day burning a few more thousand acres. Each day on the Huck Fire was the same, a heavy smoke inversion in the morning that would burn off in early afternoon, and the fire activity would pick up with fire runs moving through acre after acre of lodgepole pine until the sun began to set. At sunset the fire would lie back down with another inversion setting up after dark. Some days air support could not fly, and we had to rely on pack animals to bring in supplies. The packers and their horses and mules got so tired they could not keep everyone supplied. We ran out of hot food for two days and had to rely on MREs and went without water for a day.

We were into our sixteenth day of hard work, spiked out in the back country. My cold had finally run its course but not eating or sleeping well was beginning to take its toll on me. Every time there was a break, many us napped curled up around our packs.

While working the fire line on day seventeen, we came across the carcass of a moose just off the line. We wondered how it had died and walked over to take a look. The vegetation around the moose was trampled down, and the moose was partially eaten. We were wondering what had fed on it, when we heard a rustle and saw two bear cubs sitting on branches in a nearby pine tree. I had about one second of, "That's cool, two bear cubs," and then reality hit me. Bear cubs usually mean a full-grown sow lurked nearby, and that spelled trouble. I saw some movement in a thick grove of pine trees below the cubs and realized the sow was there. I saw that unmistakable hump on the shoulders and made out a round face staring at us. "Oh shit, a grizzly bear!"

We all froze, not sure if we should back off, stand our ground or try to climb the nearest tree. But, the bear did not charge. She did not even let out a *whoof*. She had eaten so much moose she could hardly move, and she seemed content enough to tolerate our presence. It was a stand off. I got on the radio and reported the bear and dead moose. Overhead called back and said two park rangers were going to be heading in to deal with the bear and for us to back away. So we went back to building line, laying hose and going about our business, constantly glancing over our shoulders to keep an eye on the bear. The cubs stayed in the tree, while mom dozed down below. The rangers showed up later in the day. Instead of closing the trail—normal protocol—and leaving the bear alone, they chased her off. With a rope, they dragged the carcass out of the way but where the bear could find it. The bear, normally the highest priority, took second fiddle to the fires.

On day eighteen, September 6, the stage was set for lighting the fire. Overhead was worried about another cold front that was supposed to move into the area in a couple of days with high winds. They hoped to nail this fire before the front hit. The green light was given to start the back burn and a hotshot crew in the next division began back burning along the line moving north to south. Meanwhile, in the early afternoon when the inversion lifted, a helicopter flew into the area with ping-pong balls filled with a napalm-type fuel. Helitack folks began dropping the balls deep within the line close to the wildfire. The back burn began to do its job, consuming fuel and moving uphill towards the wildfire.

The hotshot crew just kept on burning. It was a race to get the entire six miles of line burned in one day. They did not get to our division until mid afternoon but didn't hesitate, just continued burning along the fire line. I could see black plumes of smoke in the distance get closer and closer as the back burn continued down the line. After six days of preparation, the back burn was happening. Fuels were so dry that most trees immediately torched off, and the back burn made big runs up the slope above us. Ash rained down around us, and spot fires started showing up just outside the fire line. We had to hump to catch them. In one place a burning snag fell, rolling down the hill spewing fire everywhere. Several of us had to jump to get out of the way. It crossed the fire line and rolled into a meadow just below and started a small fire. We immediately ran down the hill, whooping like Indians, and jumped on the fire, knocking down the flames and putting a line around it. I glanced over at Jim, who had had the bad day on the Huck Fire to see how he was handling this. He had a big smile on his face and, seeing me looking at him, said, "The fire, at least, isn't shooting bullets at me. Shit, I can beat this. This is great!"

He had overcome his fear. The past eighteen days probably had been the best therapy he could have had. The Yellowstone fires had brought suppressed memories to the surface. He had been able to hit his fears head on and finally won. His biggest fear in Vietnam was fighting in dense jungle, unable to see the enemy and expecting at any second to have a bullet come slicing through the air with his name on it. We were not at war getting shot at, at least not in Yellowstone, and I didn't tell him about the incident in California in 1987. Perhaps he could die in flames, but at least that was something he could see.

Others on the crew were becoming stressed out, having a hard time of it because of the extreme fire behavior of the back burn that day. Later on, when the back burn pushed the line pretty hard, several looked as if they were ready to bolt and head for a safety zone. It was my turn to try to hold the troops together. We were not in danger; there was no need to run, but several who had never been on a fire before had second thoughts. Jim came to the rescue. He talked to them, joking the whole time, keeping the rookies close by and making them feel safe. He had become one of the strongest on the crew.

Meanwhile, the hose lay was charged and running, working as perfectly as a Rolex watch. Each pump station had two people, one operating a radio, the other the pumps. Firefighters along the line were spraying water, knocking down flames and beginning to mop up hot spots. They would direct which way to send the water by opening and closing valves; the two manning the pumps could send water in either direction.

The hotshot crew back burned well after dark finally stopping around 11:00 P.M. The air temperature had dropped into the twenties, and the fire had lain down for the night. The word went out on the radio to head back to camp. In one day, we had back burned about 15,000 acres along four miles of line. That was a record for me. Most of the fires I had fought in my twenty years of firefighting were smaller than 15,000 acres, and we burned that much just to stop a fire that was over 100,000 acres in size. It was definitely not a burning bush I could put out wearing shorts and flip flops.

We had been out for eighteen days, and I had not had a hot shower the whole time. I had long since run out of clean underwear, socks, and shirts. Back at camp, we were told our strike team was flying out the next day, September 7, for some R&R.

We spent the next morning mopping up hot spots along the line. Another cold front had moved through, and the winds had picked up, but the wind was blowing from the west, pushing our fire away from us. Our fire was moving to the southeast, and our line was holding. Elsewhere in Yellowstone on September 7, it was a different story. The North Fork Fire near Old Faithful almost burned Old Faithful Lodge down that day. In 1989, I met a married couple who worked out of Old Faithful in 1988. The wife had been on the roof of the Old Faithful Inn watching the flames come roaring down the hill towards them. The husband was out with a fire crew trying to keep buildings in the area from burning. In the *National Geographic* article about the Yellowstone fires was a picture of the fire burning just beyond the lodge, and, if one looks closely, several yellow-shirted people can be seen on the rooftop. She was one of them. Watching the wall of flames bearing down on the area, she was thinking there was no way the lodge or any other building was going to survive and wondered if any humans were going to survive as well. Tears came to her eyes as she stood up there with some overhead folks watching the world around them burn. They left the roof top, heading for safety sure the lodge could not survive. Her spouse, down below with other firefighters, battled the mighty beast head on with water and foam. During the worst part of the fire at Old Faithful Inn that day, there was about five to ten minutes when the day turned to night due to dense smoke, and firefighters and visitors trapped by the fire fell to the ground to find fresh air. They were safe from the flames in the large parking lots and open areas, but the fiery inferno scared the hell out of all of them.

Talking to the two in 1989, they confessed they had not been convinced they would live when the fire surrounded them. There was no place to go, no oxygen to breathe. It was entirely up to the fire, whether they lived or died. They were ringed in by fire. Just when everyone thought their world would end, the smoke began to lift and the air began to clear. The wind had shifted, and the fire front was moving away from Old Faithful. Firefighters got off the ground and went back to work. Several buildings burned in the Old Faithful area that day, but the famous Old Faithful Lodge survived. Looking on a map of the fires, it looked as if the Old Faithful area was the hole in the donut. The fire had burned all around the area.

No firefighters died on September 7, but my friends at the Old Faithful Inn who had survived said they would always remember that day. The couple from old Faithful went through the fire together, and, when I met them the next year, they seemed to be one of the most together couples I knew.

As for us on the west side of the Hellroaring Fire, on September 7, we kicked butt into the middle of the afternoon, cleaning up hot spots along our fire line. Around 2:00 P.M. we were told to report to a nearby meadow with our fire packs ready to be flown out of the back country. A Chinook landed in the meadow, unloading two fresh crews and picking up our strike team. Getting on last, and sitting in the rear, I could once again look out the back door. Once we were airborne and above the tree tops, I could see the smoke column that had burned around Old Faithful. The sky was full of smoke and fires were still burning everywhere. It looked as though the thousands of us out on the line in the past eighteen days had done nothing to stop the fires. However, our fire was burning away from us, and it looked as if our six-mile line was holding. We landed at the air strip outside Gardiner and everyone but myself, my assistant crew boss, and the other crew boss and assistant loaded up in a bus and headed for a place called Chico Hotsprings. The four of us headed into the ICP to turn in crew reports and check in with the overhead folks. Walking into the building, I went to the rest room to wash my face and hands. That was the first time I had seen myself in a mirror for days. My face was covered with a five-day-old beard, blackened with ash, my clothes were blackened, and I realized for the first time I had a rather strong smell. It had been a hell of a good time. We heard about Old Faithful, and all I could do was shake my head and hope no one had been injured.

After checking in, the four of us were driven to Chico Hotsprings. I headed for the showers and felt hot water for the first time in a couple of weeks. The best part of Chico Hot Springs however, was not the hot showers but the hot springs. Chico sits over some thermal springs, and they have a large swimming pool full of hot water. Slipping into the hot water, my body just unwound. I almost fell asleep floating in the water. Chico also had a bar. Later that night after a good meal, we were all in there slugging beers, enjoying life, and listening to Country Western music. It was a Wednesday night, but there were many locals in the bar, and we had one hell of a good time. I called home for the first time in ten days and caught up on the news. I slept late into the next day, catching up on sleep, but, when I got up, I found out our R&R had been cut short.

That afternoon someone showed up from the ICP. Everyone was predicting the mother of all cold fronts to hit the area the next day, September 9. All hell was expected to break loose. The cold front was supposed to bring sixty- to seventy-mile-per-hour winds, and the fire would be threatening Yellowstone National Park's headquarters and permanent housing at Mammoth Hot Springs. Nearby Gardiner, Montana, was also in the path of the fire. Everyone expected the worse after what had happened at Old Faithful, Cooke City, and West Yellowstone. All available crews were needed back on the front lines.

On the morning of September 9, the winds were already blowing hard. We loaded up onto a bus and headed back into the action. Driving into Gardiner, I saw car after car of locals heading out of town, their vehicles filled with whatever they could carry. The entire town of Gardiner was being evacuated. Everyone I saw had a worried look. They looked like war refugees on the road trying to get away from the front while troops headed into action. The sky over Gardiner had turned a sick yellowish-green from the smoke and clouds. The smoke blotted out the sun and it seem like evening instead of morning. All the fires in the Yellowstone area had blown up and were burning thousands of acres. They staged us at the airport in town with the intention of flying us to initial attack hot spots, but the wind was too strong, and the ships were grounded. Instead we drove to the high school and unloaded. The high school was at end of the town limits. The wilds of Yellowstone National Park started just on the other side of a fence. The winds were blowing forty to sixty miles per hour by mid-morning, and we could see flames burning over the top of a mountain southwest of town heading our way. I could see bright red flames mixing with black smoke licking the sky. If this world ever faces a nuclear holocaust or the impact of a comet, it will probably look like September 9.

Police cars drove around town with sirens and loud speakers blaring, telling people to evacuate the town. This was going to be Custer's Last Stand. It was our job to stop the beast from entering the town. Our strike team, one hotshot crew, a couple Native American crews and a group of engines was the only thing between the fire and the town. Firefighters stood or sat, watching the fire burning on the mountains outside of town. Most of us were quiet, watching what turned out to be the North Fork Fire in one of its finest hours. The North Fork Fire had burned through the park and was now reaching its northern boundary. The wind stiffened but started to shift from the south to the north. The air temperature dropped, and I suddenly realized that some of what I thought was smoke was actually low-lying clouds; all the signs indicated snow or rain on its way. The relative humidity climbed as the clouds dropped lower. The wind began blowing the fire back on itself, and the danger to the town appear to be over. We all relaxed. Someone got a football from the high school, and a group of firefighters started playing touch football on the high school football field. One minute we faced the beast and the next played touch football.

As the sun set, the clouds lowered to the mountain tops, and the flames licking at the sky disappeared, as snow — the first snow fall since the storm on Memorial Day — filled the sky. On September 10 the snow and rain became serious, and fires all over Yellowstone only smoldered. I heard a report that snow was falling heavily at Old Faithful.

Since we were not in the back country and our twenty-one days were up, they demobbed us on September 10. That afternoon I found myself on a plane en route to Stapleton Airport, Denver. I had been gone from my family for twenty days. After disembarking from the plane, passengers in the terminal looked at us as we passed because we were still dressed in Nomex. Several asked if we had been to Yellowstone. When we said yes, they wanted to know what it was like. It was as if we had been to a war and won—heroes coming home. It made the old chest swell, brought out the pride.

"Damn, it feels good to be a firefighter and a American," Jim said, as we walked through the terminal. I suspect he compared our hero's walk through the airport with the unpleasant one made when he returned from Vietnam.

Getting back home and settling into the family life, I thought I was done with firefighting for the year. I was ready for winter and looking forward to peace and quiet, but just two weeks later, I got the call that they still needed crews in Yellowstone. The weather had warmed, and the fires were still actively burning. Shortly I was again on a bus heading north with another crew. This time I was dispatched to the Clover Mist Fire, my fourth fire in Yellowstone. After the September 10th storm, the summer was finishing out in typical fashion with a warm late summer, early fall. The U.S. Forest Service was still kicking the fire beast and being very active on fire suppression. The National Park Service had backed off and was into rehabbing the fire lines and cleaning up the back country. Late in the day, we arrived at a place called Crandel, the ICP for the Clover Mist Fire. The place looked like an 1800s mining town instead of a temporary fire camp because of the plywood shacks with stove pipes jutting out of the roofs. We checked in at what looked like a hotel lobby and had a shack assigned to us. Our shack—a tent with plywood sides and a canvas top—had plenty of room for the twenty of us. In the center of the shelter stood a wood stove, and I thought, *It's like we're going to be here for the winter.*

Even though the days were warm, the nights dipped into the teens, and the wood stoves were needed.

We spent fourteen days at Crandel, most of the time doing mop-up and rehab work. The intense fire behavior of August and early September was gone. The fire was slowly dying, giving way to winter. Several 206 helicopters flew us into the back country almost every day to work hot spots. Some of the firefighters had been working fires almost non-stop since April. It had been a long fire season.

Wildlife abounded in the area. I observed elk, mule deer, and a fox just driving from fire camp to the fire. For the first five days, we hiked about one mile up a hill to get to the fire in our division. The first morning out on the line, I hiked into a dense grove of large unburned pines and fir trees to check for spot fires, while the crew was busy mopping up some others. Once inside the grove, I heard a deep-throated hoot. Sitting in a nearby tree was a great gray owl. It was the first great gray I had ever seen. The owl was huge in comparison to the great horned owl and had a gorgeous facial disk. It sat in the tree watching me. I watched it back. It brought back memories of the golden eagle I had seen in Bryce Canyon years before. Things had changed a lot for me since that day. I didn't want to disturb the owl from its roost, so I backed out and continued on my way. Every morning for the next four days, I would see or hear the owl. It sometimes even followed us, flying from tree to tree as we walked.

The remarkable thing about the Yellowstone fires was that no one was severely injured or died even during the worst of the fires. Many firefighters had to run to safety a number of times, but only three had deployed their shelters, and that had been a bad decision made by a park ranger. The ranger jeopardized the life of two people and himself by staying behind at a back-country cabin to protect it as the fire burned through the area. He thought they would deploy their fire shelters and be safe versus flying out of the area. He broke one of the cardinal rules of firefighting—a fire shelter is not considered a safety zone, only a last resort. Several other people had been with him when fire threatened the cabin, including a friend of mine. They elected to leave by helicopter, having sense enough to recognize the danger. The three who stayed behind, ended up in their fire shelters. They survived but received some burns. The poor ranger got his already cooked butt roasted some more by his supervisor when they got back to civilization. He clearly should not have put the three of them in danger.

In late September overhead folks were patting themselves on their backs for having an almost injury-free episode with the fires in Yellowstone. Everyone thought for such an intense fire season and number of close calls, it was remarkable that no one had die. That all changed on the Clover Mist Fire at the very end of the fire season.

On the Clover Mist Fire, our crew spent many days in boggy meadows trying to put out smoldering peat. Isolated trees or clumps of trees mostly grew along the edges. The peat would burn around and under many of the trees, making them extremely unstable. I could push over a three-foot diameter spruce with one hand because the roots were burned out or there was nothing holding the roots of the tree in place. Some trees looked unscathed above ground—still green even—but below ground was a different story. If a strong gust of wind blew through the meadow, trees would start falling. I saw a number of them fall during the time we were assigned to the fire. Every morning at the briefing, the safety officer told everyone to watch out for falling snags. However, it was almost impossible to not work around them. I had everyone work in teams of two so one could look out for the other. But sometimes, no matter how careful one is, fate can deal an ugly hand.

Most crews were being flown into the back country each day in 206s. Each morning three of them would fly into an open meadow and spend an hour shuttling crews to various places in the back country. While the helicopters flew in and out, picking up firefighters, a red-tailed hawk would perch in a nearby tree. The noise and rotor wash from the helicopters would scare up meadow voles, sending them in a panic across the grass. The hawk would swoop down and catch one. I kept expecting the hawk to be killed by a rotor, but it always stayed far enough away. I was amazed how the hawk figured out that the helicopters were creating easy pickings for a breakfast, but day after day for two weeks as we flew in and out of the meadow the hawk was always there.

After picking up firefighters, the helicopters used burned meadows as helispots, landing and taking off a number of times each day to drop us off and pick us up. As in our division, the next division over from ours ferried in firefighters by 206s in strings of six firefighters per load. The firefighters would wait off to the side until the entire crew showed up, so they could start working. As a 206 took off, the rotor wash apparently caused an unstable tree to topple. The firefighters had their back to it and, due to the noise of the helicopter, never heard it falling. The tree hit one of them, instantly killing him.

A freak accident had claimed a firefighter. The word quickly spread throughout the divisions. We were devastated. The overhead folks decided to pull everyone in from the lines and reassess the safety situation. Back at fire camp, everyone was quiet. The crew who had lost the firefighter took it hard. Overhead brought in trauma specialists to talk with the crew about the death.

We wondered if the accident could have been prevented, but there didn't seem to be a clear answer. Firefighting is not a safe profession. That was why we got hazard pay. In the case of the fallen firefighter, no cardinal rule had been broken. He had just been in the wrong place at the wrong time. That death was hard to swallow, and I just wanted to see the summer end and the country covered with a blanket of snow. It was time to go home and be with my family.

After fourteen days, the weather turned even colder, and clouds moved in from the north. Dark and low, the clouds settled over the mountains around us. It had a feel of permanence this time. Winter was finally going to dominate the land, and the 1988 Yellowstone fires were being put to bed. The day we left, Crandel ICP was being dismantled. The "mining camp" in a matter of a few days would cease to exist. Loading up on the bus that would take us home, I looked to the west were the Clover Mist Fire had burned. The land was interlaced with burned, partially burned, and unburned forest. Low lying clouds enshrouded distant mountains, and snow began to fall. The landscape looked great. The fire left a natural mosaic pattern. When firefighters fought fires, the fires often ended up as circles of burned vegetation surrounded by intact forest because we built fire lines, then burned all the fuel inside the line either by the fire itself or by back burning. Because firefighters, even the hoards present, had had so little effect on the Yellowstone fires, the fires left that natural mosaic, and that may have been the best thing that had happened to the Greater Yellowstone area in a couple hundred years.

The 1988 fires were a wake up call for the National Park Service. Throughout the Park Service, but particularly in Yellowstone National Park, the fires generated research on what affect the fires had on the ecosystem and also helped to initiate state-of-the-art fire monitoring and fire management programs in all national parks. One of the discoveries from the research in Yellowstone was that 1988 was not the first time that a large area of the park had burned. In the 1700s even more of the park had burned in one summer. Of course, in the 1700s, no one tried to suppress the fires. What happened in 1988 was a natural occurrence. Every two to three hundred years, the conditions are going to favor large fires in the greater Yellowstone area. What was also learned in 1988 was that, even if everything possible is done to suppress a fire, it does not mean a thing. Under the right conditions the woods are going to burn.

11

May you live all the days of your life.

— Jonathan Swift (1667 to 1745)

Colorado 1994

O n a Saturday morning in late March, the phone rang. The last person I expected was someone from Northern dispatch. They were looking for a crew boss to take a Type II crew to Michigan. I would have thought Michigan was still buried under two feet of snow in late March. Apparently they had had a dry winter, and a couple of kids had built a campfire the day before to roast a few hot-dogs. It had been a warm day with strong westerly winds. The camp-fire became an 800-acre weenie roast, burning down two cabins and threatening a small town. Eastern deciduous woods have different burn periods than the conifers in the West. Between the time the snow melts in the spring—particularly when there has been below normal snowfall—and when the trees leave out is a small window of from two to six weeks when the woods are dry, and the fire danger can rise quickly. The 800-acre fire had burned on U.S. Forest Service lands, so they called for reinforcements, including a Type I overhead team. Type I teams usually are only used when a fire was large or, in this case, threatened a community. This Type I team was from Colorado, and, not unusually, overhead teams use resources from their region, hence why I got the call. Three hours after the phone call, I was on a

164

plane with my crew and the Type I overhead team, heading for Michigan. We arrived on scene in the late afternoon, and even before we had left the bus, the sky clouded up, and it started to rain. We found ourselves sitting in a bus at a staging area watching the rain pelt the windows. Besides the Type I overhead team, the forest service had called in five hand crews. It was the first fire of the year for all of us, and everyone was itching for action, but as quickly as the fire had started, it died. By the time we got there, there was no smoke visible in the air; the fire was out. The fire went from a raging crown fire, threatening a town one day to ashes the next. We sat around in buses reading, sleeping, waiting to find out if we were just going to turn around and go home or be kept for pre-suppression work. Overhead decided to release everyone but our crew, and we spent the next five days in pre-suppression, doing project work, working in cold tem-peratures and rain in the woods of Michigan. Apparently the fire sea-son in Michigan was over that year almost before it really started. Leaving a fire crew around for initial attack, was more of a political move to let people sleep better at night than to serve any purpose for fire suppression because, during the five days we were there, it rained every day. We returned to Colorado five days later never having seen smoke let alone flames.

The winter and spring of 1994 had been drier than usual in Colorado, and by May the live fuel moisture in trees was low. Fire overhead folks from Colorado and BIFC try to forecast months ahead of time what the next fire season is going to be like, and by May they all were nervous about the fire danger in Colorado and other places in the West. Since my job does not revolve around fire, I usually do not even think about fires until late summer, but by early June, fire-fighting seemed to be all I was doing. There had been a number of small fires along the front range in Colorado that kept local initial attack resources busy. I ended up on several of them. Most were just one- or two-shift fires, but they seemed to come one right after the other. It was difficult for me to get my other work done because of fire suppression work. Meanwhile, the fire season was going gung-ho in New Mexico and Arizona, and it already seemed like late summer with the number of fires burning. Resources starting to stretch a little thin. The Alpine Hotshot crew that works out of Rocky Mountain National Park had been in Arizona since early June experiencing some intense fire behavior on fires in the Chiricahua Mountains in southeast Arizona.

In late June, all hell broke loose in western Colorado. A large fire broke out near Paonia and threatened several developments. Resources were stretched even thinner. Along the front range in Colorado, overhead folks were reluctant to release resources for fear of a big fire breaking loose and threatening communities. Firefighters in the area hung loose waiting for the call, while resources were being flown in from other parts of the country. We watched the news and read the situation reports. On July 2, a number of new fires broke loose because of lightning. One, the South Canyon Fire, near Glenwood Springs, Colorado, came into existence then. It was small and not threatening any structures at the time, and many other fires were and demanded more attention. No one was sent into suppress the South Canyon Fire, so it slowly began to build in size. Meanwhile, I was still at home watching the news. I felt frustrated; I wanted to be in on the action. I talked to my park's fire management officer about putting together an all NPS crew as we had in 1988.

By 1994, Type II crews were composed mostly of interagency personnel. After the 1988 fire season, the National Park Service realized their firefighting organization was behind other agencies in qualified personnel, equipment, and management planning. There was a strong push to form better working relations with other agencies, and the Park Service became more involved with fires outside park boundaries. After 1988, it was more common to see Park Service personnel on a hand or engine crew with forest service, Bureau of Land Management, state and county firefighters than just a crew of Park Service employees. Since we had only five firefighters obligated to an interagency crew, the fire management office agreed to pull together a Park Service crew and had a crew by the end of the day from Rocky Mountain National Park, supplemented with several firefighters from Great Sand Dunes National Monument. I was put on the list as the crew boss. The crew went on the board as available on July 5. I got a call the first night we were available; the next morning the crew was on a bus, to be dispatched to the west slope of Colorado to a fire near De Beque. Passing through Glenwood Springs in the morning, and just west of town, I could see smoke from the South Canyon Fire. A mountain called Storm King had a good smoke column rising into the air. Driving along I-70, I noticed a BLM truck parked on the road shoulder and a man inside talking on the radio. It was hard for me to drive by a fire without stopping. My gut feeling told me to stop and talk to the guy. "Hey, here we are, a fully equipped crew, self-contained. Put us to work." But our assignment was the De Beque Complex, not the South Canyon Fire, so we drove by without stopping.

Over the years, I have come close a few times to having the fire beast bite me, and July 6, 1994, was one of those times. Sometimes, just a small thing changed could make a difference between life and death—like hesitating at a stoplight when the light turns green and missing a broad-side crash as a car runs through the red light. That one-second hesitation let you live. If we had stopped to talk with the individual in the truck outside Glenwood Springs, there is a possibility I might not be alive today.

When we arrived at De Beque and checked in at the ICP, I found out we had been reassigned to the South Canyon Fire near Glenwood Springs. The fire was kicking up, and they needed resources. *Damn*, I thought. *We should have stopped and talked to that guy in the truck. If I had, we would probably be building line already, instead of having to turn around and waste precious time driving back the way we had just come.*

On my way back to the bus, I ran into some friends from another crew and stopped to talk to them for a few minutes. They had been out on assignment for two weeks already, and had a couple of days of R&R. While talking to my friends, someone from overhead ran up and said, "There's been a change of plans."

Instead of heading back to Glenwood Springs, we were to continue on to Western Slope Dispatch out of Grand Junction and check in with them. I told him that seemed a waste of time to drive farther west to Grand Junction only to turn around and drive back to Glenwood Springs. The guy just shrugged his shoulders and said, "Perhaps they have a higher priority fire for you."

Now I was thinking I should have just walk directly to the bus and driven off instead of stopping to talk to my friends; the overhead man would not have caught us, and we would have been able to drive back to Glenwood Springs. But orders were orders, so we loaded up and headed west instead of east. We arrived at Grand

Junction in the early afternoon and immediately were caught in the maze of a major fire dispatch center. Fire crews and supplies were coming and going out of Grand Junction. The place buzzed with activity. The airport was loaded with air tankers and planes were coming and going. A dry cold front had passed through the area, bringing only wind, not rain. The wind was gusting to forty miles per hour at Grand Junction, and a fire just west of town was putting up a good smoke plume. The air tankers were flying retardant to several fires. Upon landing at Grand Junction, they seemed to be taking off as fast as they were refueled and a new load of fire retardant stored in their bellies. Walking into Western Slope Dispatch to check in, I noticed several dispatchers working the radios, and the radio traffic was extremely busy. It seemed as if every fire in western Colorado had blown up, and firefighters were scrambling. I was frustrated for missing so much action. We could have been on the South Canyon Fire up on Storm King by now battling the beast. I wanted to get going, but, once we were checked in, instead of sending us back to Glenwood Springs, overhead hung on to us in case they needed initial attack on some new fire. Also, several fires had blown up, and a number of people were calling for more resources. Little did anyone know that, at that moment, about 100 miles away on Storm King Mountain near Glenwood Springs, fourteen firefighter's lives were going to end.

After hanging out for about an hour, we finally got our fire assignment, the Rabbit Mountain Fire near Craig, Colorado.

"What happened to us going to the South Canyon Fire?" I asked.

"The Rabbit Mountain Fire blew up and is threatening some oil and gas wells up there," the dispatcher said. "They only have one hand crew on a 1,000-acre fire and need a couple more. The South Canyon Fire has the Prinville Hotshots on it and one other Type II hand crew with a couple more crews already en route."

I said, "Yeah we could have been there hours ago if we hadn't come here."

He shrugged his shoulders and answered a ringing phone.

I headed out the door but quickly found out there was no bus to take us. The bus we had been on had left, so we were staged near the airport right where I had been sitting in 1987 waiting to go to

Northern California. Here I was doing the same thing, waiting to head out on a fire, while private citizens were coming and going out of the airport. The only thing that seemed different sitting there at the airport waiting in 1994 was being seven years older. I watched the air tankers come and go. They were beautiful prop planes, grabbing air as they climbed, heading off to face danger and support the ground troops, while another lumbered in after dropping a load of retardant.

The sun was beginning to set when we finally got a bus. The fire west of town had covered the sky in smoke, and the setting sun was a large, deep-red ball on the horizon. It was easy to look directly at it because of all the smoke. The sun colored the clouds in yellow to red that made for a spectacular sunset. Walking towards us in single file, with the sun a red ball in the background, was a tired hand crew of twenty firefighters that turned out to be the Colorado River fire crew I had been with a couple of times while working at Canyonlands in Utah. They had just gotten off helicopters and were dirty from a hard day on the line. Everyone's clothing, face, and hands were blackened with soot, dirt, and ash. I knew the crew boss, and we chatted for a few minutes. They had been kicking butt for almost three weeks on a number of fires in the Grand Junction area. The crew was tired, but their spirits were high. He asked if I had heard anything about the South Canyon Fire. I said no, except a hotshot crew was on it with another Type II crew. My friend said he had heard the fire had blown up, and some firefighters had had to scramble to get out of the way. I was not alarmed; confusion is often the name of the game when a fire rocks and rolls, but usually everyone shows up okay. As I was getting on the bus, I glanced over at a few people standing near one of the air tankers that had just taxied in after dropping a load of fire retardant. The pilot stood with several other people, and he looked pretty upset, looking at the ground and shaking his head. The others were not talking, just shuffling their feet. *Jeez,* I thought, *it looks like a funeral over there. What the hell is going on?* My gut tied into a knot, and I got a bad feeling that something was not right. I wanted to go over and find out what it was, but rumors and gossip can run rampart on fires, and often what you hear is not exactly true. We also had to get going.

A few hours later, in a small town between Grand Junction and Craig, we stopped for gas. We unloaded to buy snacks and use the restrooms. Inside the filling station, the person behind the counter asked if we had come from the fire where the firefighters had died.

"What?" I said. "What firefighters had died?"

She pointed to a TV set behind her. A reporter was talking about Storm King Mountain and the fourteen fatalities that had been confirmed. My crew suddenly hushed as we watched the news. We were supposed to have been on that fire. We drove through there that morning, and I had almost stopped. If I had, we might have ended up on the mountain with the others. Call it fate, but we were in Grand Junction when the fire beast ate fourteen firefighters. Now I realized what the pilot and the others had to have been discussing around the plane. The pilot turned out to be the last one to dump fire retardant on the fire as it blew up and ran up the mountain engulfing the firefighters. He had watched it happen from the air and could do nothing to help save them.

Meanwhile, back at my park, our fire management officer and others thought we were on the South Canyon Fire. They had gotten the word from Northern Dispatch that we had been assigned to it. He was scared that the fatalities had been us. He was on the phone trying to find out the fate of my crew, worried sick about us. No one had released the names of the ones who had died. He stayed up late that night, unable to sleep, thinking the worse. Family members were calling in to him, asking if we were okay. But we had been on a bus heading for Craig while all this was going on, having no idea people worried about us. We were nowhere near South Canyon, but family and friends back home thought we were in the middle of it.

We arrived in Craig well after midnight and bedded down at the BLM District Office. The dispatcher at Craig didn't know much more than some firefighters had died. The next morning when we got up, we found out that fourteen had indeed perished, twelve from the hotshot crew and two smokejumpers. Some of the elite had died, wildland firefighter's best. I called the fire office back at the park to check in, and, after finding out he had been worried, I called my wife to let her know I was all right.

I lucked out that day. We could have been on that mountain that afternoon instead of in Grand Junction if things had been just a little bit different. If I had stopped to talk to that guy in the BLM truck outside Glenwood Springs that morning, I would have learned we were supposed to be there and stopped instead of going on to De Beque. We might have been there before the hotshot crew and might of been flown up to that ridge.

Reading the report later that fall, I found out the firefighters had disregarded some watch-out situations and broken some fire-fighting orders. That is not to say what led to their deaths, but they did have warning flags that trouble was brewing. If they had heeded the warnings a little earlier, they might have been able to get out of there and lived. For any firefighter, it is hard to back off until the world blows up, then six words, "We better get out of here," voice the only thought on everyone's minds. No one wants to back off and then realize later it was the wrong decision. Our strike team leader in California in 1987 had wanted us to stay and fight when the Navajo crew boss and I were thinking retreat. Tom had been right, and we stopped the fire, but what if he had been wrong? It had been a dangerous call and put us in jeopardy for a time. If we had backed off, the fire would had gotten out of control and probably would have burned up some homes. We were the heroes that night in California, and we also lived. I am sure the hotshot crew and smokejumpers on the Storm King Fire had been thinking the same thing. Those firefighters on Storm King unfortunately played the wrong hand, staying down below the ridge too long and paying for the mistake with their lives.

Anyone fighting fires year after year like a hotshot crew has pushed the envelope. The odds are in our favor, but if someone does it too many times, eventually they get bit. Standing on that ridge in Bryce Canyon when lightning was popping around me didn't mean I was going to be hit by lightning, but the odds were a lot higher than if I was down below in the ravine. Fight fire aggressively but with safety in mind is the first firefighting order. There have been times over the years when many, including myself, have backed off and let safety take the driver's seat, but, more times than not, fighting fire aggressively does the driving. I have lucked out over the years with only a few close calls. But, how many more close calls are left in my bag before my luck goes belly up?

Western Colorado has claimed a number of firefighters over the years especially in the gamble oak country from Glenwood Springs to Grand Junction. The explosive nature of gambel oak is what got the hotshots and smokejumpers that fatal day in July 1994.

The live fuel moisture was very low in the oak, and when the cold front passed through with its associated winds, it turned a small fire into a raging inferno that burned a whole mountain side in almost a wink of an eye. Once the fire blew up, a galloping horse would probably not have been able to get out of the way, let along firefighters trying to run up a steep mountain side.

That people died on Storm King Mountain took the wind out of my sails in 1994. I had been battling the fire beast for eighteen years by then. For the first time, I really began to wonder if it was worth it. How many years off my life had firefighting taken? My lungs sometimes felt as if I, a non-smoker, had been smoking cigarettes for years.

In 1994 my life seemed to be a different crossroads. My spouse sprang a surprise on me in May announcing that she was pregnant. She had been moping for a couple of years about our two boys not being babies anymore. She missed having a baby to cuddle and kiss. I said she had me, but she said I was too hairy and had whiskers. Through her pregnancy that summer, she was as happy as a meadowlark singing on a warm spring day. She was going to be a mom again. As for me, I was freaked out; I was forty-five years old and going to be a dad again. I didn't know if I could handle diapers, sleepless nights, crying and someone needing lots of attention.

Then I began to think about the years when my boys were young and the fun things we did. Having someone run up to me when I came home from work yelling, "Daddy!" Someone to climb into my lap and snuggle while I read him a book. Giving me a kiss before falling asleep and saying things like, "Your are the best daddy in the whole wide world," or "I love you." It melted my heart to realize I was going to get to experience all that again. I was going to have an excuse again to ride a Merry-Go-Round, or play hopscotch, marbles, swing on a swing set, go to Disney World and ride Dumbo, or any of the other countless things that a dad can do with a child. So, once the shock wore off, I began to get excited. I secretly wished for a daughter, since I already had two sons. She would be Daddy's little girl! The princess of the house. I would wait on her hand and foot. Spoil her rotten. So my thoughts started wandering, while fighting fires during that summer of 1994. I sure as hell did not want to die.

Meanwhile, we had a fire to fight, so we got the details from the dispatcher at Craig, loaded back up into the buses and headed for

Rabbit Mountain. The Rabbit Mountain Fire had burned about 1,000 acres of piñon/juniper. The day the South Canyon Fire blew up, the Rabbit Mountain Fire was also rocking and rolling. A friend of mine was the only one on the fire that day, calling the Western Slope Fire Center asking for reinforcements. When the fire blew up, it trapped him in an open area near some oil pumps and storage tanks. The area was large enough that he did not have to deploy a fire shelter, but he was trapped with no way out and did have to hunker down and move from one side to the other as the fire burned around the open area. He definitely did not lay out the checkered cloth and have a picnic. He spent the night in the open area, unaware that firefighters had died on Storm King. When we got there and started talking about Storm King, he wanted to know what had happened. He was devastated because he knew some of the hotshot crew and the smokejumpers when I told him the names of those who had died. He had fought fires with them, drunk beer with them and shared war stories. Standing in a circle beneath a cloudless sky in Western Colorado with piñon/juniper trees torching off behind us, we took our hard hats off, lowered our heads and had a moment of silence before hitting the fire line. It was a fitting place for a small ceremony, out in the wilds of Colorado almost on the Utah border, miles from any town. The Rabbit Mountain Fire still blazed away, sending a smoke column thousands of feet into the air. A couple of ravens circled overhead, croaking in their deep raspy voices and flew off in search of thermals near the fire. I sent out a silent greeting to the ravens, wishing them the best. We put our hard hats back on, picked up our tools, and headed down the partially constructed fire line to finish the job we were hired to do. The battle raged on.

We dug a fire line the rest of the day working until sunset. Air tankers out of Grand Junction flew the fire throughout the afternoon, knocking down hot spots with retardant. Every time one of those bombers flew into view, we stopped to watch. It was a beautiful sight to watch the planes lumber overhead loaded with retardant, slowly swinging around to make a run on some part of the fire. Often a small scout plane circled overhead to lead the big bomber in its run—a hummingbird followed by an eagle. For me, it was comforting to see the bombers fly into view. Sometimes they didn't do much because the fire was just too hot, but, by just being, they supported the ground troops in an age-old symbiosis dating back to World War I.

Because firefighters were scarce, only three hand crews worked the Rabbit Mountain Fire plus a few overhead folks. Usually on a 1,000-acre fire there would be more people. But, because this fire was in piñon/juniper, the fire was almost history by the second day. After the cold front had passed through, the winds had died down, the temperature dropped, and the rh rose. If wind didn't blow in piñon/juniper, fire usually can't jump from tree to tree because of the lack of understory vegetation and the wide spacing of the trees. No wind, no fire. By sunset there were only a few hot spots still burning, and they were all lined. We walked back to fire camp as the sun began to sink in the West. We had a great view of western Colorado and the Book Cliffs of Utah from our location. The sunset was another brilliant display of red. I watched the sun set behind the Book Cliffs and realized it really felt good to be alive.

The fire camp had been set up at the end of a road overlooking a ravine with the Utah state line about a quarter mile away. One group of firefighters rigged up a slingshot between two trucks and began lobbing apples and rocks into the ravine. Several groups broke out Hacky Sacks and began playing, while others worked on saws, sharpened tools, read, talked or dozed, a typical scene in any fire camp. The death of the firefighters from the day before still hung in the air. Talking with a firefighter from one of the other crews, I found out he had come from Wisconsin and a couple others from my mother's hometown of Beaverdam. They knew my uncle and aunt who lived on a farm just outside town. Firefighting, like war, brings people together from all parts of the country.

The next day we worked only half a day before the fire was declared contained. We loaded up and drove back to Craig. The cold front that had contributed to the death of the fourteen firefighters on Storm King changed the weather, and the fire danger in Colorado dropped. Overhead started demobbing people. Since there was no other place for us to go, we headed home.

There was about a two to three week reprieve with little fire activity around the country. Fire caches were restocked and firefighters geared up, ready for the rest of the season. Ceremonies were held in Glenwood Spring honoring the fallen firefighters. Firefighters from around the country flew or drove there to participate. The news media ate it up; for a while it was headline news. While the fire season geared down in Colorado, New Mexico, and Arizona, it was just getting started in the northwest. In late July, wildfires started in Idaho, Montana, Washington, and Oregon. Firefighters again where in demand. The big push to fall and winter was starting. When large fires start burning in the northwestern states, they usually stay active until cold weather puts them out.

I had a family reunion coming up in early August in Wisconsin. When fires broke out up north, the urge was strong to skip the reunion and make myself available, but my sails had deflated somewhat, and anyway I thought the fires were still going to be burning into late September. I had plenty of time to get into the thick of things. In earlier years, I would have skipped the reunion and headed into the woods, but I decided I would spend some time with my family and take the two-week vacation. We headed for Wisconsin, even though two days before we left, I received a call to take a crew to Idaho. "Sorry dude," I said. "I have two weeks of approved leave, and I am outa here." For the first time in years, I spent two weeks in August on vacation and did not think about battling the fire beast even once. It felt great!

As I figured, after the reunion, the fires still burned hot and heavy up north. The first crews out were coming up on their three weeks, so I knew there would be a big turnover, and those of us who hadn't been out would be mobilized. Almost to the day, one week after being back to work, I got the call to head to Idaho as a field observer. Field observer, my favorite job. A person in that position can be a line scout, weather observer, mapper, lookout, and fulfill a number of other jobs—like the scouts from old cavalry days, the mountain man (or woman) out in the hills by him or herself—showing up back in camp late in the day to provide the latest information to the general. I also liked being independent of the fire line mentality. Not having to dig line all the time, back burn or mop up was a welcome change. The disadvantage of being a field observer was that it could be one of the more hazardous jobs in firefighting. Often a field observer ends up out on point. Out ahead of the fire crews, they flag line or scout out the fire. Sometimes there is no fire line between the fire and the observer. If a fire blows up he or she could be in danger. The field observer spends time also looking for safety zones. The fire crews rely on the field observer for pointing out those safety zones, as well as keeping them informed on weather conditions and fire behavior. I usually called in every hour to the ICP with an update on dry and wet temperatures, relative humidity, wind speed and direction, and fire behavior. Sometimes I ended up on a mountain top high above everyone else, where I could keep an eye on what the fire was doing down below. If the fire started to make a run or increase in activity, I was usually the first to know it. The field observer has to be at least crew-boss qualified because of the responsibility of protecting the other firefighters as well as having an understanding of fire behavior and an awareness of the changes in temperature, wind, or rh, and what effect all that might have on the fire. When people asked me what I thought about being a field observer, I'd say it was a horrible job, dangerous, and should be avoided, but, while all that was true, the real reason was that I wanted the job.

I found out I was heading to the Chicken Complex in Idaho above McCall. Most of the fire was burning in the Frank Church's River of No Return Wilderness. The fire also threatened a small community called Warren. The forest service was being smart and limiting suppression activities mostly to protecting commercial hunting lodges located in the wilderness, other structures, and communities like Warren, located just outside the wilderness. The fire for the most part was allowed to do its thing inside the wilderness.

On a Saturday afternoon, I flew out of Stapleton to Boise, Idaho, the home of BIFC. When I got there, as usual when fires were running out of control, the place was hopping with activity. I checked in and found myself an hour later loaded in a van heading north.

Fires sometimes have interesting names. The Chicken Complex was one of them. The driver told me the fire had started on a mountain called Chicken Peak. Several lightning fires had started in the area and had burned together, eventually becoming one fire. The fire so far had burned about 50,000 acres and still had not been brought under control.

As was usually the case, I got to the ICP about 3:00 A.M. and had to be at briefing by six. So I got less than three hours of sleep. I sure wished overhead folks would let firefighters sleep in their first day, but a fire was not a vacation, so I was up and ready to go at 6:00 A.M. The first shift was usually the killer for me because of lack of sleep. On big fires, I got into a routine fairly quickly. I usually got six, maybe eight hours of sleep a night, after the first shift.

Overhead was a Type I team from the Carolinas, southern folk with heavy accents. I liked listening to these guys talk, hearing them say "Oookay" or "Afffirmative" in a thick drawl that would drag out over the radio. It brought chuckles to those of us from the West, plus they had some great expressions like, "The fire is digging taters!" That meant it was rocking and rolling in my language. I spent the first two weeks with the team before their three weeks were up, and they headed home. Enjoyable bunch of people and knowledgeable about fire.

The first day on the fire, my assignment was to flag out a fire line along a ridge top for a couple of miles. The fire burned down below the ridge in a drainage bottom. The terrain was so steep with dense fuels, it was not worth it to send anyone down to try building line any closer. The drawback was that the fire was at the bottom of a steep hill, and there was plenty of unburned fuel between it and me on the ridge top. The fire behaved itself until the early part of the afternoon when the rh dropped into the low twenties and the wind picked up from the southwest. The fire blew up and made a run for the ridge. The call went out over the radio to pull firefighters off the line back to safety zones, but I was a mile out in front of everyone else and would not be able to make it back. I was on my own. Looking at a map, my only option was to continue along the ridge to an old burn from a few years before, and then out to a logging road, where I could be picked up by a vehicle. I was in dense lodgepole pine and did not have good views of the fire burning up the ridge behind me, but I could hear it and see the smoke column over the tree tops. I was worried about spot fires starting in front of me cutting me off from safety, because I was running the same direction the fire was burning. The fire was definitely "digging taters" that afternoon. I sure did not want it to dig any of mine. I stopped flagging line and just moved along at a fast clip, finally coming out into a wet meadow. I could see flames behind me torching through the tree tops shooting a hundred feet or so into the air. The head of the fire was not far behind me. The unmistakable sound, like the roaring of a locomotive, could be heard through the trees, and I could feel the heat from the fire. The fire was licking my heels. I didn't have much time.

The map showed the old burn just on the other side of the wet meadow, so I struck out through the meadow skirting some beaver ponds. Scrambling up a steep incline on the other side, I glanced back and saw the fire burning along the edge of the meadow where I had just been. There was enough distance between me and the fire with a wet meadow in between to make me feel safe. The fire wanted to follow, but there was not enough wind to carry it through the wet vegetation or start a spot fire on the side where I was standing. Instead it started to fan out along the edge looking for some way to skirt the meadow. I laughed at it and said, "Not this time, you dog!" I turned and burst through a narrow band of dense live trees into a blackened forest of standing dead trees—the old burn. There were live tree seedlings two-feet high scattered amongst burned trunks. The forest was regrowing out of its ashes. I could see the logging road a hundred yards off and, working my way through dead and downed logs, made it to the road. Sitting down, I drained a canteen of water. I watched the fire as it burned through the woods from where I had come. It was always interesting to watch a rip-roaring fire from a safe distance. The division boss showed up in a Hum-V. The National Guard had been called out to work as ground support and had a number of the "Hummers" available for use. So my first day on the Chicken Complex had me scrambling, and it was not the only time.

Overhead on the Chicken Complex seemed paranoid; so far in 1994, thirty-three people had died fighting fires. It was one of the worst seasons for fatalities in the history of firefighting. By late August, everyone was counting the days until winter. It had been a long season for me, starting in Michigan in March. The Chicken Complex would not die, however, and blew up somewhere almost every day, threatening structures and the firefighters trying to protect them. I spent considerable time during those three weeks on a mountain top acting as lookout, doing weather observations on the hour and keeping crews informed about the fire. I had great views into the Frank Church's River of No Return Wilderness whenever the smoke lifted. As in Yellowstone in 1988, the smoke inversion would usually be heavy in the morning and break for a few hours later in the day. The fire would punch through the inversion in the afternoon and burn up a few more thousand acres before lying back down in the evening. The fire went from 50,000 acres, to 60,000, 70,000 and, by the second week, had burned over 80,000 acres.

During the second week, I teamed up with another field observer. They flew us in by helicopter to the top of a mountain called Pilot Peak. A fire lookout tower situated on top provided an incredible view of the Frank Church's River of No Return Wilderness. The lookout had been abandoned due to the fire danger, so no one was home. The days of folks operating lookout towers were dwindling. Due to budget shortfalls, lookouts around the country could not be staffed.

After the helicopter dropped Mike and me off, we climbed the fire lookout and went out on the cat walk to have a look around. It brought back memories of the Gila. I wondered what Bob and Shelly were doing, since I had not been in touch with them in years. I wanted to stay at the Pilot Peak lookout and spend the afternoon kicked back enjoying the view, but we had a job to do. Our assignment was to flag a fire line from the mountain top down to the north fork of the Salmon River. Checking out the topographic map, and from what we could see from the fire lookout, this mountain was no easy hill. It went from about 8,000 feet above sea level to 3,300 feet in three miles. I was glad I would be heading downhill and not up, though I was nervous about the fire burning about halfway down the mountain. The relative humidity was dropping and the temperature rising. The fire beast was about to wake up and start consuming fuel. Once we started going downhill, it would be a bitch to come back to the top of the mountain. Our only means of escape at any sort of fast pace would be downhill towards the fire or traversing along a contour line to another side of the mountain. I thought about the South Canyon Fire. I was violating some of the same watch-out situations those guys did the day they died. Safety zones and escape routes not identified, heading downhill with the fire below, unburned fuel between me and the fire because of heavy forest—I could not get a good look at the fire down below, and no one else was watching it for us. Terrain and fuels made escape to safety zones difficult. I was thinking, "Here I go pushing the envelope again. I sure don't want to screw the pooch."

I probably should have spoken to Mike about it, but I didn't and let fate play out its hand. The sky was clear with a few small puffy cumulus clouds, and the temperature was in the seventies. From the mountain top, we had an incredible view of the wilderness all around with a river far below, winding through a steep-walled canyon. It was a breath-taking view and a great day for a hike. Mike looked at me and said, "Ready?" I think he had the same concerns I had.

Jokingly I said, "I was born ready!" Inside I was saying, *Yeah right.* We had just started down a ridge flagging line when the ICP dispatch called and said they wanted us back at the fire lookout to direct some heavy helicopters dropping water and fire retardant on the fire below. That was just fine with me. I did not have to be the weenie who chickened out even though it was a fitting move being on the Chicken Complex Fire. At least from the mountain top, a helicopter could fly in and get us if the fire blew up. Being half way down the mountain in dense forest would have been a different story.

We spent the rest of the day doing weather observations, directing Sikirsky 5-64E Sky Cranes and Chinook helicopters making water and fire retardant drops on the fire below us. The Chinooks were military ships, the same as used in Yellowstone, but the sky cranes were private. The sky cranes cost big money, thousands of dollars an hour to fly. Mike and I dragged chairs out onto the catwalk and kicked back, enjoying the view and our role as air traffic controllers. This is definitely the way to be fighting a fire, from the director's chair. However, dropping retardant on the flames down below seemed like a waste of taxpayer's money to me. Mike and I both thought that, without ground support to fight the fire, the retardant was not going to do much. The flames were just too hot, the fuel moisture too low. Unbeknownst to us, the overhead folks had a reason for doing the bucket work. They were planning an attack. They wanted to fly in three hotshot crews the next day and build line down the mountain. The reason we were flown to Pilot Peak was to flag a line — until we were told to stay at the lookout. The bucket work held the fire in check and pre-wet fuels. So, there was some order to the madness after all. The Sky Crane and Chinooks kept dumping retardant all day long, spending a good chunk of taxpayers' change. The Chicken Complex was a multi-million dollar fire, and $50,000 dollars or so of air support that day was only pocket change.

A helicopter flew in to pick us up as the sun started to set behind the mountains to the west. The big ships were done for the day, too. In the helicopter, flying a few thousand feet higher than the mountain tops around us, I could see two other fires burning within fifty miles of us. They were almost as big as ours, putting up good columns of smoke—a typical late summer in Idaho. Getting back to the ICP, I found out about the plan for the next day. Apparently there was some expensive timber earmarked for logging on the mountain-side outside the wilderness. The effort would be to save the timber so cutters could come in and log it. This was the reason for the retardant drops. Hotshot crews would be used to build fire line. Mike and I were to go with the three hotshot crews to help with the operation. Tomorrow was going to be an interesting day.

That night I called home to find out how my family was doing. The fire camp had a few phones set up, and we were allowed a three-minute phone call. Shortly before I had left for Idaho, my wife had a couple of tests done to check the health of our unborn child. We also wanted to know the sex—none of this waiting for the baby to pop out in the birthing room to find out. I wanted to know how we should decorate the nursery, with lace and pink ribbons or blue ribbons. I was hoping for the pink. So when she answered the phone, I said, "Hi! How are things? Is it a boy or a girl?"

She said, "Your wish has come true. It's a girl."

I could imagine her smiling on the other end of the phone with that cute dimple of hers showing in her left cheek. I jumped up from the table, "Yahoo, it's a girl!"

Everyone around me thought my wife had had a baby. They slapped me on the back, and someone crammed a cigarette in my mouth. "No, no," I said, "not yet. She's still pregnant, but she just told me that we're going to have a girl."

Everyone went back to what they were doing. My wife and I spent our last minute on the phone talking about names and how to decorate the baby's room. I hung up with a big smile on my face. I was a happy camper. I lay in my sleeping bag that night thinking about how my life was going to change and wondering what our little daughter would be like. I always had wanted a little girl, and now my wish was coming true. I drifted off to sleep thinking about dolls, tea sets, a club house, white lace, and a little blue eyed, blond-headed girl.

The next day dawned clear. The inversion had not set up as it had the previous night, and, as a result, the fire had remained fairly active through the night. The rh had not risen significantly overnight, and the temperature had remained relatively high. It looked as if it was going to be a warm day. The three hotshot crews and overhead met at the helibase, and five National Guard Black Hawk helicopters flew in to load us up for the trip to Lookout Mountain. Flying over the fire en route to the helispot on the mountain peak, I could see that the fire was already fairly active with an occasional tree torching. It was about 9:00 A.M. We unloaded and gathered around beneath the fire lookout. The folks in charge planned out what we would do. As they discussed their options, I pulled out a belt weather kit and took a weather reading. The air temperature was seventy-two degrees, the wind blew from the southwest at fifteen to twenty miles per hour. The rh was in the high teens. The fire behavior guru from overhead had come with us. He looked at the weather observation data, and his eyebrows rose. I suspected he was thinking the same thing I was—if we started digging line downhill, we would be in deep doo-doo. The fire was going to raise its ugly head today.

Meanwhile, the hotshot superintendents and other overhead folks were thinking about which ridge to build the line down. They were thinking attack. From our vantage on top of the mountain, we could not see the fire very well. Everyone was nervous because we had no one below the fire to see what was happening. There was a small inversion down at the bottom of the mountain, and the smoke was dense, preventing any helicopter from landing. The only way to get anyone down there was to walk. Since my job was field observer, which is lookout, I felt obligated to get down there. I volunteered to hike down, get below the fire and act as lookout for the troops. Everyone else thought it was a good idea. I put on my fire pack and dropped off the mountain top, heading down a ridge, one ridge over from where the fire was burning. I was going to drop from about 8,000 feet to 3,300 feet in about three miles. Working down the ridge, the trail occasionally flattened out and offered a great view of the fire below and a panoramic view to the south. In places, specifically on the flat areas huge, beautiful conifers grew straight up, with three- or four-foot-diameter trunks. These trees had been around for at least a couple hundred years. I could see why someone wanted to save them, but it was rather sad to think they would be logged. I could not see the fire very well most of the time because of dense timber, but I could see when the smoke changed from gray to black. I was about half-way down, when the radio traffic began to pick up substantially from my compadres on the mountain top. The fire was torching trees and beginning to make short runs up the mountain towards the hotshot crews. The division boss got on the radio and called the ICP, saying they were going to back off and not start building a fire line down the mountain. *That,* I thought, *was a very wise move.* He said they would hold for a little while to see if they could build line that night. Now I was in a pickle, down the mountain by myself. It was too late for me to head back up. The mountain was getting steeper, and shortly I found myself having to cling to vegetation to keep from sliding. I got into an area with loose soil and rocks. The footing was horrible. I slipped several times, sliding down the mountain in dust and rocks. Building line in this stuff would be hazardous, especially at night. I called on the radio and gave a report about the difficulty.

The ridge I was following snaked closer to the fire, and I was beginning to see flame and thick black to dark gray smoke tinged with yellow indicating flames within the smoke column. The smoke told me the fire was really cooking. I figured I better start humping it downhill a little faster. I wanted to get below the flames before it really started moving uphill. I was just above the main part of the fire and could see plenty of flames. For some reason, perhaps because of the danger I was in, the colors of the flames seemed very bright—dark red to orange—almost as if the flames had been digitally enhanced. Flames angrily licked around the trunks of some very large conifers burning heavy brush and grass. The fire wanted to get into the tree tops and was trying to find a way to do it.

Suddenly the fire roared from the ground into the tops of the trees. The wind affected little at ground level beneath the trees, but when the fire leaped into the tree tops, the wind fanned the flames, and the fire became a running crown fire roaring up the mountain towards the fire crews above. I started moving very fast downhill while the fire started moving very fast uphill. Calling on the radio, I told everyone the fire was coming their way. The division boss got on the radio and said they needed to be air lifted off the mountain ASAP, and he told me to head for a nearby ranch, where an open field offered safety.

I wished I could fly like the eagle and falcon. I sure wanted to be somewhere else. The fire roared by me one ridge over and jumped onto the ridge I had been going down, a hundred yards or so above me. I scrambled down a rocky chute kicking large rocks loose that bounced downhill and out of sight into dense timber. The mountain finally leveled off. I was at the bottom. I found a small stream with a road next to it. Another part of the fire had been milling around down along the road. Some of the vegetation had burned, so I could run into the black if necessary. I looked back up the mountain. The entire mountainside above me was engulfed in flames. Those beautiful conifers through which I had walked were gone, consumed by fire. The radio traffic blared non-stop, and the fire crews above were in a full blown retreat. The hotshot crews started back burning to slow the fire down so the helicopters could land and get them out of there. I hurried down the road, ending up in an open meadow. I could see the buildings of a ranch in the distance, but I knew the owners had evacuated the area days before.

The first wave of helicopters with rescued firefighters from the mountain top started coming to the ranch, landing in the meadow. The pilots decided that flying back to the helibase was too far. They had almost seventy people to fly off the mountain, and the fire was coming too fast. The meadow was the closest place to drop the troops and fly back for more. Almost in a hover the Black Hawks unloaded firefighters and immediately took off, heading back to the mountain top. The five ships were lined up behind each other hovering in the air while one ship loaded. The last ship out had the overhead folks and some hotshots from the Boise Hotshot crew on board. The superintendent from Boise was burning out around the helibase and literally tossed a fusee at the fire as he jumped on board. The helicopter lifted off with the main part of the fire a short distance away. A close call by anyone's standards, even for a hotshot superintendent. Meanwhile, I was sitting in the meadow watching the entire south side of the mountain burn. We were close to the north fork of the Salmon River, and the fire was also burning on the other side of the river up another mountain. We had fire around three sides of us. It was as if the world were on fire. Flames leaped hundreds of feet into the air, and the smoke column rose thousands of feet above us. The roar of the fires was almost deafening. After getting everyone off the mountain, the helicopters started transporting us from the meadow back to the helibase, snaking their way around the columns of smoke. We were bounced around by erratic winds created by the fire. The main smoke column went twenty to thirty thousand feet into the upper atmosphere. In places flames raced up steep slopes, jumping from tree top to tree top. No one would have been able to outrun that.

Another close call, another group of firefighters pushing the envelope. No one talked about how close it had been. It was just another typical day for the firefighting elite out doing what they were told and thinking they could do it. But a day with relative humidities in the teens, with winds, warms temperatures, and dry fuel, was not the conditions needed for digging fire line down a steep mountainside towards a fire. In this case, everyone recognized the danger in time, but it could have been sixty lives lost if they hadn't.

Typical of times before on a project fire, the days started running together. I would get up, eat, go work, come back, eat and go to sleep. Over the two weeks, fire crews continued to improve the fire line I flagged my first day of work. It was the last line of defense before reaching the community of Warren. The overhead folks wanted to back burn along the line, but because of a south facing slope and dry fuels, the spotting potential was extreme. Every time they tried a back burn, even at night, spot fires started outside the line. In frustration, they decided to wet the entire fire line near Warren with fire retardant and called in air tankers. The plan was to wet vegetation on the outside of the fire line one day and then back burn the next.

I was working as lookout on a nearby mountain top and had a great view of the entire operation. About mid-morning when visibility finally improved, a small scout plane came into view, flying in from the southwest, and set up shop above the fire. The plane flew along the fire line while waiting for the air tankers to show up, checking for dangerous areas. The tankers also came in from the southwest and, following the directions laid out by the scout plane, they began dropping retardant along the fire line from west to east. The scout plane would take the lead, flying along the line and pull up where they wanted to dump the retardant. There was a PB47-2 Type I air tanker, a CL-215, a Grumman Type III ship and even an old B26 Type II tanker. All day long, the planes flew by my mountain top, slowly working down the line. These propeller-driven air tankers have character. No computer flew that plane. It was a pilot, working in harmony with the plane making it do what it was supposed to do.

Occasionally a tanker came so close I could easily see the pilot.

Sometimes the planes would be at eye level off the side of the mountain. It reminded me of the eagle I once saw flying along the edge of the plateau years before in Bryce Canyon. I felt the same type of attachment towards the tanker as I did with the eagle. These large prop planes seemed to be a part of the sky, using the air currents to their advantage, unlike jets that cut their way through the air.

When they painted the fire line on my mountain, I had to move a short distance off the line to keep from being covered in retardant. The bombers flew by almost directly overhead, and I watched as the retardant dumped from beneath the plane, covering everything in a slippery red goo. The tankers kept it up all afternoon, finally finishing by sunset. Pre-wetting the fuels was a good idea, but the timing was poor. A cold front moved in that day, and it started to snow just after sunset. During the night, it snowed enough that the moisture washed the retardant away and one whole day of flying was wasted. About $100,000 or so of retardant washed away that night. The next day would have been a good day to back burn, but everything was too wet and too cold. By the next day, it got hot and sunny again and an attempt to back burn started some spot fires across the line, so the back burn was stopped. Winds blowing from the south, southwest were dry and warm and quickly dried out the fuels. All that could be done at that point was to keep improving the line and wait for the fire to reach it.

Near Warren the fire finally came calling one afternoon and made a run up through a drainage to the line. I was sitting on the ridge top watching the fire building below. As typically happens on steep, south-facing slopes, the fire, in its race to the ridge top, followed a drainage and looked pyramid-shaped, wide at the bottom, but when it made a run for the top it narrowed significantly. Once it reached the ridge top, it fanned out, widening again as it continued burning down the other side. The fire was too hot to launch a direct attack, so the word went out to retreat. Crews headed for their buses. The fire hit the line in a narrow section about 100 yards wide and never slowed. Several overhead folks were cut off when the fire hit the line, and they had to drive out into a meadow to hunker down until things got mellow again. A helicopter flew in some hot meals, soda, and water, so they sat in their trucks that evening watching the fire burn up a couple thousand acres while they ate. I watched from a small knoll back at fire camp. Fortunately, where the fire made its run was not towards Warren.

The fire was fascinating to watch. The downside was that the slop-over burned up a bunch of hose, one water pumpkin, and six Mark-III pumps. Someone was going to have to fill out a lot of paperwork.

I was run off a ridge two other times in the next five days with the fire pushing the line each time. The overhead folks were good about making the call to pull the troops off the hill when necessary. There were no structures to protect, so they didn't put fighting the fire aggressively in front of safety. Along the fire line, the timber grew thick in places, and no natural safety zones existed. Safety zones had to be built with bulldozers, but they were never big enough. They were really only shelter-deployment zones. No one wanted to test them out, so overhead made sure no one had to be in one of those areas when the fire headed towards the line.

Every couple of days, another cold front rolled through, causing winds to increase and temperatures to drop but offered very little precipitation. Winter was coming but not quickly. One morning after a little dusting of snow, I drove out to a rocky point at the east end of the fire line. The point looked out over a roadless wilderness. The mountain peaks above tree line were covered in snow, and the mountain sides and valleys below the fire were shrouded in a thick blanket of smoke. It reminded me of when I use to live in New England; it looked a lot like the hills of Vermont and New Hampshire on a cool early fall morning, with fog in the valleys and the hilltops in sunlight. While sitting at the rocky point, the sun rose above the distant mountain tops and painted the snow-covered peaks in pink. Small groves of aspen, their leaves already turned golden, sparkled with frost and snow in the early morning sunlight. I heard an elk bugle from a meadow not far away. The elk were beginning their rut. The Chicken Complex had burned almost 100,000 acres, but wildlife carried on their lives regardless. As in Yellowstone, they just walked out of harm's way to where the fire had not burned. Elk, deer, and bear would particularly enjoy the next spring in the burned areas because fire stimulated new succulent, nutritious plant growth.

I sat down amongst the rocks out on the point and watched the sunrise. The pink color and shadows brightened into white light. It was a quiet morning, no wind. The fire activity would stay low for the day. I wouldn't have much to do, and it gave me a chance to enjoy the moment. I sat cross-legged, placed my hands palm up, closed my eyes and meditated. A wave of warmth passed over me, and I smiled. I thought about my future with my new daughter, still in the womb of my love. What kind of a life would she have? I prayed her world would be full of warmth and happiness.

On my nineteenth day on the fire, the weather warmed, and we were back into active fire behavior. A 100,000-acre fire does not die a quick death. No matter what we tried to do, this fire would burn until snow blanketed the ground and smothered it. I found myself working as a look out on a mountain top along one of the hottest sections of the fire. Several fire crews were working the fire line below while I sat out on point, watching the fire burn in a drainage down below. The temperature began to rise, and the rh was dropping. *Here we go again*, I thought.

The smoke in the drainage below began changing from gray to black. I saw several fingers of trees that ran from the drainage bottom several hundred vertical feet in elevation to the ridge top, a distance of about half a mile. From all the signs I was seeing, the fire was going to come up one or more of these fingers, and if it did, it would hit the line hard. I called the division boss and recommended helicopters start dropping buckets of water and retardant. He hiked to my location, took a look and agreed with me. Getting on the radio, he called the helibase, asking for air support.

Shortly thereafter, two sky cranes flew into view, and I directed them to the hot spots. They dropped retardant for a couple of hours, but the fire just kept building. The fire was just too hot and the fuels too dry. Once again when the rh dropped below twenty percent, the fire raised its ugly head. A gust of wind came up the drainage and kicked the flames into the tree tops. From my viewpoint, the orange flames licked the air well above the tops of the trees, hungry for more food. I got on the radio and explained the situation to the division boss, who had gone back to direct the fire crews. He worked his way over for another look and saw the fire boiling up below, starting to make a run towards the line. He called the troops back to a safety zone.

I kept my position so I could keep an eye on things until everyone made it to the safety zone. Air tankers were ordered in, their ETA about fifteen to thirty minutes. I figured the fire would be on the line at about the same time. Word came over the radio that everyone was safe, so I abandoned my position and started moving quickly down the line for the nearest safety zone. The fire licked at my heels. Moving through a thick grove of trees, I could see flames in the tree tops just below the ridge. I picked up the pace. Coming over a small knoll, I had the shit scared out of me by a small fixed winged aircraft flying at treetop level right down the line towards me. I ducked as it went over, it seemed that close. I recognized it as the scout plane for the air tankers. I had not heard them over the roar of the fire. I knew an air tanker was not far behind, so I bailed off the fire line into some thick brush outside the line and kept moving downhill. Ten seconds later, a tanker flew overhead and dropped a load of retardant right where I had been standing. I would have gotten the full force of the load right in my face. A load of retardant has been known to break windshields on vehicles and snap trees. It's heavy stuff, especially if dropped as low as the plane was flying; coming down at over a hundred miles an hour, it can pack a good punch. It might have killed me if I had been standing on the knoll.

The pilot flying the B-26 made a perfect hit on the fire, knocking the flames out of the tree tops. Another tanker came in and made its drop. The two planes made two runs each and stopped the fire from spotting over the line. Once the planes cleared the area, the firefighters moved back in and mopped up the hot spots. It was a perfect example of air support and ground support working together to stop a fire.

My last day on the Chicken Complex, I spent walking down into the drainage that had burned the day before to look for hot spots. I worked my way down the steep ridge, and the ash was almost a foot deep in places. Everything organic had burned. Large burned-over conifer trunks jutted into the sky, their branches bare of needles. The trees, thirty feet or more in height, were burned from top to bottom. Bark falling from the trees left bare yellow wood behind that conflicted with the black. Boulders scattered around the hillside had pieces of rock flaked off because of the heat. Even though I know fire does good things, I was still saddened to see such magnificent trees die. Still, I knew the trunks would someday make good cavity nesting sites for birds and other animals.

That night back at camp, I started the demob paper work, getting ready to head home the next day. By 9:00 A.M. the next day, I was in a van heading towards McCall and on to Boise. The van pulled into McCall where we had to go through another check out. After three weeks in the woods without a day off, it was great to see a town again. Later that day, I was on a commercial jet flying back to Denver. Staring out the window, I decided it was time for me to spend more time at home and less time firefighting. For eighteen years firefighting had played a major role in my summer months. I decided it was going to only play a minor role from now on. As I drove up the driveway of my home that evening, my two boys ran out the door waving hello, with our two dogs following close behind barking. My spouse stood in the doorway smiling, the dimple in her cheek showing. The bulge in her stomach had grown. My daughter was safely tucked away inside. I hugged everyone and kissed my wife. It was great to be home.

Back at work three days later, I heard that one of the Black Hawk helicopters at the Chicken Complex had flipped over at the helibase, killing an overhead person and severely injuring the pilot and support crew. The person who died was the thirty-fourth to die fighting fires in 1994. I knew the overhead guy and was saddened.

12

There is no Greater Weakness than Stubbornness
If you cannot yield, if you cannot learn that there
must be compromise in life - you lose.

—Maxwell Maltz

Colorado and Nevada 2001

While monitoring a 100-acre wildfire burning in sagebrush, piñon, and juniper on the west side of an unnamed mountain near Elko, Nevada, I could see six other wildfires burning within a fifty-mile radius of me. It had been hot and dry for a couple months. Recently a cold front had passed through several western states bringing only wind and dry lightning with little rain. Twenty large wildfires burned in seven western states. The interagency fire suppression effort had reached level five, the highest level. The fire I observed only had one engine on it with three firefighters working along the bottom of the fire trying to keep the flames from backing downhill and crossing a road. The head of the wind-driven fire burned towards the top of the mountain. Since the fire threatened no homes, few resources had been committed to suppressing it. Firefighters, by early August, had been stretched thin. About 12,000 firefighters battled the beast throughout the West. The military had even mobilized a division to assist in the firefighting.

I thought the year 2000 had been a bad fire season, but 2001 seemed likely to set the record. Looking around the landscape where the fire I watched was burning, I was saddened by what I saw. As far

as I could see in any direction the fuel beneath the trees and few existing shrubs was an annual exotic grass called cheatgrass, *Bromus tecto-
rum*. Fire frequency—both wild and prescribed—livestock grazing,
and human development had drastically altered what was once a vast
sea of about 155 million acres of sagebrush and other herbaceous
native vegetation in six Western states. Nevada used to have the
largest acreage of Great Basin sagebrush, but, unfortunately, a significant portion had grown to cheatgrass. I knew from other fires I had
worked in other Western states—Idaho, Wyoming, Colorado, and
New Mexico—that Great Basin sagebrush and sagebrush steppe had
been disappearing. Many fire managers, ranchers, and other land
managers with whom I had talked said a problem existed but that it
was not severe—millions of acres of sagebrush still grew. Thoughts of
the demise of the passenger pigeon came to mind when I heard
someone say we had plenty of anything left.

To many people who live in the West, sagebrush is the symbol
of the true West, representing wildness and open spaces. Humans are
few and widespread, living in small towns; only cattle and sheep, an
occasional windmill or stock pond indicate any semblance of civilization. The state of Wyoming boasts fewer humans per square mile than
any other lower forty-eight state, and they have a large portion of the
sagebrush steppe.

Before European settlement, early explorers of the inter-
mountain West encountered a landscape dominated by shrubs and
found grasslands chiefly limited to hillsides and moist valley bottoms, with forests growing at the higher elevations. Forbs and peren-
nial bunch grasses grew in great abundance in the understory
beneath the shrubs. Wildlife that had evolved with the shrub habitat
abounded. Some scientists believe that the high density of shrubs
indicated fire came infrequently to this habitat. However, by 2001, the
shrub habitat is being replaced with a monoculture of exotic cheatgrass. Fire frequency has significantly increased. The monoculture of
cheatgrass is not as valuable to native wildlife.

Nature's alliance with fire can be seen in ecosystems throughout the West. Fire frequency in pristine sagebrush is estimated to be
twenty to twenty-five years in dry areas and sixty to 110 years in wetter habitat. Unfortunately, cheatgrass has altered the fire frequency,
and now fires burn through these areas sometimes annually or often

at five-year intervals. Sagebrush habitat cannot recover this quickly and, apparently, is being lost. At this point, it is not economically feasible to replace millions of acres of cheatgrass unless a scientist can find some form of biological control and then figure out how to reseed vast areas with native plants. Because of the fires, the seed bank in the soil is currently lost, and without human help there is no chance for recovery.

Ponderosa pine, which is common in Colorado, Utah, and Arizona, are the most fire-dependent kind of forest in the United States. Fire frequencies of five to thirty years are needed to keep these forests healthy. In healthy forests, most fires usually take the form of ground fires that burns in patchy mosaic patterns leaving most of the large mature trees untouched while clearing out the undergrowth. Forests that are denied fire, however, become prime for catastrophic wildfires because of unnatural fuel buildup. That is where the dilemma lies. Many mature stands of ponderosa are choked with dense young trees. There fires often become crown fires, destroying the older trees as they burn. California chaparral, another habitat that has evolved with fire, sees explosive fires that clear hillsides with a frequency of twenty to fifty years. Lodgepole pine and spruce-fir forests have a fire frequency of maybe 200 to 400 years; tall grass prairie is visited by fire every five years or so, and Boreal forest every twenty-five to 150 years. Unlike in the West, the Appalachian Mountains mixed forests see only a mosaic pattern of fires that tends to be rare. Unfortunately the vegetation with the highest fire frequency is located where many Western cities or towns and private landowners have built homes. Every summer during the fire season, communities are threatened from wildfires, and some homes are lost.

Prescribed fires and wildland fires in shrub habitat have been a concern of mine since 1994. The 1994 fire season saw a big turning point for fire management. The huge loss of acreage, homes, and human lives forced federal and state agencies to rethink how they managed fires. Discussions about wildland fires for resource benefit, prescribed fires, forest thinning by cutting trees with chainsaws dominated. Land managers began to plan for more prescribed fires.

In Rocky Mountain National Park, I worked closely with the fire management officer in developing burn plans. Burn plans were also being prepared in other parks, by the United States Forest

Service, the Bureau of Land Management, and by state and county offices. By 1996, everyone wanted to be doing prescribed burning, and fire plans were proposed for burning more acres. In the National Park Service, fire managers had written into their performance evaluation that they were supposed to burn a certain amount of acres per year. Funding was made available to them based on the amount of acres burned. The fire manager who burned more acres got more money. For them to have a satisfactory annual evaluation, they had to take bigger risks. It was not uncommon to hear about a two- or three-thousand-acre prescribed fire somewhere, the bigger the better. An acquaintance of mine with the Bureau of Land Management boosted how his agency had changed thousands of acres of piñon/juniper forests to grasses.

At first I believed the new era of prescribed fires was a good thing, bringing forests, shrubs, and grasses back into a more ecological regime, but after monitoring vegetation changes in upland shrub habitat at Rocky Mountain National Park and seeing thousands of acres of nothing but cheatgrass in places like Idaho and Nevada, I began to worry that excess prescribed burning and burning certain habitats went to the opposite extreme—too much too fast without fire managers really thinking about the ecological consequences. "Lets get smoke in the air," had become the battle cry.

Where I worked, prescribed fires were being applied mostly in upland shrub habitat where it intermixed with ponderosa pine. Because of a number of variables, I saw the shrub habitat two to three years post burn, shift to grass, forb habitats to grass and forbs. Prescribed fire, in my opinion, was not bringing the habitat back into ecological balance, but was shifting the habitat and not allowing it to return to shrub or forb before the next fire occurred. Fire managers with whom I talked were asking what was wrong with that. More grass and forbs were good for wildlife. My argument posed that changing the shrub habitat too quickly might court ecological disaster.

Rocky Mountain National Park has some of the best antelope bitterbrush habitat in Colorado. This shrub community is considered rare and imperiled in Colorado because of housing development, invasion by exotic plants, browsing by livestock and wildlife, and prescribed and wildland fires. Certain songbirds and other wildlife are specialists who breed only in this habitat. In Rocky Mountain National Park, antelope bitterbrush is the mule deer's primary source of food during the winter. The vegetation monitoring I was doing in the park indicated that, if the present frequency of prescribed fire continued in antelope bitterbrush, the shrub might be almost gone from the park in five to seven years. All the remaining antelope bitterbrush fell within burn areas identified for prescribed fires. The natural fire regime in the park would probably never burn so much antelope bitterbrush and sagebrush in such a short time. Any natural fire in this habitat probably burned in patchy patterns at best, leaving behind unburned vegetation that could grow into burned areas. From the prescribed burns with which I was involved, a spring fire burned just under fifty percent and a fall prescribed fire burned almost all the shrubs. Antelope bitterbrush can survive fire by resprouting. About half of the burned antelope bitterbrush did resprout. However, elk browsed heavily on the new twigs. Often three years after a prescribed fire, little antelope bitterbrush and no sagebrush could be found. The shrubs could not grow quickly enough to reach a size to withstand grazing pressure.

Rocky Mountain National Park used to have wolves and grizzly bears and Native American hunters, all of which helped keep the elk population low enough that vegetation remained vigorous and could survive a fire. Wolves and grizzly bears were extirpated from Colorado before Rocky Mountain National Park was established. The present elk population is protected from hunting and, with no wolves or grizzly bears to prey on them, remains at high levels.

I noticed that the lower intensity of the spring burns left behind a mosaic pattern of burned and unburned shrubs and appeared to be the best fire prescription, but one fire manager, after seeing a prescribed burn in the park that left behind unburned patches of shrub, stated the firefighters should go back and burn all the remaining shrubs.

Fire managers who have fought fires their entire careers were used to seeing a blackened landscape, and they believed that was the appropriate prescription. "Burn it all!" In 1977, I pledged to protect the wildlife and vegetation in the national parks in which I worked and, because of my concern at what I saw in Rocky Mountain National Park and elsewhere in the West in the 1990s, I became an outspoken opponent of burning upland shrub habitat under fire pre-scriptions that charred most of the habitat. I was not opposed to burn-ing in shrub habitat but just how it was being done. A prescribed fire should leave behind a mosaic pattern of burned and unburned shrubs verses a blackened landscape. But right now few critics speak out as to how prescribed fires are being applied because of the loss of fire-fighters' lives and the disasters that have occurred to communities throughout the West as a result of wildfires. I quickly found out that I almost stood alone in voicing any concerns. My stubbornness got me into trouble, and I was shunned. One fire manager said all of Rocky Mountain National Park was threatened because of fire sup-pression, but I don't believe this is the case. Scientists and fire ecolo-gists with whom I have spoken indicate that the natural fire regime in spruce-fir and lodgepole pine forests in the park, which represents over fifty percent of the landmass, have not been suppressed to any great degree. They believed fire frequencies remain close to normal. Only fires in ponderosa pine have been significantly suppressed, but ponderosa pine represented a small portion of the forest in the park. Other scientists express concerns about the loss of upland shrub habi-tat not only in the park but throughout the West. This issue has had a great difference of opinion between scientists and land managers.

After seventy-five years of fire suppression, fire managers believed large-scale prescribed fires were the panacea to restore the natural fire regime. I find it hard to convince fire managers that too much fire too soon was not a good thing, particularly when each fire season seemed to be worse than the preceding one. Trying to take too many risks with prescribed fire got the National Park Service and the Bureau of Land Management in trouble in 2000 when the Cerro Grande fire and a couple other prescribed fires burned out of control and destroyed homes. In 2001, some fire managers went back the other way and began suppressing all fires, even some that should be allowed to burn for resource benefit. A wildfire allowed to burn nat-urally can be a good thing if under the right conditions. Instead, fire managers rely heavily on fuel thinning by cutting trees with chain-saws.

At Rocky Mountain National Park, stubbornly expressing my concerns despite the criticism actually paid off, and fire managers now recognize the importance of shrub habitat such as antelope bitterbrush and have adjusted the fire prescription so this habitat type will be protected. Other natural resource specialists in other national parks are also working more closely with fire managers. Rare and unique plant communities, like antelope bitterbrush, are now being carefully studied and prescriptions designed that will not drastically alter these unique plant communities. Wildlife biologists at Rocky Mountain National Park are developing an elk-management plan that considers the role of fire and the elk's impact on vegetation after a prescribed fire, particularly on their winter range, which is where the antelope bitterbrush occurs.

Congress' solution to the disasters after the 2000 fire season and after many Western governors complained about hazardous fuels and out-of-control wildfires threatening communities was to budget large sums of money for reducing the risk of wildland fires. In 2001, Western governors have now developed a ten-year plan that will protect homes by implementing an ambitious program of fuel thinning and prescribed burning. Federal agencies have developed an interagency national fire plan and initiated a national fire program. Congress and the president gave the federal agencies millions of dollars in 2000 and 2001 that is now being devoted to reducing hazardous fuels in high-risk areas such as around communities built amongst dense forests or that border national parks, United States Forest Service and Bureau of Land Management lands where heavy timber exists. Fuel thinning by cutting trees with chainsaws and using prescribed fires, including resource-benefit fires, are occurring all through the West.

Unfortunately the Cerro Grande Fire that occurred in New Mexico in 2000 made many fire managers gun shy, and they are not all "fighting the good fight" and are putting out some fires that should not be suppressed. Prescribed fires are also occurring in low-risk areas because they are the safest to do, but these may not necessarily reduce the risk of catastrophic fires. Fires are being suppressed in denser forests because fire managers don't want to lose their jobs. I consider this practice like looking for a lost quarter in good light regardless of where it was actually lost. Some fire personnel lost their jobs, took early retirement or were forcibly moved because of the Cerro Grande Fire. Fire managers do not want to risk their careers by letting certain resource-benefit fires that fall within a prescription continue to burn. I can't really blame them. I don't want to lose my job either.

Instead of prescribed burning, fire crews at Rocky Mountain National Park are cutting trees just inside the park boundary in high-risk areas. Using chainsaws in recommended wilderness in a national park seems contrary to the philosophy of the National Park Service, but times have changed. Natural regulation—the "hands off" policy—which use to govern the management of most national parks since the 1960s seems outdated, and hazardous-fuel reduction along park boundaries with chainsaws seems appropriate. However, the buffer zone currently being created will not stop a running crown fire. For most parks like Rocky Mountain National Park that have gateway communities built up right to their boundaries, a thinned forest along the park boundary is a good-faith effort. These buffer zones of thinned forests carry a lower risk than prescribed fires, but a prescribed fire to reduce fuel loading further in the interior of the park should follow the thinning. Few fire managers in these high-risk areas are willing to take the risk, and put their careers on the line, by setting a prescribed fire.

Adjacent communities need to take some responsibility and develop fire-safe environments. City and county planning commissioners should force developers or private landowners to build homes away from dense forests without some forest thinning and away from boundaries of national parks where dense forests grow. If a wildfire starts in a national park and escapes, burning into adjacent communities that have not taken the proper precautions, the National Park Service should not be held responsible, particularly if the park has tried fuel reduction along its park boundary and further in the interior by fuel thinning and prescribed fires. In some places, homes exist that should never have been built; they stand in high-risk areas.

The present administration is in favor of "hands on" work in national parks and on other public lands. My concern is that Congress and the present administration may expect too much too soon. It is going to take ten to twenty years of active management using carefully applied prescribed fires, fires for resource benefit, and hazardous fuel reduction by cutting trees before some sort of balance is achieved. This cannot be done in two to four years. Congress may get impatient and take away the millions of dollars presently available before any noticeable results are achieved, and all the work presently being accomplished maybe for naught.

Meanwhile, my firefighting days are coming to an end. I now spend more time working closely with fire personnel in Rocky Mountain National Park to recognize trees important to wildlife such as snags with tree cavities. The supervisor for the fuel-thinning crews and I have surveyed forest stands and identified important trees, flagging them so they will not be cut down.

There are also prescribed fire protocols being developed today that some firefighters see as silly. A firefighter with the Bureau of Land Management has come up with this list of protocols after witnessing a porcupine being killed by a prescribed fire. The porcupine, a rather ponderous rodent, could not move fast enough and died right in front of several firefighters. A simple walk through the burn area before the match was lit might have saved the porcupine's life. Some firefighters say the loss of an animal like a porcupine is a risk that should be accepted. I think we should make an effort to protect these animals. Birds, deer, elk, coyotes can either fly away or run fast enough to get out of the way of fire; some species can't. Firefighters should make a good-faith effort to find these species and move them. From my perspective, a prescribed fire is different than a wildfire or a fire for resource benefit. Fire managers dictate when, how and where the prescribed fire will burn. Therefore, there should be some responsibility for wildlife survival.

I also have a serious concerns about the privatization of public land in the West. Critics say the federal government has not done a good job, so let private industry take charge. In my opinion, that puts the fox in the hen house. I hope the general public is not bamboozled into thinking that making United States Forest Service, Bureau of Land Management, and National Park Service lands private land will solve any problems—what an ecological disaster that would be.

Fire management has become more complex, the risk is higher and we know that what is done today will effect plants and animals for decades to come—in the case of cheatgrass, perhaps forever. I just hope that in thirty to fifty years, if I am still alive in this wonderful world, I will not stand on a mountain side in Nevada and see seas of cheatgrass instead of sagebrush.

Epilogue

uture years with fire might be worst as global warming continues to screw up weather patterns, El Nino has its effect, and urban interface in the mountains gets worse. Fire suppression encourages the growth of denser fuels. Wildfires seem to be getting bigger, harder to control and more dangerous.

It is important that any land-managing agency start active fire management programs, but they need to consider rare and imperiled plant communities and the effects the shift in vegetation will have on wildlife. The public is being educated that fire can be a friend and is an important part of the woods, prairies, and meadows. People who live in the mountains are also being educated to understand their need to be prepared, to clear brush and trees away from their homes, keep log piles at a safe distance. Such homes should landscape with short grasses and forbs and should be built out of stucco, cement, brick, or steel, not wood. Every home owner should insure that roads and driveways are wide enough to accommodate fire engines and fire-support vehicles. It's usually a good idea to make roads loop rather than have one way in one way out. When a fire is rocking and rolling, firefighters have to make quick decisions whether a house can be saved or must be sacrificed. This is usually based on the firefighters' safety. The more a home owner can do to make his house and site safer for firefighters, the better the chances that he will have a home after the fire. Remember, in the West, the statement isn't *if* a fire is ever going to burn through a wooded area but *when*.

In the fall of 1996, at the Pearl Street Mall in Boulder with my spouse and my bouncing, bubbly two-year-old daughter, I observed some yellow-shirted firefighters walking down the sidewalk. The firefighters were men and women twenty years or so younger than I. I knew most of them. They had been on a small fire just west of town and had come to get ice cream after their shift. They were dirty from a day of mopping up fire and reeked of smoke and sweat. I smiled as I watched people's heads turn as they walked by. Those who recognized them as firefighters smiled or greeted them as they passed. They walked by us, but I didn't say anything. They didn't recognize me. Laughing amongst themselves, they were compadres, buddies, equals, and damn proud to be firefighters. I thought, *Yes, firefighting has a glamorous side,* and I was glad that I had been a part of it.

Appendix

The Incident Command System

Wen on a small fire with three people, organization is not really that important. There is still one person who is the Incident Commander (IC) and the other two listen and carry out the IC's orders. As a fire grows in size, organization becomes critical. Firefighting has evolved significantly in the past 100 years with most of the changes occurring in the past fifty. The roots of present-day firefighting started during the Civilian Conservation Corp (CCC) era. They modeled their organization after the military, so it is natural that today the Incident Command System in firefighting is also similar to the military—pyramid shaped with the grunts (firefighters, digging-in-the-dirt folks) at the bottom and the Incident Commander at the top. The complexity of the fire organization is based on the size of the fire. The small fire I was on in Utah had three of us. I have been on fires when I was the only one. On large fires or complexes of multiple fires, there are branches and divisions composed of thousands of firefighters.

All fires start out small and are usually attacked with a small contingent of initial-attack firefighters. These usually consist of local people from a park, forest, county, or volunteers from a rural fire department. The crew is often composed of two to three people driving a wildland fire engine. These engines are usually four-wheel drive and are smaller in size than the typical structural engine used on house fires. Sometimes initial attack is with a nearby staged heli-tack crew or could be smokejumpers if the fire is in a roadless area or access is difficult. The initial-attack firefighters are first on scene, and the one with the most experience and training becomes the Incident

Commander. He or she is responsible for sizing up the fire and calling in by radio to a central fire dispatch center regarding the location, size of the fire, the fuel type (heavy forest, light, grass, shrub), slope, aspect, wind speed, wind direction, access to the area, any structures in the area, fire behavior (smoldering, active flames), and color of smoke. The folks back at dispatch will use the information to assist the IC in determining if other resources are needed. The initial-attack crew oftentimes will take fire weather information, such as a dry temperature, wet temperature, and relative humidity (rh) from the fire's location. Based on the preliminary information, which is passed by dispatch to a fire management officer or forest supervisor managing the area with the fire, a decision will be made between the IC and others if the initial-attack personnel can handle the fire or more resources are needed (i.e., firefighters, engines, helicopter, air tankers). Sometimes the fire is first scouted by a fixed-wing aircraft, and information is passed on recommending what resources will be needed for initial attack.

The IC, after sizing up the fire, will decide if the fire should be attacked directly or indirectly. If possible, the fastest way to put out a fire is by a direct attack, which is treating the fire as a whole on all its burning edges, usually working directly along the edges of the burning fuels. If the fire is moving too quickly, flames are too high, fire behavior indicates unsafe conditions, there is a very steep slope, or anything else that could jeopardize the safety of the firefighters, they will fall back and do an indirect attack. An indirect attack is a method of suppression in which the control line is located along natural firebreaks, favorable breaks in topography. As a fire grows in size and fire behavior intensifies, the indirect attack moves farther away from the head of a fire, which is usually the hottest and most dangerous area in the direction the fire is heading. Firefighters in an indirect attack will try to flank the fire eventually pinching out the head of the fire. This leaves unburned fuel between the fire line and the fire that is in itself a safety hazard. Oftentimes this unburned fuel is intentionally burned by firefighters in a "back burn." The set fire burns vegetation into the wildfire and, the firefighters hope, stop the fire.

When building any fire line, the first thing that should be done is find a good anchor point so the fire cannot hook around the firefighters. This anchor point might be a boulder outcrop, the bottom of the fire on a hill, or edge of a lake. The plan is to entirely circle the fire with a fire line starting from the anchor point. On initial attack, this might be a narrow scratch line to mineral soil, just enough to slow the fire down but maybe not stop it. In the beginning, initial attack forces, instead of building a fire line from an anchor point, may move around putting out hot spots or active parts of the fire, trying to stop it from spreading. Then they can go back and begin to build a fire line that will stop the fire. A proper fire line dug to mineral soil is usually about one to two feet wide. Fuels such as shrubs and trees are cleared away on average about one and one half times the height of the surrounding vegetation. Often this is done with hand tools, such as shovels, chain saws, and pulaskis, but sometimes bulldozers are used in non-wilderness areas or on fires that are threatening human lives or homes. For example, in 1988 bulldozers were used in Yellowstone National Park in roadless areas to try and stop the North Fork Fire from burning down the community of West Yellowstone. However, the fire blew over the dozer lines like they did not even exist. Bulldozers could have bladed a fire line one-half mile wide, and it still would not have made any difference. Using bulldozers in national parks or wilderness areas for wildland firefighting is not ethical in the philosophy and policies of the National Park Service, United States Forest Service, or Bureau of Land Management, but when the fire is rocking and rolling, threatening human lives or structures, bearing down on some community and making the bear dance, most ICs throw all thoughts of a National Park or wilderness area policy out the window and use whatever tool they think will stop the fire.

A fire line that is one and one-half times the height of the surrounding fuels varies depending on the types of fuels. Down the middle of the line is the two- to three-foot-wide line dug to mineral soil, but either side is cleared wider. In shrub habitat, this may be only the three-foot-wide line, but in heavy forest with large trees this could be 100 or more feet wide. For example, if the trees were ten feet high the fire line would need to be fifteen feet wide. All brush and trees are cleared on either side of the dug line leaving only grasses or other low growing plants.

While the firefighters are working, the IC responsible for the firefighters' safety, continues to size up the fire, keeps an eye on the fire behavior for any change that might spell a blow up, takes weather readings and keeps dispatch informed of the situation. The IC, as well as the firefighters, should be aware of safety zones, where firefighters can find refuge if the fire blows up and endangers them. The IC also seeks water sources, looks ahead of the fire for fuel types and may begin calling for additional resources, such as more firefighters, engines, or maybe an air tanker for cooling the head of the fire or prewetting fuels in front of the fire.

Nationwide about ninety-five percent of all wildland fires never exceed what is called a Type IV level of complexity. This would be defined as fires less than one acre in size and composed of one or more burning trees. A Type IV fire can be up to about ten acres, and usually involves anywhere from one firefighter to maybe a single task force of a bulldozer, fire engine or two, and a squad or two of firefighters. A squad is composed of five firefighters and a squad boss. A Type IV fire also lasts only one operational period (i.e., one burn period from 9:00 A.M. to 6:00 P.M.) and normally does not require a written action plan.

If the fire has grown larger than ten acres and is not contained or controlled by the initial attack force, additional resources are needed. The fire becomes an Extended Attack Incident and is upgraded to a Type III fire incident, which is normally less than 100 acres in size. Firefighting resources on a Type III fire vary from several single resources to several task forces or strike teams, but the incident is expected to be contained or controlled still within the first operational period.

At some point the fire will be contained (a fire line is built around it) or controlled (the fire is contained and there is no danger of the fire escaping) or a decision is made to make the incident a Type II organization if the fire grows beyond 100 acres in size. A Type II fire needs a written action plan. Logistics are now getting complicated. All of the command and general staff and support positions are filled, and the fire complexity exceeds the capability of an extended attack organization. A Type II fire can be thousands of acres in size involving many resources. The number of personnel on the fire during any one operational period is less than 500 firefighters and less than 1,000 personnel total. Divisions are usually formed in a Type II fire. A division divides the fire into geographical areas of operation. A Type II fire has an overhead staff composed of the IC with logistics, operations, planning and financial support. The number of staff can vary but could be up to a couple hundred.

Under extreme fire conditions, when fuels are very dry, the weather is hot, the relative humidity is low (usually below twenty-five percent in the West and thirty percent in the Southwest), the wind is high, and the fire can grow from one tree to hundreds of acres within minutes, thousands of acres within an hour. The pucker factor rises significantly. When a fire goes from one hundred to one thousand acres within minutes, this is often called a blow-up. The fire, when it gets into the tree canopy — actually burning above ground — becomes a crown fire. When moving fast, it becomes a running crown fire. Flame lengths can reach two to three hundred feet, and the fire can move faster than a human can run. Spot fires can occur a quarter to one mile out in front of the fire. No one or at least no one with any brains wants to be in front of a fast-moving crown fire. When a fire blows up and grows rapidly in size, threatening humans or their habitation, the fire is usually classified as a Type I incident.

There is a gray area between a Type II fire and when the fire reaches a complexity that requires a Type I classification. Type I fires are usually large, or maybe a complex of fires, and require well-qualified personnel at the IC and command/general staff level, the top dogs of overhead folks in firefighting, the most qualified personnel from all agencies. The number of personnel on the fire often exceeds 500 per operational period and total personnel will be over 1,000 firefighters.

In Type III to Type I fires, the basic foundation is built on hand crews. The hand crews are made up of twenty people, similar to a platoon in the military. A crew boss is directly responsible for the crew. This person has a lot of training and been on a number of fires. He or she is responsible for the safety and well-being of the crew, record keeping, and many other tasks related to the crew. Often there is a crew boss trainee, someone who has the training but not enough time on the fire line supervising a crew. Under the crew boss and crew boss trainee are three squads, each squad made up of five firefighters and one squad boss and often trainees. Amongst the crew, there are usually several people who are trained in chain saw use and water pumps. There may also be an emergency medical technician (EMT) and sometimes even a paramedic. Each crew can be self-contained and, on small fires, works directly under the IC. The IC on Type IV and possibly Type III fires are often the crew boss.

Today, unlike when I was on my first fire season in 1976, all firefighters have to go through basic training. This is usually a three- to five-day course, where they are taught the fundamentals of firefighting. This includes the different types of tools to use, fire line construction, some basic information on fuel types, and fire behavior. Most important, the trainees are taught fire safety, such as the ten standard firefighting orders, the eighteen "watch-out" situations, and LCES (lookouts, communication, escape routes, and safety zones). Watch out situations are the red flag warnings that indicate danger could be brewing. Over the years, the firefighters who have died usually break one or more of the firefighting orders or watch out situations. Some of the common denominators of fire behavior on tragedy fires are:

- Many fatalities happen on smaller fires or on isolated portions of larger fires.
- Most fires are innocent in appearance before the "flare -up" or "blow-ups."
- In some cases, tragedies have occurred in the mop-up stage.
- Flare-ups generally occur in deceptively light fuels.
- Fires run uphill surprisingly fast in chimneys, gullies, and on steep slopes.
- Some suppression tools, such as helicopters or air tankers, can adversely affect fire behavior.

Fire safety is always an issue but, most firefighters who have seen a lot of action at one time or another have "pushed the envelope," and violated a couple of rules. It is hard not to do that sometimes, but we all hope that luck is always in our favor. Hell, the first fire order is, "Fight fire aggressively, but provide for safety first." There is a fine line between aggressiveness and safety. It is almost an oxymoron.

The following are the standard firefighting orders:
- **F**ight fire aggressively, but provide for safety first.
- **I**nitiate all action based on current/expected fire behavior.
- **R**ecognize current weather conditions and obtain forecasts.
- **E**nsure that instructions are given and understood.
- **O**btain current information on fire status.
- **R**emain in communication with crew members.

- **D**etermine safety zones and escape routes.
- **E**stablish lookouts in potentially hazardous situations.
- **R**etain control at all times.
- **S**tay alert, keep calm, think clearly, act decisively.

"Watch Out" Situations

1. Fire not scouted or sized up.
2. In country not seen in daylight.
3. Safety zones and escape routes not identified.
4. Unfamiliar with weather/local factors influencing fire behavior.
5. Uninformed on strategy, tactics, and hazards.
6. Instructions and assignments not clear.
7. No communications link with crew members or supervisors.
8. Construction line without a safe anchor point.
9. Building fire line downhill with fire below.
10. Attempting frontal assault on fire.
11. Unburned fuel between you and the fire.
12. Cannot see main fire, not in contact with anyone who can.
13. On a hillside where rolling material can ignite fuel below.
14. Weather is getting hotter and drier.
15. Wind increases and/or changes direction.
16. Getting frequent spot fires across line.
17. Terrain and fuels make escape to safety zones difficult.
18. Taking a nap near the fire line.

LCES

LCES is a system for operational safety. In the wildland fire environment where the four basic safety hazards confront firefighters —lightning, fire weather, timber, rolling rocks, and entrapment by running fires—LCES is key to safe procedures.

L—Lookouts
C—Communication
E—Escape Routes
S—Safety Zones

All firefighters should know these rules forward and backwards and be aware of what could happen if they violate one or more.

Beyond basic firefighting, numerous other fire courses are offered. Any firefighter who uses chain saws or water pumps has to go through a three- to five-day training course for each tool, besides the basic firefighting courses. Squad bosses need the basic firefighting courses, saw and pump courses, and maybe a few others, including a squad boss course, as well as having several fires or seasons of firefighting under their belts. The crew boss has all the training of the firefighters, squad bosses, plus a crew boss course, a fire behavior course, air operations, and fire business course, to name a few. The same applies for the trainee. The crew boss has a number of fires and fire seasons under his or her belt. The people who become crew bosses have had close to two months of training and at least a couple of years of fire seasons behind them.

The hand crew is the digging-in-the-dirt, get-down-and-dirty part of firefighting. Fire crews, like fire complexities, are divided into two types, Type I or Type II. A Type I crew is the elite crew (the hotshot crew). These people eat, drink, sleep, and have sex thinking about firefighting. Firefighting is their main job and every day while not on a fire, they physically train. These are the crews who are usually out on the point of a fire line doing the hardest or most dangerous work and usually working the hottest part of the fire. They are often times the safest crews because their crew boss (called a superintendent) and foremen have had many years of firefighting, and they know what a fire can do if it blows up.

There are other types of elite firefighters such as smokejumpers, helitack, and engine crews. They usually do not make up a twenty-person crew but may be eight or ten people for smokejumpers, three to six people for helitack, and three people for engine crews. These people are similar to the hotshot hand crews in experience and physical conditioning. The difference is often instead of walking to a fire, they jump out of a perfectly good aircraft or are flown in by helicopter or drive an engine. Smokejumpers and helitack have an advantage over hotshot crews in that they can be on a fire scene rather quickly. They are often used in areas of the west where roads are lacking or the fire is on top of a mountain making access from the ground harder.

To be on a hotshot crew (or any other elite crew) men and women have to be in top physical condition. All go through the same conditioning during the first part of the summer. They run, lift weights, and do aerobic conditioning. The ones that cannot make it during the training period are left behind and have to find other employment. The smokejumpers have to go through parachute training. In a "good" fire season, some of these elite fire crews, when they become available, head out on fires and are basically gone until the end of the fire season. They go out on twenty-one-day assignments then come back to their duty station for at least two-days rest. They will then become available again heading out for another twenty-one days. In some years, they will amass over 1,000 hours of overtime between the months of May and September. That is beyond the forty-hour workweek. That can average out to a workweek of eighty-eight hours, week after week for four to six months. These people have to be in good shape. After a hard season, many of them head to an island in the Caribbean or some ski area to unwind and spend their overtime money.

The level below the elite crews is called Type II crews. A Type II crew is usually a pick-up crew made up of firefighters from several different agencies, or a Native American crew from one or more reservations. One crew could have firefighters from a state or county, the U.S. Forest Service, National Park Service, Bureau of Land Management, and so on. These firefighters often fight fire as a side duty and not their primary work. A Type II crew could be an off-season school teacher, wildlife biologist, park ranger, heavy-equipment operator, or business person. Like a hotshot crew, each time a crew goes out, everyone used to have to commit to a twenty-one-day assignment. In 2000, it was changed to fourteen days with an option to extend it to twenty-one. However, when they come back to their duty station they might head back to their primary jobs. The next time a hand crew goes out, even though it might have the same name and originate from the same area, it could have a different crew boss and firefighters. Type II crews will often do everything a hotshot crew will do, and be made up of firefighters in as good physical condition as hotshot crews, but they are often used for the less threatening jobs and often end up doing the dreaded "mop up."

Once the fire has burned through a particular area and has a fire line around it, fire crews will begin the mop up stage of the operation. Sometimes on a large fire, portions are being mopped up at the same time as the fire is spreading in other areas. When mopping up after a fire, fire crews spend time putting out smoldering tree stumps, burning needle duff, grass, cow pies, anything that has some coals or heat. This is a tedious, boring job, but at the same time very important. Without mopping up a fire, the fire could easily blow up again. Firefighters have been killed during mop up, so there is still an element of danger.

Mopping up along the fire edge, cooling the fire and slowly working into the interior, the fire is eventually contained. Containment means there is a control line around the fire and any associated spot fires. This can reasonably be expected to check the fire's spread. There still could be pockets of fuel burning in the interior of the fire when it is contained. When the perimeter spread of a wildfire has been halted by natural or man-made barriers and has remained under control throughout the first succeeding burning period, the fire can be considered controlled.

The hotshot crews, smokejumpers, or helitack often times get out of the dirty job of mop up, instead moving on to another part of the fire or a new fire that is "rocking and rolling" — lots of heat, lots of flame. They have the true glamour jobs. Many Type II firefighters, like myself, look up to these elite people for guidance and support when working side by side on a fire.

When a fire warrants more than one hand crew, two crews can form into a strike team. Usually two crews are only called a strike team on large project fires. The strike team will have a strike team leader who supervises the two crews. The crew bosses now report to the strike team leader, who in turns reports to the IC or a division boss. As the fire continues to grow in size, the complexity of fire personnel increases. For example, a fire that is 100 acres or so could have two or more crews (at least forty firefighters), an IC, several engines composed of two to three people each, perhaps a bulldozer or two, one or more helicopters dropping water and moving supplies around, people providing food and supplies, a time keeper, and logistic foreman.

As mentioned earlier, as the fire grows, the area it covers can be divided into divisions, such as Division A and B. Each division will now have a division boss, with hand crews, engine crews, dozers, dozer bosses, maybe a field observer and fire behavior specialist. Everyone in the division reports to the division boss, who then reports to the IC or overhead folks in Operations. From divisions, the fire could develop into branches with several divisions below each branch. There is usually a branch chief for every branch. Divisions and branches can also be formed when there is a complex, i.e., more than one fire.

Besides different types of hand crews, there are different types of fire engines classified from a Type I to Type XIII engine. Type I, II and III engines are the structural engines usually found in urban areas and used to put out structure fires. Type IV to XIII engines are usually the wildland fire engines and often have four-wheel drive and are designed for off-road travel. The Type XIII engine is the smallest with a twenty-gallon water capacity, about 200 feet of one and one-half-inch diameter hose, and 200 feet of one-inch hose with a crew of two firefighters. In addition, there are water tenders. Large water trucks that engines can draft out of to fill their tanks.

The entire fire organization falls under the Incident Command System (ICS). The same organization is used all across the country not only for fires, but for hurricanes, tornadoes, any natural disaster. It is also used for law enforcement problems or events. The advantage of the ICS is that no matter where one goes in the country the organization is the same, and any person assigned to an event knows how he or she fits into the organization and to whom they report.

A fire, as it continues to grow, can demand from a few firefighters to hundreds in just one day. All these firefighters need transportation, food, supplies, and tools to name a few things. Without a good ICS, fighting the fire would be chaos, and firefighters would be in danger. It is not to say that even with the ICS a fire can't be chaos in the beginning, but at least it is organized chaos—the perfect definition of an oxymoron. Any firefighter who has been on initial attack or the early phases of a large fire knows what this is. The overhead team needed to pull the chaos together usually do not get to a fire until the second day or late at night on the first. Many large fires do their worst damage during the first day before the troops get organized and enough resources are on hand. I have been on a number of fires over the years that burned thousands of acres the first day and only a few hundred over the next week or so because adequate resources had been organized to battle the beast.

About the Author

Jeff Connor has been a public servant with the federal government for twenty-three years in the roles of park ranger, wildlife biologist, and Natural Resources specialist. He has been involved with forest fires (suppression, prescribed fires, and wildland fires for resource benefit) since 1976, qualified as a crew boss, engine boss, strike team leader trainee, Incident Commander Type IV, field observer, line scout, fire monitor, fire management officer, and para-archeologist. In the course of his career, he has worked in five national park units: Bryce Canyon National Park, Canyonlands National Park, Arches National Park, Natural Bridges National Monument, and Rocky Mountain National Park. He also served as a wildlife biologist with the Bureau of Land Management in New Mexico. While in the service of the federal government, Connor climbed mountains, rafted rivers, explored caves and trapped the following animals for study, inventory, and research: big horn sheep, elk, mule deer, black bear, rattlesnakes, amphibians, fish, bats, rodents, birds (raptors and songbirds). As a hippie in the late sixties and early seventies, he hitchhiked across the country and has lived in the Caribbean and Mexico and in a commune in New Mexico and spent time in Cape Cod, Massachusetts.